In the Mouth of the Dragon

In the Mouth of the Dragon

*Memoir of a District Advisor
in the Mekong Delta, 1971–1973*

JOHN B. HASEMAN

with thanks
for your support and
interest.

John Haseman

McFarland & Company, Inc., Publishers

Jefferson, North Carolina

LIBRARY OF CONGRESS CATALOGUING-IN-PUBLICATION DATA

Names: Haseman, John B., author.
Title: In the mouth of the dragon : memoir of a district advisor
in the Mekong Delta, 1971-1973 / John B. Haseman.
Other titles: Memoir of a district advisor in the Mekong Delta, 1971-1973
Description: Jefferson, North Carolina : McFarland & Company, Inc.,
Publishers, 2022 | Includes index.
Identifiers: LCCN 2022034655 | ISBN 9781476688909 (paperback : acid free paper) ∞
ISBN 9781476646800 (ebook)
Subjects: LCSH: Haseman, John B. | Vietnam War, 1961-1975—Personal
narratives, American. | United States. Military Assistance Command, Vietnam.
Advisory Team 88 | Military assistance, American—Vietnam (Republic)—
Bến Tre (Province) | Vietnam War, 1961-1975—Campaigns—Vietnam
(Republic)—Bến Tre (Province) | United States. Army—Officers—
Biography. | BISAC: HISTORY / Wars & Conflicts / Vietnam War
Classification: LCC DS559.5 H3735 2022 | DDC 959.704/38 [B]—dc23/eng/20220722
LC record available at https://lccn.loc.gov/2022034655

BRITISH LIBRARY CATALOGUING DATA ARE AVAILABLE

ISBN (print) 978-1-4766-8890-9
ISBN (ebook) 978-1-4766-4680-0

Front cover: ARVN Captain Tan (left) with the author
in August 1971. Background: the area where the Mekong River
splits into the Hàm Luông River and the Mỹ Tho River
(both photographs from the author's collection)

Printed in the United States of America

*McFarland & Company, Inc., Publishers
Box 611, Jefferson, North Carolina 28640
www.mcfarlandpub.com*

This book is dedicated to the thousands of Americans who served as advisors in Vietnam. Advisors were the first in and last out, and served with courage and dedication. And to the hundreds of Vietnamese officers and RF/PF soldiers with whom I fought the enemy for 18 months in the heat, rain, mud, and water of Kiến Hòa Province: You inspired me to do my best. I so deeply wish the outcome had been better.

Acknowledgments

I did not undertake this book project by myself. I owe thanks and a deep debt of gratitude to many people who pushed me to start the book in the first place, as well as to the many friends who helped along the way with suggestions, contributions, corrections, and assistance.

The book began back in 2011, when all six of my siblings and their spouses attended a ceremony at the Defense Intelligence Agency, where six of us were inducted into the Defense Attaché Service Hall of Fame. My family surrounded me at the reception afterwards and claimed forcefully, "You never told us about any of this." That morphed into, "Start writing before you forget everything, and by the way, you can start with Vietnam because you never told us anything about that either." Well, I am a good brother, so I started writing and produced three locally printed, picture-heavy 8½ × 11-inch "books" about my two Vietnam assignments and one on Burma (my most difficult post–Vietnam assignment). It took me more than five years and a lot of false starts, but my family was with me all the way. So my heartfelt thanks, love, and affection go, first of all, to Paul, Vivian, Lynn, David, Sanny, Joan, Katrina, Ruth, Charles, and Debbie for putting my fingers to the keyboard and getting the entire show on the road.

I took the "family only" photo and prose book of "Vietnam II" to one of the annual reunions of Counterparts, an organization of former advisors in Southeast Asia (www.counterparts.net). From them came more support and frequent urging that I turn the family book into a "real book." My grateful thanks to every member of Counterparts, all of whom have done great things as advisors, but only a few have written of their experiences "because I didn't do anything special and, besides, who cares?" Well, they did do special things, and we share a background of work out in the boonies with Vietnamese tactical units but especially out in the districts from the Mekong Delta to the Central Highlands to the DMZ on small advisory teams trying to make a difference. Thank you, guys, for keeping the pressure on. In some ways my story also tells your story.

A few advisors have written their story before me and thus helped spur me along to tell the advisors' stories. John L. Cook, way back in 1973, wrote *The Advisor* about his district-level advisory assignment. I read that book almost nonstop, seldom putting it down, and said to myself, "Damn, that guy just wrote my book."

My friend Andrew Finlayson, Colonel USMC (retired), a Counterparts member, wrote two books about his Vietnam experiences: *Killer Kane: A Marine Long-Range Recon Team Leader in Vietnam, 1967–1968*; and *Rice Paddy Recon: A Marine Officer's Second Tour in Vietnam, 1968–1970*, both published by McFarland. Thank you, Andy, for your encouragement.

Another good friend, Terry Turner, also a member of Counterparts, writes under the pseudonym David Donovan. In *Once a Warrior King: Memories of an Officer in Vietnam* (McGraw-Hill, 1985), he tells about being the chief of a small MAT Team on the Plain of Reeds who, as a young lieutenant, was ordered to become perhaps the most junior district senior advisor. Terry also authored *Counterinsurgency: What the United States Learned in Vietnam, Chose to Forget and Needs to Know Today,* also published by McFarland, and which draws on his own experiences, as well as those of many Counterparts members (including me), and describes how the lessons we learned a long time ago in Vietnam are still important today.

Thanks, folks, to you and other advisors who wrote about their advisory duty and showed me the way to tell a story that needs telling.

This project brought me back into contact with former colleagues on Advisory Team 88, some of whom I had neither seen nor contacted since 1973 and some of whom have remained friends in touch over the many years. You will read of their experiences in this book. My thanks to former Sergeant Robert "Ike" Isenhour; Colonel (retired) George B. "Byron" Reed; Colonel (retired) Roger H.C. Donlon (CMOH); Brigadier General (retired) Robert L. "Steve" Stephens; Captain Mike Delaney; Captain Brian Valiton; and Captain Ed Blankenhagen; former Deputy Province Senior Advisor Mr. Norris Nordvold and many others who remain unnamed for personal privacy reasons, all of whom shared memories and recalled events from our time together in Kiến Hòa Province more than 50 years ago.

Over the years, I wrote separate articles about some of my Vietnamese counterparts, and I wanted to include parts of those articles in this book. I owe great thanks to *Vietnam Magazine* and *Infantry Magazine* for giving me permission to use those materials. You will see them throughout this book, along with notes with complete credit details. A third journal, *Asian Affairs*, ceased publication many years ago, but I add my thanks to that magazine as well.

Most of all, I am thankful for my memories of the hundreds of Vietnamese officers, NCOs, and the unsung heroic RF and PF soldiers with whom I served and fought, laughed and cried, and who walked with me in the sun and the rain in Hàm Long and Mỏ Cày Districts. This is their story, not mine.

Table of Contents

Table of Contents

Preface

This book is not about me. It is about the dedicated, courageous Vietnamese officers and soldiers with whom I worked and supported as we fought against the common enemy.

It was my honor to work with dozens of courageous Regional Force (RF) and Popular Force (PF) soldiers, most of whom were defending their own homes and villages. The vignettes in this book are filled with descriptions of bravery, stoicism, pain, and dedication. These people were not fighting to defend the leadership of the Republic of Vietnam or the concepts of nationalism and democracy. They were fighting for their family, for their friends, for their neighbors. Like the American soldier, bless every one of them; they fought for the soldiers on their left and right, their hooch-mates, their outpost mates, their friends. And unlike American soldiers in Vietnam, they often fought with their family members almost literally by their side, who often lived in the same small muddy outpost as the soldiers. I am determined to tell THEIR story.

Several of these chapters are about my individual counterparts. I was able to tell their stories in several articles published in professional journals in past years. In this book I paraphrase those texts because I want you to know their personal story. Details on accessing the original article are included. I thank *Vietnam Magazine* and *Infantry Magazine* for giving me permission to include some of those words in this book. These sections are very important to me, and each time I read them again I feel emotions quickly rise and tears flow.

This book is also about an American advisor who worked at the district level in Vietnam's Mekong Delta region at a time when the number of American military personnel declined precipitously—1971 to early 1973. The chapters about my life as an advisor are descriptive of my surroundings with my Vietnamese counterparts. Circumstances like mine and my colleagues on Advisory Team 88, Kiến Hòa Province, were completely different from those experienced by American soldiers during their arduous assignments in a large combat unit or as support troops in comfortable base camps and cities. An advisor's surrounding environment, living conditions, and tactical operations were different from those described in any number of excellent books written by Vietnam Veterans whose service was on the ground with an American tactical unit or in the air piloting helicopters or working with air force fast movers providing tactical air support.

In telling my story as an advisor, besides emphasizing my Vietnamese counterparts, I also tell about some of my Advisory Team 88 comrades at the province level and on other district advisory teams. Several of them have contributed their experiences to this book. Many had experiences just like mine but have not written of them. Some were wounded in action, and some were killed in action. All of them gave great service to the United States of America.

My personal library of books about Vietnam War history and memoirs once reached more than 500 volumes. I was struck by the fact that, in all of my bookcases, there were fewer than a dozen books written by advisors who had lived and fought out in the districts with the Vietnamese RF/PF soldier. That's why I sat down and wrote this book. It has taken me more than 50 years to organize my thoughts and memories, and I am sure I have left out too much that I just plain forgot.

In telling about my experiences as a district advisor in a dangerous province, you will find no blood-and-guts combat descriptions. There were plenty of those events, but I lack the memory, and the words, to recount the description of what happened in those frequent short and sharp contacts with the enemy. It is more important to emphasize the unique relationship between advisor and counterpart and how, together, that unusual combination worked well, at least in my case.

Everyone's war was different, depending on where one was assigned, whom one worked for and with, and when in the war those experiences took place. I know that many advisors had a much more difficult experience than I did and experienced far more brutal combat. Likewise, many advisors lived in cities and towns, had access to air-conditioning, a real bed and mattress, and not much risk to life and limb. Everyone's war was different. I'm just telling about my experiences and those of my Vietnamese counterparts, and if I have misled or offended anyone in the telling, I apologize.

Introduction

This book is about my 18 months as a district-level advisor in two districts in the Mekong Delta of the Republic of Vietnam from July 1971 to February 1973. It has been difficult for me to commit all of these memories to paper. Although 50 years have passed, the memories are still sharp in some ways but very hazy in others. I can remember highlights—for 10 percent of those days—but I have difficulty remembering what I actually did for much of the other 90 percent. I thought it best to write down what I can, now, before everything fades away.

During and right after my advisory assignment in Vietnam, I started writing down "bullets" of remembrances under the general rubric of "Happiness Is…." From time to time I also wrote down longer memories, never more than a short paragraph in length. These very short vignettes appear throughout the book. I have separated these soon-afterwards "happiness" items and identified them to you by using periods before them (….) and italic font. Then, as best I could, I filled in as many details as I could remember.

This is the first time I have tried to put my personal experience into an organized written form. I did not take enough pictures. I did not keep a diary. I seldom carried a camera on combat operations—it was one more thing to carry, a few more ounces of weight, and I didn't want to worry about ruining it while wading across canals, through the mud, and falling off monkey bridges. I have virtually no photographs of any combat experiences or enemy contacts because either I did not carry a camera on those operations or mostly because taking pictures when I was trying to fight back or control air strikes was last on my list of things to do. I've taken the pictures I have and tried to match them with experiences, memories, and events I still recall. It's mostly accurate but is by no means complete.

I write in military-ese because the story flows better using military terminology and acronyms, considering that is how I thought of those events or experiences at the time, and it is more natural to tell the story that way. I have tried to list all of those non-civilian terms (see

Appendix IV: Military Terminology) so I don't have to keep explaining them chapter after chapter.

I am sure that I have permanently blocked out some unpleasant experiences from my memory bank. When I recall difficult times, I tell the story with what seems like unusual restraint—that is because I guess it is still too difficult for me to relate what really happened, what I really saw. There are no blood-and-guts accounts of firefights and violence in this book. Even in my first contact, I remember it in slow motion. I honestly do not remember what those four dead enemy soldiers looked like or who shot them. Instead of making something up, I have "down-described" it.

Every person's war in Vietnam was different. Everything depended on where you were, when you were there, and who you served with. Two people in the same place at the same time will remember things with different details and from differing viewpoints. That is the way it was. I tried to do my best in this telling, and I apologize in advance if I missed telling it exactly right. I wish I had stayed in better contact with my American comrades-in-arms in Kiến Hòa Province and told a broader story of what it was like to be an advisor in a rural district of a dangerous province.

One question that friends and family usually do not ask but strangers do is, "What was it really like in combat?" This is a very difficult question to ponder and to answer. It is not something I am comfortable discussing with anyone who has not also been in combat. It is especially difficult to talk about it with family and close friends. It has taken almost 50 years for me to attempt to put "pen to paper" to sort out what it was like *at the time* but to explain it in "today" time. So here goes.

My first assignment in Vietnam, December 1967 through November 1968, was with the 9th Military Intelligence Detachment, 9th Infantry Division (summarized in the Prologue). It was not too dangerous. I was always stationed on a large U.S. base camp or city—successively Bearcat, Dong Tam, and Mỹ Tho. The main threat was from enemy mortar attacks on the base camps and from ambushes as I rode from place to place on the road network. I saw some blood but not much.

I was never in combat during my year with the 9th Infantry Division. I chafed at snide remarks about "MI pukes" that implied we deliberately avoided contact with the enemy. I carried a very large chip on my shoulder because of those disparaging comments.

So, what changed when I arrived in Kiến Hòa Province and lived in a small, barely secure Vietnamese compound, with no large tactical units (U.S. or Vietnamese) around, and confronted lots of enemy soldiers in a province always in the bottom five, security-wise, in the entire country?

To this day, I don't know. Somehow the once-shy, never-in-good-shape, nonathletic, glasses-wearing guy turned into a tiger (Big Grin). I lost about 40 pounds from a change in diet; the rigors of the hot, humid climate; and the arduous physical activity involved in day-to-day work. I found muscles I didn't know I had, trained them, and in short order I was in the best physical condition of my entire life.

Intellectually and realistically I knew I was always in danger, either from a mortar attack, ambush, booby traps and mines or from a confrontational firefight with the enemy. I enjoyed the environment and reveled in my situation. As one of my shortest vignettes reveals, at one moment I was at peace with the idea that I might not leave Kiến Hòa Province alive. It did not bother me.

Most of the district-level advisors in Kiến Hòa Province went to the field on some form of operation. I looked forward to my turn and sought out opportunities to accompany my counterparts to the field, whether on a simple visit to a village office or on a search operation looking for contact with the enemy. My counterparts took a few weeks to get used to me and to decide I was to be trusted and would be an asset in the field. After that, they automatically assumed I was willing to go on operations of any kind.

When we got into a firefight, I felt the adrenaline flow, and yes, I was scared. But I knew what I was doing. I had gone through infantry training (a long time ago). I had the right equipment. I knew my weapon, and I was a good shot. I trusted the soldiers I was with in the field. It was second nature to me how to act, or react, when danger struck. (Read Chapter 6, titled "First Contact.") The atmosphere and description of 30 minutes of close combat in that situation says it all.

At 6'2" I was always the tallest and largest person on tactical operations, so I was a natural target. I made it easier for the enemy because I always carried the advisory team's PRC-25 radio and added another antenna to the command group silhouette.

I have no idea how many enemy soldiers I personally killed. The maximum confirmed number might be four enemy soldiers, all in that "first contact" incident when my counterpart insisted that I was the one who had shot them. In subsequent contacts I fired my rifle at the enemy but do not know if I hit anyone. However, an aggressive employment of air strikes, particularly during the three months I served as district senior advisor in Hàm Long, would have resulted in the deaths of dozens, if not hundreds, of enemy soldiers. That never bothered me in the slightest. They were enemy soldiers doing their best to try to kill me.

I am absolutely, positively confident that I never even once caused an innocent civilian to die.

I did not have to deal with wounded or dead American soldiers, which might have made a difference in my attitude. Instead I dealt on a regular basis with wounded and dead RF and PF soldiers. I felt they were my soldiers and felt the same sense of responsibility for them and the same outrage and sense of loss when one of them died. I shed a lot of tears over the bodies of RF/PF soldiers killed in outposts or when helping with first aid for soldiers suffering from grave wounds before a medevac helicopter arrived.

I never took things for granted. I respected the enemy, whether local VC or invading NVA soldiers. They were good fighters, and they endured great physical discomfort and hardship. On the other hand I despised the Viet Cong Infrastructure (VCI), whose tactics of terror and torture were despicably carried out against unarmed local officials, schoolteachers, and their families. Perhaps I transposed them in my mind during tactical firefights.

I do not have bad memories or nightmares. I have suffered a light case of PTSD for the rest of my life since Vietnam. Exposure to Agent Orange caused cancer which, hopefully, has been in remission for more than ten years now. Memories of my 18 months as an advisor in the Mekong Delta reoccur all the time. The impact is obvious.

A word about peoples' names. The main purpose of this book is to tell the stories of the brave and dedicated RF/PF soldiers and ARVN officers and NCOs with whom I worked on a daily basis for 18 months. I must also be conscious of the political realities in Vietnam and the terrible conditions inflicted on "our side" survivors during years of brutal incarceration in so-called reeducation centers. The passage of 50 years, and the fact that most of my counterparts were roughly my age, means that those who have survived are in their 70s and 80s, and their previous status is well known to contemporary Vietnamese security interests. I am using the real names of most people, American and Vietnamese, who I know were killed in action during the war or have since passed away over the years. I also use the real names of some Vietnamese counterparts whose status I am sure is known to security offices. My understanding is that the status of former ARVN personnel and RF/PF soldiers is well known, and any punishment has long since been imposed on them. Nevertheless, there are some Vietnamese who had close associations with Americans, or who had special roles or intelligence connections, who might not be known to government authorities. I have given pseudonyms to them and have identified them throughout the book by "not his real name." I have also protected them by not using photographs of them in this book. I use pseudonyms for some Americans identified in this book with "not his real name" in order to protect their privacy. Those still living have given me permission to use their real names. I am grateful for their assistance in remembering what happened in Kiến Hòa Province all those many years ago.

A short note about the "f-word." You will see it only a few times in this book. It is not in my personal vocabulary. In this book it is either a direct quote from another person or a descriptive phrase so inherent in use that it only makes sense to include it. My apologies if anyone is offended.

The 18 months I spent as an advisor remain among the most ingrained memories and recollections of my entire life, so obviously it had a huge impact on me. Sometimes it seems like it was only yesterday. So be it.

Prologue

My first Vietnam tour of duty began in November 1967. It was not a surprise. In discussions with the Military Intelligence branch assignments officer, he told me I was due for a Vietnam assignment. If I volunteered, I could choose the type of assignment I would get. I volunteered, specified assignment to a tactical command and, at all costs, no assignment to MACV Headquarters or one of the several military intelligence commands already in Vietnam. The assignments officer kept his promise—I was assigned to the 9th Military Intelligence Detachment, 9th Infantry Division.

Departure from home was more emotional than I expected. My father, a retired colonel who had served in both New Guinea and Europe during World War II, cried and said he should go instead of me because he knew what war was like. My youngest brother, age nine, stood up tall, stuck out his hand for a farewell handshake, and said, "It's been nice knowing you." Mother and my other five siblings were all trying to hold back tears, mostly unsuccessful. I was a wreck.

Departure from Travis Air Force Base, California, was hectic but organized. The charter flight stopped for refueling in Honolulu, Guam, Clark Air Base in the Philippines and arrived at Bien Hoa Air Base in Vietnam early in the morning. Getting out of the airplane, through processing, reclaiming luggage, all the while dealing with the heat, the humidity, and the new and totally strange smells was a madhouse. Shortly I was on a bus with heavy wire mesh on the windows and driven to the 90th Replacement Battalion reception station on the huge Long Binh base camp. It took three days, but my orders to the 9th Infantry Division were confirmed. Soon I was on a two-and-a-half-ton truck for the relatively short ride to Bearcat, the division headquarters southeast of Long Binh.

I procured a ride to the 9th MI Detachment, and there I was, standing amid a small pile of baggage and field gear in front of the detachment orderly room. I went inside and met the detachment commander, first sergeant, and company clerk. I put in a month of work as an administrative officer and then became chief of the Interrogation of Prisoners of War (IPW) section. I settled in; learned my job; met my lieutenants, NCOs, interpreters, and the attached ARVN MI Detachment; and got to work.

As Christmas 1967 neared, I sent my Christian interpreters home for a week, and then a month later, as Tết neared, I sent my Buddhist interpreters home for a week. And then came the 1968 Tết Offensive. As enemy attacks hit all over the Mekong Delta, I had two interpreters at work. One of them went with the ARVN MI Detachment and one of my American NCOs to Long Binh, where they interrogated captured and wounded Vietcong POWs right on the field of battle. The detachment commander sent me and the other interpreter, together with one G-2 section officer and our own dedicated helicopter, and we flew all around the Delta trying to compile an enemy order of battle. It took us three days. Then back to Bearcat and 24-hour days of interrogations in the MP POW cage and in the hospital.

At the end of February, the CO called me into his office and told me the assistant division commander at the division's forward base camp at Dong Tam was unhappy with his tactical intelligence support. He reassigned me as Commander (Forward) of the 9th MI Detachment, and I left immediately. Dong Tam was to be the new division headquarters, built on sand dredged out of the Mekong River, west of the Định Tường Province capital of Mỹ Tho, about 35 miles southwest of Saigon. I took charge of the IPW interrogators and the counterintelligence special agents at Dong Tam and the brigade base camp at Tân An and kept the title of IPW Section Chief for organizational accounting.

I reported to the unhappy Assistant Division Commander, Brigadier General William Knowlton. He gave me my marching orders: get the information organized and reported as quickly as possible; type up the written reports later. He was very supportive of the importance of intelligence and our work. He was an inspiring boss to me, a young captain in a chaotic wartime situation. I consider General Knowlton to be the finest military boss of my 30-year army career.

Since we were an ad hoc organization with no direct support elements, I put my NCOs to work scrounging up everything we needed and my best personal style to work at smoothing feathers. We had our own much-too-large barracks building for the 25 of us—U.S. army officers, NCOs, Vietnamese ARVN interrogators, and ARVN interpreters. We wrested enough sandbags to build two bunkers for protection from the nightly mortar attacks. We traded captured souvenirs to the medical company to keep the barracks building and to the military police company for use of their mess hall. The artillery folks agreed to maintain our jeeps.

We worked our asses off on prisoner interrogations, counterintelligence operations, and liaisons with intelligence organizations and advisors for the 7th ARVN Division, Định Tường Province, the Navy Intelligence Liaison Officer, and the CIA, all in the city of Mỹ Tho. We used an acquired Boston Whaler with a "borrowed" Special Services outboard motor and went back and forth to Mỹ Tho on the Mekong River, considered much safer than the single gravel road.

In June 1968 the entire 9th Division headquarters moved to Dong Tam. I had to adjust to the presence of a new detachment commander, the obnoxious division commander, and the division staff. I adjusted poorly, unable to accept with equanimity the poor senior leadership that replaced the now-departed people who had worked for BG Knowlton. I had to change from being in charge of our ad hoc but well-received operations to the spit and polish of the new environment. The detachment commander did not like me spending evenings teaching English conversation to the ARVN MI Detachment Commander, nor did he like me socializing with the interpreters who had worked for me in both Bearcat and Dong Tam. I was not a happy camper.

When General Creighton Abrams took over as COMUS MACV, he instituted a new policy as a component of his emphasis on Vietnamization. He directed that all U.S. commands establish a full-time liaison with the Vietnamese officials, ARVN units, their American advisors, and other intelligence components operating in the same province. For the 9th Infantry Division that meant the city of Mỹ Tho. The detachment commander assigned me as the 9th Infantry Division Liaison Officer, and in August 1968 I moved to Mỹ Tho. I was released from the tight constraints of Dong Tam.

It was like night and day—throw me into that briar patch! I was given housing in Embassy House, the CIA station office and billets. In addition to those highly professional intelligence officers, the Province Reconnaissance Unit (PRU) advisor also lived in Embassy House. My primary assignment was to work in the Provincial Intelligence and Operations Coordination Center (PIOCC) that was charged with responsibility for the Phoenix/*Phụng Hoàng* program targeted against the Viet Cong Infrastructure (VCI). My American cohort was the captain who served as the Province Assistant Intelligence Advisor (S-2). Our nominal boss was the major who was the Advisory Team S-2.

I thoroughly enjoyed the new environment. I found the advisors with whom I worked and lived to be thoroughly professional colleagues, cooperative workers striving toward a common objective. My routine included attending the daily afternoon wrap-up briefings at the Seminary, where most of the advisory contingent lived. I enjoyed working with the advisors and made a firm decision that if and when I received a later assignment back to Vietnam, I wanted to be an advisor.

My assignment ended in November 1968. I returned to Dong Tam about a week before my DEROS, reclaimed my downstairs room in the officers BOQ, and prepared for departure. I was so disillusioned with the poor leadership of the second half of my 9th Infantry Division assignment that I made the decision to take a break and requested a two-year release from active duty in order to pursue a master's degree at the University of Kansas in Lawrence. I had over five years on active duty under my belt and fully anticipated a return to active service once I had attained my master's degree.

My academic year began in January 1969. The cold, windy winter climate in Kansas was a shock to the system. My degree program was a pleasant two-year stretch of academic classes, a three-month summer internship, and a final semester of distance learning and periodic scheduled on-campus seminars. The GI Bill covered most of the costs, and the army was kind enough to fund TDY travel to attend the on-campus seminars. I earned a master's degree in public administration and managed to coexist with the civilian academic community in Lawrence.

I made a formal request for recall to active duty, and the army—still in need of live captains—was happy to comply. In June 1970 I returned to active duty and attended the Military Intelligence Officer Advanced Course at Fort Holabird, Maryland.

And so began the next leg of my 30-year military career.

1

So, You Want to
Be a District Advisor?

In June 1970 I returned to active duty as a senior captain after completing the on-campus portion of my master's degree program at the University of Kansas. I spent the first nine months attending the Military Intelligence Officers Advanced Course (Career Course) at Fort Holabird, Maryland.

During the Career Course, I contacted the MI branch assignments officer to get an idea of my next assignment—I assumed that I would be headed back to Vietnam for a second tour of duty in the war zone. I recalled the rewarding three months I had experienced during the time I had been detached from the 9th Infantry Division as liaison officer to the American advisory teams in Mỹ Tho (recounted in the Prologue). I admired their work, and those three months had given me a good idea of how I wanted my second assignment to go.

By 1970, the American military situation in Vietnam had changed. The drawdown of U.S. military units was well underway. "Vietnamization" and a much-needed emphasis on the Phoenix/*Phụng Hoàng* program against the VCI created a high demand for MI advisors. I immediately volunteered for assignment as a *Phụng Hoàng* coordinator, so I knew early on that I was going back to Vietnam as an advisor. I graduated from the Career Course in March 1971.

After completing the Career Course, I joined several classmates to attend the three-month Military Assistance Security Advisor (MASA) course at Fort Bragg, North Carolina. Our class ran from 29 March through 27 June 1971. The course was designed for officers projected to become intelligence advisors to support the Phoenix/*Phụng Hoàng* program to attack the VCI. The course combined six weeks of basic Vietnamese language with blocks of instruction dealing with the *Phụng Hoàng* program (from now on referred to as PH), the advisory system and chain of command, and the science and tactics of intelligence support to counterinsurgency operations. The course was a shorter parallel to the Military Assistance Tactical Advisor (MATA) course for combat arms officers headed to District Senior Advisor (DSA) slots.

While at Fort Bragg, we were allowed to select one of the four geographical Corps areas in Vietnam as our destination. This Corps selection was "guaranteed" as one of the benefits of volunteering for the PH advisory program. The destination Corps headquarters would then make assignments to a province after in-processing and interviews. Because of my prior experience in the Mekong Delta, I chose IV Corps, figuring that my knowledge of the region would be beneficial both to my advisory assignment and to me.

Back to the Mekong Delta

By late June 1971, I was finally finished with almost three years of school at the University of Kansas and army courses. I was eager to get to Vietnam. After a short farewell visit with my family near Fort Belvoir, Virginia, I headed west to Travis Air Force Base and another contract charter flight to Saigon. The flight left Travis on 7 July 1971. I was one of the more senior officers on the big 707 aircraft—a captain with more than five years in grade—so I got to sit in a window seat toward the front of the plane. I don't remember our route. Nor do I remember the folkloric, steep, rapid descent onto a runway at Tân Sơn Nhứt Air Base. But I definitely remembered the unique smell of Vietnam that smacked everyone in the face the moment the aircraft door was opened!

On my earlier assignment I had gone to a U.S. Army Vietnam (USARV) tactical unit and had been processed at USARV's 90th Replacement Battalion at the huge military base at Long Binh. This time, as a MACV assignee, I was processed at MACV Headquarters adjacent to Tân Sơn Nhứt Air Base. I was billeted at Camp Alpha, which I remembered well as the start and end point for R&R travel. The processing was much the same—I received combat gear, an M-16 rifle, and a steel bunk and mattress in the wood-and-screen-sided officers open-bay BOQ to await my assignment orders. I filled out a lot of paperwork and attended several days of briefings inside MACV Headquarters.

When we received our Corps assignments, several of them were screwed up. Although "guaranteed" assignment to IV Corps, I was initially told I was going north to II Corps in central Vietnam. A classmate who had requested II Corps was told he was going to IV Corps. The two of us quickly went to the admin office and got ourselves "traded" to the correct region we had selected. My friend ended up in Phú Yên Province, where he lived in an air-conditioned trailer on a district advisory team just outside the province capital of Tuy Hòa. As for me, once I left those briefings at MACV Headquarters, the only air-conditioning I experienced was when I went out of Vietnam on R&R. Everyone's war was different!

Soon I was on a plane from Tân Sơn Nhứt Air Base flying to Cần Thơ, the location of IV Corps Headquarters. The table-flat green mosaic of rice paddies contrasted with the ribbons of brown water ranging from huge branches of the Mekong River to tiny canals tying everything together. I had seen this frequently during my prior Vietnam assignment and remembered it well. Once in Cần Thơ, I spent several days in a small commercial hotel that was used as officers' billets while the personnel office went over my records. In the process I was reunited with "Skoshie," an ARVN sergeant who had been one of my interpreters in the 9th MI Detachment in 1968. Now he was assigned to IV Corps headquarters. He also had his own business as the owner of several small hotels, including the one where I was billeted. He leased some of his hotels to the Americans and some to the dollies—"short time" hotels. Skoshie always was an operator.

As part of the processing sequence of interviews, I recounted my experience and knowledge of the northern IV Corps provinces where the 9th Infantry Division had operated. That prior experience certainly guided the personnel section—I was assigned to Kiến Hòa Province,

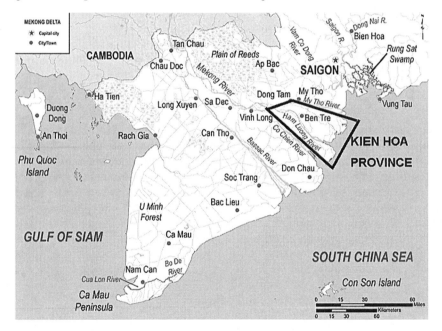

Map 1: Location of Kiến Hòa Province (Library of Congress).

directly across the river from the former 9th Division base camp at Dong Tam. So about a week after arriving in Vietnam, I was riding to Bến Tre in an Air America Porter aircraft, which could, and did, land and take off in a very short distance. One time a pilot took off *across* the runway in Cần Thơ just to show me how nimble his airplane was.

Kiến Hòa Province Welcome

It was July 1971, the rainy season, when I arrived in the small military airstrip serving Bến Tre, the province capital, at about 1000 hours on a hot, humid morning. An admin NCO met the plane, I tossed my luggage into the van and hopped in for the ride to the Advisory Team 88 compound. The narrow, paved two-lane highway was crowded with bicycles, trucks, military vehicles of all types, animals, and pedestrians.

The van driver dropped me off at the MACV province advisory team compound. It occupied a large city block next to the Bến Tre River and across a narrow side street from the province chief's official residential compound. The advisory team compound was a crowded complex of many single-story buildings, the lower half built of whitewashed cement block and the upper half heavy-screened, louvered windows, with sheet rock or tin roofing to shed rain. A small Vietnamese-style villa housed the small team club, mail room, and the compound store. A high stucco wall topped with sharp, pointed steel arrows ran all the way around the compound. A wide main street sidewalk ran from the main gate on the side-street entrance into the compound, with perpendicular branches to billets and offices. The mess hall and billets for officers and NCOs lined both sides, with supply and administrative offices behind.

When I entered the main gate into the compound, the NCO on guard duty directed me to the mess hall, the first building on the right. The advisory team administrative officer came in and introduced himself. He brought me a welcoming cup of coffee and briefed me about Advisory Team 88, the personalities on the province team, and the general situation in the province. He took me on a quick tour around the compound and pointed out the important offices I would be dealing with in the coming months—the administrative office, the logistics and supply area, and the club. Then he escorted me outside and across the main street to the large province headquarters compound and dropped me off at the small side building holding the province PH coordinator's office. Major John McHaven (not his real name), the province PH coordinator and a fellow MI branch officer, was glad to see me and gave me a warm welcome. He went right into a concise briefing on the PH program in Kiến Hòa

Province, details of his job and mine, and what would be expected of me at the district level. He told me that I was assigned to Hàm Long District. The current PH coordinator there was due to depart in two days on his DEROS move home, and the district senior advisor (DSA) was on his 30-day home leave. "We've got to have an officer out there," he said.

Anticipating a concern I had, he explained the officer rating system. He was "coordinator" of the PH program and thus a member of the province staff. My efficiency reports would run through the operational chain of command—rated by my DSA, and my senior rater would be either the province senior advisor (PSA) or the deputy province senior advisor (DPSA). With no further ado, he walked me across the province headquarters complex to the senior advisors' offices at one end of the province headquarters building and introduced me to the Advisory Team 88 DPSA. I reported, "present for duty, sir," to Lieutenant Colonel William Tausch, an infantry officer on his second tour of duty in Vietnam. He commanded all the U.S. military personnel on the advisory team because the PSA was a civilian. He apparently held an abiding mistrust of MI officers in general. His greeting to me was not auspicious.

"Oh, great," he said, "just what I need, another fucking MI officer."

He was more pleased when I showed him the 9th Infantry Division patch on my right shoulder that signified my prior combat duty with that unit, and I told him about my previous assignment across the river at Dong Tam and Mỹ Tho.

Usually new arrivals to Advisory Team 88 got an immediate interview with the PSA and then a two- or three-day orientation trip around to the eight districts that still had advisory teams. However, I was told there would be no time to do this because of the rush to get me to Hàm Long. The PSA, Mr. Albert L. "Buck" Kotzebue, returned from home leave a week or so later, and I met him then. I never did get that orientation tour.

Major McHaven then took me to the nearby heavily fortified joint U.S./Vietnamese tactical operations center (TOC) for a quick orientation, then back to the compound for lunch. I met many of the province team members over lunch and got warm welcomes from everyone. With 170 military personnel assigned to Advisory Team 88, and a good number of them assigned to jobs in Bến Tre, names and faces were hard to keep straight. Chief delight: meeting the PH coordinator in Giồng Trôm District, who told me that one of my interpreters from the 9th MI Detachment, Sergeant First Class Hồ Văn Bé, was assigned to the Giồng Trôm District advisory team. I immediately made plans to meet SFC Bé, and at my urging, within a month or so, the Hàm Long DSA and Giồng Trôm DSA arranged a trade of interpreters. Sergeant Bé would remain with me for the rest of the time I was in Kiến Hòa Province. After lunch, the admin officer took me to his office for a detailed

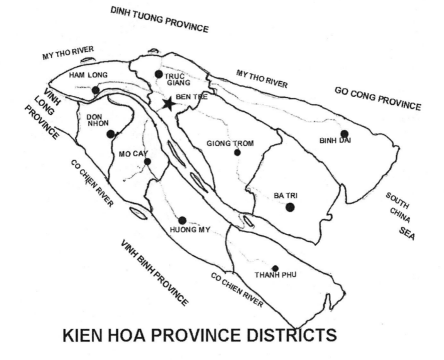

KIEN HOA PROVINCE DISTRICTS

Map 2: Kiến Hòa Province with district boundaries (expanded by author from cover page sketch, *Advisory Team 88 Kien Hoa Province Briefing Folder*, Bến Tre, Vietnam, undated).

briefing on advisory team strength and the locations of everyone assigned at the district level. Like my PH briefing, it was a concise introduction to Kiến Hòa Province and the people I would be working with.

Introduction to Kiến Hòa Province

Kiến Hòa Province (its name was changed to Bến Tre Province after 1975) is located in the Mekong Delta approximately 85 kilometers (50 miles) southwest of Saigon. In 1971 (and until roughly 2008) it was accessible only by boat or air. Three main branches of the Mekong River separate the province from the "mainland" of the rest of Vietnam. The only approved vehicular and passenger ferry route to and from Kiến Hòa Province was from the city of Mỹ Tho (capital of Định Tường Province) to the Kiến Hòa Province ferry landing at Tân Thạch. The river was a couple miles wide at that point, and the ferry route zigzagged around the ends of two large riverine islands.

Several ferries constantly shuttled back and forth at the same time, and dozens of small private boats, water taxis, and sampans also shuttled back and forth all up and down the river. As I was soon to learn, the VC/NVA also shuttled back and forth using those sampans and water taxis. The large ferry boats carried everything imaginable, from buses and trucks, military vehicles of all sizes, cars, motorcycles, bicycles, and people to animals of all sizes and shapes. It was always a colorful crossing.

The province is broken into two main segments, further divided by rivers and canals. The "upper island" included the districts of Hàm Long, Trúc Giang, Bình Đại, Giồng Trôm, and Ba Tri. The "lower island" districts of Đôn Nhơn, Mỏ Cày, Hương Mỹ, and Thạnh Phú were separated from the rest of the province by the Hàm Luông River. The only approved ferry connection went from just west of Bến Tre across to Thanh Tân village in Mỏ Cày District. The Cổ Chiên River formed the southern boundary of the province, across from which is Vĩnh Bình Province. There were no government-approved ferry crossings between Kiến Hòa and Vĩnh Bình provinces. Kiến Hòa's westernmost district, Đôn Nhơn, had a land boundary with the Vĩnh Long Province district of Chợ Lách. (After 1975, Chợ Lách was transferred to Bến Tre Province.)

The Mekong River has nine mouths to the South China Sea as it spreads out to form the huge rice-rich Mekong Delta. The four major rivers are split by large riverine islands where the rivers meet the South China Sea, which provides for the total of "nine mouths." The first split is at Phnom Penh, Cambodia, where the Mekong River separates into the northern Mekong and the southern Bassac. At Vĩnh Long the Mekong separates into the northern Tiền Giang and the southern Cổ Chiên. At the western tip of Kiến Hòa Province, at Hàm Long District, the Tiền Giang separates into the northern Mỹ Tho and the next lower Hàm Luông. Both the upper and lower islands of the province are crisscrossed by lesser rivers and canals of all sizes. The entire province is flat and probably no more than one meter above sea level at high tide. All canals and rivers are tidal, which means that ease of movement across these waterways is strongly dependent on the tides, water conditions, and timing. All of those waterways were barriers to troop movement.

Kiến Hòa was one of the most populous provinces in South Vietnam, with a population in 1971 of just over 550,000. Bến Tre was the largest city (approximately 75,000 in 1971); the second-largest town was Mỏ Cày. Like all 44 provinces, Kiến Hòa was divided into districts (nine) and villages (many), both of which had political boundaries delineating their territory. Villages are made up of many hamlets, where people lived.

Throughout the Vietnam War, Kiến Hòa Province was always in the bottom five in security of all 44 provinces. The province has a long history of revolutionary and communist support. The Việt Minh communist movement began in Mỏ Cày District in the 1930s, and at the end of World War II, the Việt Minh took control of the entire province. The reasons for this included strong anti-colonial feelings against the French colonial government, a mostly poor, rural agrarian culture dominated by wealthy absentee landlords, and the geographic isolation of the province because of the several branches of the Mekong River. The National Liberation Front (NLF) was founded in Mỏ Cày District in 1960, and several senior Vietcong leaders were natives of that district. Mỏ Cày was the least pacified district in the province and the one with the most enemy-controlled villages.

Despite the low level of security in Kiến Hòa Province, in 1971 there were no regular force ARVN units stationed in the province. The closest was the 7th ARVN Division, with its headquarters in Mỹ Tho. The 9th ARVN Division headquarters was in Sa Đéc Province and later Vĩnh Long Province, and the 21st ARVN Division was further south in the Delta. The only full-time security units in Kiến Hòa Province were the large number of Regional Force (RF) companies and Popular Force (PF) platoons. Their weapons were not as new, and they lacked the heavy firepower of a main force ARVN unit. It was not until 1971 that many PF and local hamlet security forces got the M-16 rifle. I spent all of my time with the RF/PF soldiers and gained great respect for them, despite occasional problems with lack of aggressiveness and poor leadership. Although called by many American soldiers derisively as the Ruff-Puffs, I never, ever used that term.

When I arrived in Bến Tre for my one-year assignment, I did not know how my time in Kiến Hòa Province would play out. As it turned out, I extended my assignment by six months and would be assigned in two different districts and would move back and forth between them. That movement was caused by the drawdown in numbers of American troops, the fortunes of war, the strength of the enemy, and casualties on Advisory Team 88. I've tried to keep the train of events in this book in chronological order.

Bến Tre—"We Had to Destroy the City in Order to Save It"

Bến Tre was badly mauled during the 1968 Tet Offensive. Heavy fighting between the attacking VC and NVA forces and the defending ARVN units, U.S. advisors, and 9th Infantry Division units took its toll. At one point the VC/NVA had seized almost the entire city except for the large city blocks around the MACV compound, the province headquarters complex, and the province chief's residence. I had been on the ground in Bến Tre at the height of the 1968 Tet Offensive as part of my intelligence duties at the 9th MI Detachment, so I had seen the city when it was in a really terrible condition. The 9th Infantry Division officer interviewed by the press spoke the now-famous quotation about saving the city from the invading enemy forces.

When I returned in July 1971, Bến Tre was a marvel—rebuilt from 1968, the scars from that Tet Offensive all but gone. A sturdy, workaday city, Bến Tre functioned very well. Much of the downtown had been completely rebuilt, and the city still had areas of attractive older architecture, religious structures, and parks. In the course of 18 months in Kiến Hòa Province I was in the city many times for short housekeeping chores and many overnight stays associated with the monthly meetings of DSAs and district chiefs and the PH advisors.

The usual landing zone for transport helicopters, including the province swing ship and visual reconnaissance helicopters, was the advisory team's landing pad constructed on a steel pier over the Bến Tre River next to the compound. The Bến Tre soccer field, located at the entrance to the city on the main highway from the Tân Thạch ferry landing, provided a bigger landing zone used for larger helicopters and for tactical air assault formations.

When I arrived in Kiến Hòa Province in July 1971, the total number of U.S. military personnel in Vietnam was about 160,000, down from 334,600 the previous year.[1] In early 1971 there were 179 military personnel assigned to MACV Advisory Team 88. That number declined each month from casualties and as men reached their DEROS. Of that number, 70 people were assigned at the province level of the advisory team, while 46 were assigned to district advisory teams (an average of five to six men per district advisory team), and 63 were assigned to the Mobile Assistance and Training (MAT) Teams subordinate to both the province team and to individual districts throughout the province.[2] However, by the time I arrived in July 1971, that number of 179 military personnel had been reduced substantially. Most MAT Team personnel had been reassigned, and district teams were reduced to between two and four people. Several dozen U.S. civilians were also assigned to the team, primarily working on the various pacification programs. In September 1972, the latest roster I was able to find, there were only 42 military personnel, 27 assigned to the province headquarters team and 15 assigned to the districts—averaging two persons per district.[3]

Ba Tri District: Showcase for Advisory Success— and Advisory Strength Cutbacks

Ba Tri District was a showcase for successful pacification efforts in Kiến Hòa Province. It was the second-largest district in population, with almost 100,000 people, second only to Trúc Giang District, which included the city of Bến Tre. Mr. Norris Nordvold arrived in Vietnam on his first Vietnam assignment in August 1968, with the U.S. Agency for International Development (USAID), a part of the U.S. State Department. He spent several months in Saigon, but then a friend and Vietnamese language school classmate serving as DSA in Ba Tri wrangled a transfer. Mr. Nordvold became DDSA in Ba Tri to a fellow USAID colleague. The two of them made Ba Tri the first district in Vietnam to have civilians serving as both DSA and DDSA.

Mr. Nordvold noted that the coastal Ba Tri District was very flat and low-lying, and perhaps its most unusual physical characteristic was an almost total lack of trees. That greatly reduced the areas where local VC forces could hide and construct small base areas. Most VC forces in Ba Tri were moving between the Cambodian border and further south to the large VC secret zone in coastal Thạnh Phú District, across the wide Hàm Luông River. The lack of suitable secure areas for the VC was a reason for the successful district security program, which made possible a wide range of efforts to benefit the district's large and almost completely agrarian population.

Mr. Nordvold became Ba Tri DSA in August 1969 and served in that position until June 1970, when his Vietnam assignment ended. During his tenure, the district advisory team was very large, with as many as 30 U.S. military and civilian personnel in the district at any one time. Most of the American military officers and NCOs served on several MAT Teams that worked at the village level to train local forces in both military operations and pacification programs. Norris chuckled when he described the process of writing efficiency reports on the many officers and NCOs serving in Ba Tri. "Mr. Kotzebue, the PSA, flew down by helicopter and quickly trained me in the art of writing military efficiency reports to avoid them receiving pink slips out of the army."

The success of pacification and the unique situation with State Department/USAID civilians serving as both DSA and DDSA attracted many senior officers on short visits to Ba Tri, as well as famed journalists such as Joseph Alsop and author Frances Fitzgerald. The successful pacification program in Ba Tri also brought a significant reduction in the American advisory effort. When Mr. Nordvold completed his assignment in 1970, the district advisory team was closed and the many military and civilian advisors were reassigned elsewhere in Vietnam or were returned to the U.S. at the end of their assignments.

Mr. Nordvold returned to Vietnam for a second assignment in September 1971 and was assigned back to Kiến Hòa Province as director of the New Life Development Program and co-assigned as DPSA for

Development. His prior experience as a DSA gave him unparalleled experience in working with U.S. military personnel as well as supervising the variety of civilian pacification programs throughout Kiến Hòa Province. He brought incredible experience and vision to the DPSA post. Perhaps most important, he spoke fluent Vietnamese, and his prior experiences working with Vietnamese government officials in Ba Tri gave him prestige with the province chief and the many Vietnamese officials with whom he worked.

2

Settling In,
Hàm Long District

Arrival in Hàm Long

While I was getting the introductory welcome briefings in Bến Tre, the TOC radioed Hàm Long to inform them that I had arrived and would be ready for pickup in the early afternoon. Just after lunch a jeep and trailer arrived at the province team compound, and I met the Hàm Long PH NCO, Sergeant "Tag" (not his real name), and the soldier assigned as the district team's official driver, Phi (pronounced "Fee"). I was ready to go. I would experience a new situation, with fewer and fewer advisors and smaller and smaller district advisory teams. I looked forward to the challenges that would be coming.

The trip out to Hàm Long was important to me—the road to my new home and a welter of new impressions and thoughts.

... The gravel and tar paved road was a surprise, paving just finished in May ... the place in Tường Dạ where the previous DSA was killed by a command-detonated mine ... can I cut it as an advisor in a strange land? ... a lot of coconut trees ... beautiful rice fields on both sides of the road ... will I be accepted by my counterparts? ... will my previous Vietnam tour be helpful?

We passed through a succession of villages with confusing names that were to become very familiar to me in the months to come. There was a big welcome arch at Sơn Hòa village and a showplace outpost at Đu Đu Dau. Then came hardscrabble Tường Đa, right on the road and a solid D village; VC control started at the coconut trees two klicks north of the road. An Hiệp was beautiful, rice paddies on the north and also coconut trees; its church was built in 1954 by Catholic refugees from North Vietnam who were resettled here. Next was immaculately tidy An Cư hamlet with a gothic church at the head of the "street." An Hiệp Canal was spanned by a section of Bailey bridge donated by the 9th Infantry Division. Then we took a long, open

The arch welcoming visitors to Hàm Long District.

run past Quán Mèo outpost to Thành Triệu, a refugee settlement for people who had escaped VC control. The old heart of the district was two kilometers further north, in a dangerous area, and until 1969, the people were VC-controlled. A bouncy left-hand curve opened up the view of the beautiful Hàm Long Cao Đài temples, one for men and one for women. Headquarters in Hàm Long District was at a fork in the road. The paved left-hand fork led past the compound gate and continued another 600 meters to the Tiên Thủy village market on the Soc Sai River, a narrow branch of the Hàm Luông River. The right-hand fork led out six kilometers to Tân Lợi village and eventually to the tip of the province where the Mekong River split into two major branches as it neared the sea. Out in the middle of nowhere, this was to be my home. It wasn't quite what I had expected, but … I liked it already.

A watchtower rose high out of the center of the compound. The compound was low and cramped with administrative and operational buildings and simple housing for soldiers and families. We swung through the painted compound gate onto the small concrete parking area that doubled as a parade ground. The civilian district headquarters dominated the parade ground; a long row of military staff offices ran down the right side, with the TOC and district chief's quarters behind the watchtower. The large building also included offices for the district chief and deputy district chief as well as the DIOCC. The advisors' team house sat next to the district headquarters building, separated only by a narrow paved walkway. One small Vietnamese-style villa housed the S-4 office; untidy concrete and metal maintenance and supply buildings filled the left side of the compound. Behind the cement block offices and senior officers' quarters was a large area given over to housing for the junior officers and family members and rough barracks for the large complement of enlisted soldiers. The heavily bunkered TOC was behind the row of staff offices.

It was to be my home for a long time.

That weekend the advisory team held a party to say farewell to my predecessor and to welcome me. Besides the American advisors and interpreters, the team house filled up with the Vietnamese district officer corps and senior civilian officials, the men who would be my counterparts for the many coming months. I was nervous, trying to listen carefully to all of the introductions, trying to remember names and place them with faces, trying to match names and faces to their jobs. My short six weeks of Vietnamese language training at Fort Bragg seemed totally inadequate; I was very grateful for the immediate assistance of the team interpreters. It would all become very easy after a while, but the first few days were difficult.

... My discomfort on the first night in Hàm Long, a welcome party where I am under close scrutiny by all those with whom I'll be working for the next year. Easily eating all the food, not dropping my chopsticks, and being very conscious of the many eyes checking me out.

The first week or so went by quickly. My predecessor departed for home the day after the party, and I was suddenly the Acting District Senior

Morning formation in front of district headquarters almost fills the parking area/parade ground. The advisors' team house is visible at the far left.

Advisor! I spent the time meeting the Vietnamese officers who were now my counterparts. Everyone had a smile and a kind word. The graciousness of their simple welcome overwhelmed me. Although they were initially cautious with a newcomer, I was prepared for allowing a period of time to earn their trust and establish that I was an important asset to the district. Over time I established an excellent relationship with all of them. One or another of the interpreters walked around the compound with me, meeting soldiers, family members, learning the layout of the paths behind the main headquarters area. I immediately noticed the many mud bunkers throughout the housing area, which attested to the danger of enemy mortar attacks. It took a while for me to get used to the noise of outgoing friendly artillery again. At least I wasn't automatically rolling out of bed and taking cover; I just woke up. It would be soon enough to again get used to the noise of incoming enemy mortar rounds!

Two weeks after my arrival, the boss, the Hàm Long DSA Major David Kretschmar, returned from home leave. We formed an instant bond, both as boss/subordinate and as friends. He quickly began briefing me about the advisory team missions, problems, key personalities and how to deal with them, living on a small team ... anything and everything I thought I needed to know. Major Kretschmar was well-liked and respected by the Vietnamese, so his "passing me along" to them brought that same respect and friendship to me. We were all off to a very good start.

Phụng Hoàng School

With the DSA back in the district, I was able to break loose for another mandatory training requirement for newly assigned intelligence advisors. I went to the beach resort of Vũng Tàu from 31 July to 11 August for the in-country *Phụng Hoàng* School. The classes were similar to what we had received at Fort Bragg. However, the instructors were experienced advisors who had extended their assignment in Vietnam to live and work in the quiet and attractive city of Vũng Tàu and provide their wealth of expertise to the new guys. Fort Bragg taught "the book," whereas Vũng Tàu taught us "reality on the ground."

The war seemed very far away from the beaches at Vũng Tàu. Rumor had it that the VC also went on R&R there. Long known as Cap Saint Jacques, it had been a favorite getaway for the French colonials and the wealthy of Saigon since the late 19th century. Vũng Tàu was very nice. I was billeted in a comfortable BOQ; we had good chow and could eat at several nice Vietnamese and French restaurants in town if we wanted. To say nothing of going to a beach in the war zone! The white and tan sandy beaches were practically empty. The short time at Vũng Tàu was the most relaxed period of my entire Vietnam assignment.

Getting Settled In

The hustle involved in getting me to Vietnam, to Cần Thơ, to Bến Tre, to Hàm Long, to Vũng Tàu, and then finally "back home" to Hàm Long was finally completed. Now my main challenge was to get used to my advisory teammates, Vietnamese counterparts, my new surroundings, and the missions and challenges of working on a small district advisory team.

There was no district town in Hàm Long—the district headquarters compound was out in the country surrounded by rice paddies and coconut groves. The largest marketplace town was Tân Lợi, about six kilometers west of the district headquarters. The wealthiest marketplace town was Tiên Thủy, about 600 meters south of the compound. A third, much smaller market area, was Sơn Hòa, a large and prosperous village in the far southeast corner of the district.The main district compound was rectangular and contained all of the military offices, the district headquarters, housing for headquarters' soldiers and their families, and the advisors' team house.

Across the road from the main headquarters compound a row of low, one-story concrete office buildings housed the district's various civilian offices, including the *Chieu Hoi* program, Revolutionary Development Cadre, Peoples' Self-Defense Force, and Psyops. Like the buildings in the main compound, these smaller buildings did not have reinforced roofing but were surrounded by barbed wire and a protective mud berm. A smaller compound for the Hàm Long artillery section sat adjacent to the headquarters compound. This compound provided space for two 105 mm U.S. howitzers, ammunition storage, and a building that housed the fire direction center, the section chief's office and sleeping space, and additional smaller buildings for the artillery section soldiers. The artillery compound had its own main gate, and there were smaller interior gates to the headquarters compound. Like the main compound, the perimeter was enclosed with low mud berms and fenced with barbed wire, with extensive protective wire all around the sides. A separate compound for one RF company was across the road from the artillery compound. I learned that one of the RF companies was broken down into platoons that occupied larger outposts throughout the district, while one full company was resident on that compound and conducted operations from the district headquarters. The two companies rotated assignments every six months.

The advisors' team house and small compound sat to the side of the district headquarters building, separated from it only by a narrow walkway. Solidly built of cinder block and concrete walls, a row of windows on three sides provided ventilation. Heavy screens and adjustable wood louvers protected against mosquitoes and all the other bugs and also kept out the monsoon rains. The team house was an open rectangular room that measured about 50 feet by 20 feet with colored patterned floor tiles and a sloped roof with zinc and tin to shed rain. It was comfortable. The large main room had chairs and sofas to lounge in and a large dining table and chairs that doubled as the map and operations planning table. One corner housed a PRC-10 radio that provided communication with province headquarters. A small steel safe held radio codes, ammunition, and the few classified documents we had on hand. A PRC-25 radio leaned against the wall; it went on all field operations. The stove and two refrigerators were powered by gas, so when the electricity went out, the food stayed cool and the stove worked fine.

A similar but smaller cinder block building behind the team house had two rooms, one with a shower, sinks, and mirrors, and the other held a western-style toilet and a 55-gallon drum filled with water; we flushed the toilet with plastic buckets. The water for all this was stored in a rubberized water tank on top of a tower, fed by an electric pump. A rubber hose attached to the ensemble enabled us to fill the toilet room drum and allowed our houseboy to keep the outside area clean and tidy. The water was not potable but was just fine for showers and toilet flushing. Next to this building a small covered enclave with chairs and a table provided a shaded area used mostly by the interpreters and their friends for conversations and very hard-fought domino games.

Team sleeping quarters were inside a large bunker built outside the long back wall of the team house, accessed by an open door cut through the original cement wall of the main room. The outside bunker walls were heavily protected by double rows of sandbags to the roofline. The bunker roof was reinforced with PSP steel sections and sandbags strong enough to ward off enemy mortar rounds. The bunker roof inside the sleeping quarters was high enough for us to walk upright. Three pairs of double-deck steel cots and mattresses, plus a single cot for the DSA, provided sleeping space for seven people. An empty space along one side had allowed room for two more pairs of bunk beds—indicative of the size of the district advisory team only a short time earlier. As it was, it was more than adequate for the three Americans and three interpreters now making up the team. A series of barbed wire fencing separated the advisors' area from the rest of the compound and gave us a bit of privacy.

Four large wardrobes stood against the walls in the main room of the team house and were large enough for all of us to hang uniforms and civilian clothing. We had foot lockers made locally from used howitzer shell wood boxes. The team house floor was heavy-duty tile. The living room and office end had red and white pattern tiles, while the dining area and kitchen end had green and white tiles.

A good cook, Cô Bai (pronounced "Bye"), had worked for several iterations of Hàm Long advisors. She took care of our meals and did the shopping at the local market. Ông Hai was janitor, houseboy, and laundry man. He kept the house clean, washed and ironed our clothes, cleaned our jungle boots, and kept would-be sticky fingers at bay. I forget how much we paid our two-person house staff; it was not much by U.S. standards but very good by local salaries. The two of them kept us well fed, in clean clothes, and comfortable. They were honest and loyal; we never had problems with petty thievery.

Hàm Long Teammates

Now it was time to get down to business, learn about my boss, co-workers, counterparts, conditions, and operational pace. I was lucky with my boss and co-workers on this tour of duty. The two DSAs I worked for, fellow team members, interpreters, and counterparts—all were competent in their work and delightful to work with.

Major David Kretschmar, DSA, was the boss in Hàm Long. He was a graduate of the MATA course and a volunteer for the District Senior Advisor Program, which offered a number of benefits for volunteers. Among them were a number of free home leave trips with transportation paid or the offer to move the family to a nearby safe haven at government expense; many advisors' families lived in Bangkok. In return, they accepted an 18-month assignment as an advisor instead of the usual one-year Vietnam tour of duty. Members of the DSA program were supposed to get command credit for their DSA assignment and preference for a later promotion, and that brought many good officers into the program.

Major Kretschmar was an Armor branch officer, stocky of build with a great, friendly personality and professional attitude toward advisory duties. He had accepted a prior Vietnam assignment with an American armor unit and was very pleased to be an advisor on this, his second Vietnam tour. He and I hit it off immediately and enjoyed a good working relationship for the ten months we worked together.

Sergeant First Class Willie Logan (not his real name) had arrived about two months before me. He was a major contributor to our team's success. His primary responsibility was conducting training for the lowest levels of strength—the People's Self-Defense Force (PSDF). Prior to the

Major David Kretschmar relaxing in his black pajamas. Cat approves.

cutback in advisory team strength that training mission was performed by Mobile Assistance Training (MAT) teams. Those five-man teams moved from village to village to conduct combat training, maintenance training, and some local security training. They lived in the village where they worked and truly were the grass roots of the U.S. advisory mission. MAT Team IV-5 was still in Hàm Long when I arrived, but within a month or so, it was disestablished and the personnel reassigned elsewhere. SFC Logan was doing the work previously done by a five-man MAT Team. He was also responsible for managing the team house, ordering supplies and foodstuffs, and keeping a watchful eye on the cook and the houseboy. He kept the small generator in working order and worked on the outboard motor for our Boston Whaler boat. Most important, he was a great cook—whether for barbequed steaks and ribs or wonderful homemade pies.

Sergeant Tag remained with the team until his early September DEROS. Because of my TDY to Vũng Tàu, we did not have much time to work together. Tag was an intelligence analyst and worked almost full time in the DIOCC. He was instrumental in getting me introduced to the DIOCC mission and operations. Reflecting the sharp personnel cutback in the overall advisory effort, Tag was not replaced after his departure.

The Hàm Long advisory team was very fortunate to have three interpreters—ARVN Sergeants Hung and Tu (not their real names), and Mr. Toi (not his real name). At my strong recommendation to Major Kretschmar, after about two months the two DSAs in Hàm Long and Giồng Trôm arranged a trade, and we received Sergeant First Class Hồ Văn Bé, who had worked for me in the 9th MI Detachment at Dong Tam in 1968. Sergeant Hung went to Giồng Trôm District.

Mr. Toi was the *Phụng Hoàng* interpreter. He was 27, had a university law degree, and spoke and understood English excellently. He could not be drafted into the army because he had a crippled leg from a motorcycle accident and walked with a heavy limp. As an alternative to the draft, he performed required national service as a salaried interpreter for the PH program. He spent a lot of his time in the Hàm Long DIOCC, the PH Center for Hàm Long District. He regularly briefed the DSA and me about DIOCC activities. Toi insisted on doing his share of the harder physical work, so he frequently went on short intelligence operations and visits to village offices, but he could not go on long tactical operations because of his bad leg.

All of the interpreters spoke and understood English excellently, had great senses of humor, and were very good on tactical operations. We rotated field operations with all of the interpreters, where they performed as tactical NCOs as well as interpreters for the advisors.

Some advisors were uncomfortable working with interpreters, but that was never a problem for me or for my bosses. All of us had worked with interpreters in previous Vietnam assignments, so we were quite used to working with interpreters. We established a good relationship with all of our interpreters, and they themselves, as ARVN NCOs, were very professional and worked out their own good relationships with the ARVN officers.

The six-week Vietnamese language class I received at Fort Bragg before deploying to Vietnam was helpful but by no means sufficient to allow either Major Kretschmar or me to carry on a meaningful conversation with counterparts and Vietnamese civilians, so interpreters were essential for us to be effective. Many of the Vietnamese officers we worked with had some knowledge of English. Some were quite fluent, and the district chief had attended U.S. military schools earlier in his career. I depended on our interpreters in most of my conversations, both professional and personal, and they never let me down or embarrassed me.

It is impossible to overstate the important role that interpreters played in our lives. They lived with us, went on operations with us, shared danger with us, shot at the enemy with us, taught us so much about Vietnamese culture, added variety to our daily life, shared humor and sadness with us. They were in every way integrated members of the advisory team. All three interpreters had a cot in the sleeping bunker and space in the wardrobes for their clothes.

Outstanding Counterparts

I was very fortunate to work with many brave and competent Vietnamese officers—my many counterparts over 18 months, in two districts. With such a small district advisory team, we did not fuss over who was whose counterpart. Clearly the district chief was the DSA's primary counterpart. I was nominally the counterpart of both the deputy district chief and the district S-2 (in my DDSA hat and my PH hat). We shared work with both of them, as we also did with the S-3 and the S-5. We did not work as much with the S-4 and the civilian deputy district chief for Development, but when needed, either the DSA or I would easily work with them.

The Hàm Long District Chief was Lieutenant Colonel Nguyễn Văn Sơn. LTC Sơn (pronounced "shun") was a truly outstanding officer. He had been district chief for about four years when I arrived in Hàm Long. He had previously attended the U.S. Army Infantry Officer Advanced Course at Fort Benning, Georgia, and spoke English excellently. He worked very well with his American counterparts. He listened to us, asked us for comments, and consulted us regularly on pacification projects that he wanted advisory funds for and assistance to carry out. He had great drive and initiative and maintained a professional bearing and attitude at all times. He knew the district well and frequently went to the field as commander of both tactical and support operations. His staff had worked with him for many years. He knew their strengths and weaknesses and used them to maximize strengths and reduce problems. He enjoyed great loyalty from his subordinates and seemed genuinely to enjoy his assignment as district chief.

Most importantly, Trung-tá Sơn extended full professional courtesy to Major Kretschmar and me even though we were both junior to him in rank. I was to find out over time that not all Vietnamese officers were so professional in this regard. Sensitivity to the status of rank and seniority between district chief and advisors was a problem in some other Kiến Hòa districts. During the two periods of extended time when I was Acting District Senior Advisor (in the absence of Major Kretschmar), he extended the same courtesy and respect to me as he did to his more senior DSA. There were no problems caused by the difference in rank between district chief and advisors.

Interestingly, LTC Sơn had a close personal and professional relationship with President Nguyễn Văn Thiệu, built up during his ten years with the 5th ARVN Division, 1959–1968. That friendship gave him a unique sense of confidence in his position.

My relations with the other district officers were all good, but our contact varied considerably depending on the amount of time we spent together on operations or support work. For example, I had little contact with the deputy district chief. My main contacts were with the S-2 (intelligence) and S-3 (operations) with whom I went on virtually all field operations. My contact with the other staff officers, with a few exceptions, took place on the district compound when we cooperated on administrative and support issues. And, of course, because of the small size of the main compound, we frequently met socially, informally, in the course of a day's activities.

I spent more time with the district S-2/Chief of Intelligence, First Lieutenant Phùng Hữu Hương. He was the most capable of all of the district staff officers and was LTC Sơn's right-hand man—he was, in effect, the deputy district chief for military affairs. He frequently commanded field combat operations, and I went on more tactical operations with him than with any other officer. He was a very effective S-2 as well, aggressive in intelligence collection, and he demanded high standards of performance from his S-2 staff NCOs as well as soldiers on field operations. He was the de facto head of the DIOCC and PH operations although he did not maintain an office in the DIOCC. He had a particular interest in the maintenance, content, and organization of PH files, and his degree of participation made the Hàm Long DIOCC the best organized in the province.

District Chief LTC Nguyễn Văn Sơn, standing in front of the admin TOC.

Trung-úy Hương and I hit it off right away. We were the same age, we shared a military intelligence background, and our personalities meshed. I gave him one of my Military Intelligence branch insignia, which he wore proudly on the pocket of his fatigue jacket. He gave me a set of Vietnamese army captain's rank pips, which I wore equally proudly on my fatigue jacket.

My other primary contact was the District S-3/Operations Officer, First Lieutenant Nguyễn Thanh Liêm. Lieutenant Liêm impressed me from the very start by his confident attitude and willingness to discuss operational plans with the advisors. He spoke English excellently and had a pleasant, relaxed personality. Initially an engineer officer, he spent two years in the 10th Regiment, 7th ARVN Division before his assignment to Hàm Long. In addition to his operations planning responsibilities he also managed TOC operations. He was the only staff officer with subordinate officers—two young second lieutenants who were 12-hour TOC shift supervisors. He also supervised several very sharp NCOs.

The Province-Level Bosses

The Kiến Hòa Province Senior Advisor was Lieutenant Colonel (retired) Albert "Buck" Kotzebue. He was a friend and colleague of John Paul Vann and retired from active duty about the same time as Mr. Vann and went to work for CORDS. It was unusual to have a civilian PSA in such an insecure province as Kiến Hòa, but Mr. Kotzebue had plenty of combat experience. During World War II, young First Lieutenant Kotzebue led a small army patrol that became the first U.S. military unit to make contact with the Russian army on the Elbe River. He became Kiến Hòa PSA in 1968 and served in that post until spring 1973, when he was reassigned as PSA in Bình Định Province in MR II. He had a good relationship with the province chief and with our higher bosses in Cần Thơ.

… Albert L. Kotzebue, "Prince Albert," the PSA. Knows enough to stay away when you don't need him, and to be right there when you do.

There were two deputy province senior advisors—one for operations and one for development. The DPSA for Operations was LTC William Tausch, an infantry officer with service in Korea during the war and an earlier assignment in Vietnam with the 4th Infantry Division, 1966–1967. He served as Kiến Hòa DPSA from May 1971 to February 1973.

The DPSA for New Life Development was Mr. Norris Nordvold, a USAID civilian. As mentioned in Chapter 1, he had been DSA in Ba Tri District, the first district in the province to have its advisory team closed because of its good security posture. Norris was a very savvy guy who did not hesitate to travel throughout the province. He spoke fluent Vietnamese.

The Kiến Hòa Province Chief was Colonel Phạm Chi Kim, a man who got along well with the American advisors. He was held in high regard by the Vietnamese chain of command. His previous assignment was as commander of the 10th Regiment, 7th ARVN Division, which at that time had its base camp in Kiến Hòa Province.

DPSA Norris Nordvold (2nd from left), in Hàm Long with a group of unidentified visiting Congressional staffers.

Hàm Long District Background

Hàm Long District was in the shape of a riverine peninsula, with the Mỹ Tho River on the north and the Hàm Luông River on the south. Its population was about 40,000, about a quarter of which lived in Tiên Thủy village near the district headquarters. There were two other market towns. Tân Lợi was about six kilometers west of the district headquarters, and Sơn Hòa was located on a spur road just west of the border with Trúc Giang District.

The Tiên Thủy village market was 600 meters south of the compound. A typical small Vietnamese market center, it was a large square with an open-air market in the middle and rows of shops and homes on both sides. The village office and military bunkers filled the north side of the square, while small docks on the Soc Sai River bank flanked the southern open end of the square.

The daily morning market featured fresh vegetables, fish, shrimp, fruit, and meat. It was gone by about 10 a.m., and commerce moved to the two rows of shops selling dry goods, material, clothes—almost anything a local villager would need. It also provided much of what advisors needed too. Cô Bai bought almost all of our foodstuffs in the market; we supplemented with what little was available in the province compound store. We bought bulk ice from a small shop that featured stucco art above the door

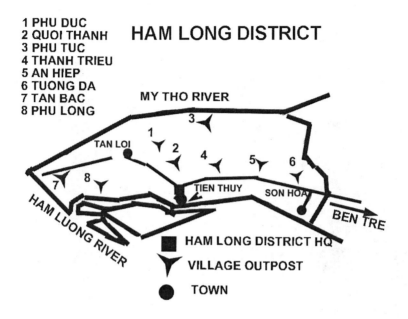

1 PHU DUC
2 QUOI THANH
3 PHU TUC
4 THANH TRIEU
5 AN HIEP
6 TUONG DA
7 TAN BAC
8 PHU LONG

HAM LONG DISTRICT

MY THO RIVER

TAN LOI

HAM LUONG RIVER

TIEN THUY   SON HOA

BEN TRE

■ HAM LONG DISTRICT HQ

Y VILLAGE OUTPOST

● TOWN

Map 3: Hàm Long District Sketch by author from tracing, with towns, village offices, and roads shown.

that showed a billiards table, pool cue, and balls—but it was now the ice plant. Most of our household supplies came from the market as well.

I enjoyed visiting the market. Everything about the hustle and bustle of this small-town hub was new and different, and it was nice to find a place to sit, enjoy something to eat or drink, and watch life going on all around me. Fortunately, the market was considered secure, but I always went armed, with an interpreter or other soldiers from the compound. They were my teachers. They seemed genuinely to enjoy explaining what I was seeing, and it was fun on their part to teach the new advisor about small-town market life in the Mekong Delta. I never tired of going to the Tiên Thủy market whenever I had some time to spare.

... Happiness Is a Măng Cầu Smoothie with Crushed Ice in a Little Plastic Bag Tied with a Rubber Band with a Straw Sticking Out of the Top.

I'm not sure how to translate *măng cầu* accurately. I think it's mostly translated as "custard apple." That is only partly accurate. The flesh does have sort of the consistency of custard, but it has smooth half-inch-long black oblong pits. It's not round but sort of "off round." It is not firm and smooth like an apple. Its green, bumpy skin looks very much like the old-style "pineapple" hand grenade. And it tastes absolutely delicious.

Tiên Thủy village and market from the air. The big river at the top is the Hàm Luông River; the small brown river is the Soc Sai River. The district compound is just out of the picture to the lower right.

Hàm Long market vendors didn't sell fresh fruit juice in a can or a bottle. They freshly squeezed or pureed fruit and poured the juice into a small plastic bag with crushed ice. They stuck a plastic straw inside and tied it closed with a rubber band that doubled as a handling loop, using some indiscernible sleight of hand, and there you have a yummy, portable drink.

Măng cầu is one of my favorite tropical fruits, along with mango and mangosteen. My very first taste of it was in Hàm Long, and I tried the juice before I tasted the fruit itself. You actually need a spoon to eat the fruit. You pull the fruit open in a messy pile and scoop the fruit off with a spoon (or clumsily, directly with your teeth). The rind is very bitter and inedible.

A lady in the Tiên Thủy market had a fruit juice and soft drink stand. She sold all the usual canned soft drinks, and she also sold fresh fruit juice. The first time I went over to look, I saw oranges, bananas, coconuts, and this strange fruit that looked like a hand grenade.

"What's that?" I asked in my best Vietnamese.

"*Măng cầu*," she responded. "Very good" (in English!).

So I asked for a *măng cầu* smoothie. Quick as a wink she opened up one of the fruits, pushed all the seeds out, scooped out the flesh and dropped it into her battery-powered blender, added some condensed milk from a can, whirled it around, strained it through a cloth (so you could suck it all up through a straw), poured it into a plastic bag about the size of a sandwich baggie, dropped in some very tiny chunks of crushed ice, stuck in a straw, and went zip, zip, zip with a rubber band to tie it all together.

Voilà! Absolutely wonderful on a hot afternoon. Every time I was down in the market, I looked to see when she had *mãng cầu*, and every time she did (fruits available varied from day-to-day), I had my *mãng cầu* smoothie with crushed ice in a little plastic bag tied with a rubber band and with a straw sticking out the top.

... Happiness Is Hủ Tiếu for Breakfast at the Hàm Long Market.

In an occasional break from a normal team house western breakfast, usually of eggs and coffee, from time to time I went to the Tiên Thủy market for a bowl of *hủ tiếu*, a hearty soup. Unlike the better-known *phở*, which is based on a tasty, clear chicken-based broth, *hủ tiếu* is based on a darker pork-based broth. It is cooked and served with a variety of goodies (shrimp, ground pork meatballs, vegetables, chunks of fish and squid). Real *hủ tiếu* soup is made with *hủ tiếu* noodles, which are made from tapioca flour instead of rice flour. I was often joined by Sergeant Bé and one or more of the MSS counterintelligence agents, which made for an interesting conversation as we enjoyed our soup, *bánh mi* ("French" bread baguettes), and Vietnamese slow-drip coffee.

Bountiful Countryside

For me one of the best parts of being a district-level advisor was the chance to live with and learn about rural Vietnamese culture. Kiến Hòa was a rural agricultural province with fertile soil and bountiful agricultural crops coupled with the myriad of Delta waterways for transportation and food. I had not experienced anything like that environment at any time in my life—until Vietnam. I took lots of pictures of ordinary scenes because rice culture, fruit orchards, and the importance of canals and rivers were all new to me. These pictures are scattered throughout the book. Security-wise we had to be alert wherever we went. The enemy threat lived full time, often "out of sight in plain view," in bucolic rural surroundings, but still I thoroughly enjoyed getting out and seeing what was going on.

I arrived in Hàm Long in July 1971 in the rainy season and left Mỏ Cày in February 1973, deep into the dry season, so I got to see the full cycle of the rice culture. The process began with preparation of the paddy and on to planting of new shoots, transplanting to the paddy, cultivation, care of the paddy, the intricate irrigation system, ripening, and harvest. The Hàm Long District compound was surrounded by rice paddies and coconut groves. Rice cultivation, up to three crops a year, provided a daily scene of rural Vietnamese agricultural society. It was a real education to watch this agricultural society go about its life.

The water buffalo was the most important possession of Vietnamese farmers. They were always attended by small children—"buffalo boys"—who were symbiotic with the huge beasts. Water buffalo had poor sight but keen smell, and they did not like western guys' smells! We always moved carefully and stayed upwind of them.

The first stage of the planting season was preparing the paddy. That meant the farmer had to burn off the dry stalks from the previous crop, plow under the stubble, smooth out the paddy, remove trash and rocks, and soften the soil with irrigation water. Meanwhile, carefully nurtured rice seedlings were hand planted in a small, well-fertilized section of paddy and allowed to grow close together to the right height for transplanting. Once the paddy was smooth and soft and covered in water, the rice seedlings were carefully transplanted one by one by hand, spaced correctly, and left to grow. Transplanting rice is backbreaking, painstaking work, mostly done by women. Each shoot is individually planted by hand to the right depth in the soft soil; the water level in the paddy is carefully calculated. Too deep and the rice plants drown. Too shallow and the rice plants die from the heat.

Rainy season, preparing the field for a new planting of rice. The boy is operating a "grader" to smooth the bottom of the rice paddy. The district compound roofs show how close he is to us. The helicopter pad is between him and the compound.

It seems like RTO Tinh and I were the only ones on this operation! See growing rice on the right-side paddy, newly transplanted seedlings at left, and paddy being prepared for a new crop, center right.

The fertile Delta soil and copious use of fertilizer allowed farmers to raise three crops a year. Each cycle is about four months, and cycles overlap. The countryside was always a gorgeous palette of various shades of green from rice in various stages of growth to vegetables, to coconut and other fruit trees. I never tired of the scenes. It made it hard to realize that danger lurked in the greenery—booby traps hidden along rice paddy dikes or underneath piles of leaves, a sniper or ambush party hiding just beyond the edge of that tree line, and bullets or mortar rounds might come flying at us from behind a hedge or tree line. It was beautiful and deadly countryside all at the same time. Rice paddies always looked pretty regardless of the season. Green newly planted seedlings contrasted with the muddy brown of the paddy water. Growing rice was a different shade of green. Mature rice had golden tips, and rice under harvest was an indescribable shade of golden tan.

… Tinh. the district chief's RTO, whose sense of humor made the long days bearable, who appears in more pictures than any other man because he was always in the right place, doing his job well.

3

Into the Field

It took a few weeks for me to get my feet on the ground. The officer I succeeded departed for home just two days after I arrived. He spent a lot of time talking to me about what was what, who was who, and how things were done in Hàm Long. I appreciated his efforts and spent the time in receive mode except for an unending run of questions. Since SFC Logan was also new, only two months on the team, I also relied heavily on Mr. Toi and SGT Tag to orient me on how the DIOCC worked (or didn't work). SGT Tag remained only a month or so before he too reached his DEROS and departed for home. The once-large district advisory team was down to three Americans and three interpreters.

Us Against Them

"Us" in Kiến Hòa Province meant the Vietnamese forces we advised and worked with and the handful of American advisors who assisted during tactical ground operations. There were no main force ARVN units in Kiến Hòa Province. Hàm Long's soldiers were all RF and PF—two RF companies and 42 PF platoons of varying strength. Virtually all of the PF soldiers were stationed in outposts. One RF company manned several of the larger outposts; the other RF company was based at the compound and deployed on mobile company- and platoon-sized operations. The two companies rotated assignments every six months or so. Hàm Long also had one field artillery platoon with two U.S. 105 mm howitzers. The 2nd Platoon, C Battery, 72nd Field Artillery was organic to the 7th ARVN Division but was assigned in direct support of Hàm Long District and on call for support to other Kiến Hòa Province areas within effective range. The young artillery section chief was superb, as were his artillerymen, who often received praise for their accuracy from ground elements as well as from USAF FACs.

The advisory team's most important contributions were to coordinate tactical air strikes, armed helicopters, medevac helicopters, "slicks" for visual reconnaissance, and the occasional B-52 strike and to assist with pacification and development projects. We also served as morale-boosting, confidence-supporting friends to our Vietnamese counterparts.

"Them" was the enemy in Kiến Hòa—the VC, VCI, and NVA. By 1971 most VC main force units were actually manned mostly by NVA personnel who had infiltrated down the Hồ Chí Minh Trail and were integrated into VC units. The actual southern VC were virtually wiped out in the 1968 Tết Offensive, when they were often the first force into a battle and were destroyed. Some provinces, however, especially including Kiến Hòa Province, still had homegrown VC units because of the province's history as the origin of the VC movement and continuing loyalty to the VC cause. Hàm Long District was part of VC Châu Thành District, roughly comprising the GVN Hàm Long and Trúc Giang Districts.

The enemy order of battle included the D-263 Bến Tre Province Local Force Battalion, the C-550 Châu Thành District Local Force Company and roughly a dozen units of village guerrillas. Their tactics included attacks against outposts, ambushes of government forces, mortar attacks, and widespread use of mines and booby traps on roads, trails, and rice paddy dikes. There was a steady supply of voluntary new VC recruits, as well as involuntary recruits who were captured by the VC and integrated into VC units against their will. We called the units VC whether or not they were really full of NVA replacements. Whether manned by southerners or northerners, the VC units were tough, well-armed fighters. I never saw any firm figures for total enemy strength, but a good estimated total of all levels of enemy strength in Hàm Long District was approximately 600 people.

Finally, we had to contend with the VCI, the most dangerous and difficult enemy to find. The VCI ran the war. They were the local enemy shadow government, recruiters, tax collectors, and intelligence agents. They were the scourge of Vietnamese government supporters in towns down to tiny hamlets, where they operated with terror, threat, and torture. Whenever there was an assassination of a village chief, teacher, or other government cadre, it was the VCI responsible for the atrocity. I respected the NVA and VC soldiers for their courage and dedication, but I felt only disgust and hatred for the VCI because of their despicable acts of terror against unarmed civilian leaders and their families. The PH program was established specifically to gather and coordinate intelligence in order to target and capture or kill individual cadre of the VCI. Like local force strength, the VCI assigned to jobs in Hàm Long District were under the rubric of VC Châu Thành District. Thus, for example, there was no VC district chief for Hàm Long, but most of the Hàm Long villages had VC village chiefs.

There were plenty of enemy soldiers of all kinds in Kiến Hòa Province. In most parts of the province, hard-core VC companies and battalions controlled large swaths of the countryside, mostly unpopulated areas but also areas with surprisingly well-maintained rice paddies, vegetable gardens, and fruit groves. In earlier years when the U.S. 9th Infantry Division operated from Dong Tam, there was usually one brigade assigned almost full time to tactical operations in Kiến Hòa Province. One 9th Division legacy I had to live with later in life was the widespread use of Agent Orange and other defoliants, which the 9th Division methodically used to strip east-to-west swaths of defoliated coconut trees and ground vegetation in Hàm Long and Trúc Giang districts near the Mỹ Tho River, directly across from the Dong Tam base camp.

Hàm Long played a major role in the VC/NVA/VCI commo-liaison network between Định Tường Province and Mỏ Cày District and other areas of the Kiến Hòa lower island and onward further south and west through the lower Mekong Delta region. Major trail networks moved east through Phú Đức and Phú Túc villages, then south through Tương Dạ and Sơn Hòa villages along the boundary with Trúc Giang District to the Hàm Luông River. One RF company occupied a series of four outposts near that primary enemy commo-liaison route. Lackadaisical leadership and the size of the enemy threat sometimes meant little progress in intercepting the supplies and soldiers moving along that route in both directions. Nonetheless, there were occasionally successful ambushes of small enemy groups moving on that trail network, mostly resulting from nighttime ambush patrols.

The primary government security operations in Hàm Long were small unit patrols and outpost construction. The strategic plan was to expand government-secured areas gradually, first by building and manning an outpost, then conducting operations against enemy trail systems and small base areas and thereby pushing the enemy into smaller and smaller safe areas and then destroying them. The enemy fought back by ambushing friendly patrols and with attacks against outposts, almost always at night. They were often successful because VC sympathizers in the local PF units manning those outposts were able to recruit or kill by surprise their fellow soldiers and then bring the VC force into the outpost, where they killed the remaining soldiers or allowed them to defect to the VC. They captured weapons, ammunition, and communications gear and then retreated back to their well-hidden safe areas. The VC never attempted to hold and man a captured outpost because they were unable—and unwilling—to withstand the artillery and air strikes that would respond to their attacks. Time after time in Hàm Long outposts were overrun in this manner.

Most outposts fought back, either because there were no traitors inside or because they had enough personnel, cover, and ammunition to drive off the attacking force. These were the real heroes of our side, RF and PF soldiers fighting in the dark against determined enemy attacks.

When an outpost was attacked, the two-tube Hàm Long 105 mm artillery platoon was always on call for direct fire support. This artillery fire often was the difference that allowed the RF and PF to win those many small battles. The district chief could also deploy a reaction force from the RF company stationed in the compound across the road from the district headquarters to rescue the outpost or intercept the enemy as they withdrew. But whenever the TOC lost contact with an outpost under attack, we knew right away that either a traitor had killed the friendly PF force or the entire outpost had defected to the VC. It made me sick inside and filled me with indescribable anger. If I had ever been given the chance to be left alone with captured VC traitors who had killed outpost PF soldiers, I might have done some terrible things.

During my tenure, Hàm Long District was considered the second-most secure district in the province. However, there was a very dark historical legacy. More American advisors were killed and wounded in Hàm Long than in any other district in Kiến Hòa Province. The last two DSAs to be killed in action in Kiến Hòa were both Hàm Long DSAs.

The greatest combat multiplier asset available to advisors was a variety of tactical fighter-bomber aircraft and armed helicopters. The province chief and PSA also directed B-52 strikes against large enemy base camps. USAF forward air controllers (FAC) from the 21st Tactical Air Support Squadron (TASS), flying in versatile OV-10 Bronco aircraft, call sign Covey, controlled tactical air support (tac air). Those tac air assets came from USAF and navy fighter-bombers, U.S. army and U.S. navy armed helicopters that were among the last American units to leave Vietnam and occasionally from VNAF attack aircraft and armed helicopters.

Phụng Hoàng Center Operations

I was assigned to Vietnam to fill a slot as a province or district PH coordinator. The plan was for junior officers—captains and lieutenants—to be assigned to district and province advisory teams to work with Vietnamese counterparts from military and police units to gather intelligence and target tactical operations against the entrenched VCI. I had attended a two-month course at Fort Bragg and spent ten days in Vũng

Tàu specifically to prepare me for this work. Each district's DIOCC was organized for multiagency intelligence collection, analysis, and operations planning. However, management, staffing, and capability varied widely from district to district.

When I arrived in Hàm Long, there was a three-man PH advisory element—the captain I succeeded, the intelligence NCO, and the PH interpreter/analyst. Counterparts on the Vietnamese side in the Hàm Long DIOCC included, nominally, the district chief as overall head of the effort. Trung-tá Sơn took a strong leadership role in DIOCC work and often attended meetings. He assigned the deputy district chief to oversee the DIOCC, but serving as the actual day-to-day DIOCC chief was an additional duty of the district police chief. Several Vietnamese agencies assigned representatives to the DIOCC. The most active were the district police, Police Special Branch, the district military S-2 section, and the Military Security Service (MSS).

For the first two weeks or so after I returned from Vũng Tàu I spent about 30 percent of my time in the DIOCC, located in a large room inside the building housing the district military headquarters' offices. Both Mr. Toi and I had desks there. Trung-tá Sơn had instituted an interesting requirement by assigning a VCI "counterpart" to each of his primary staff officers, both military and civilian. They were required to know the contents of the dossier on their counterpart and to report statuses, updates, and changes at every DIOCC meeting and to recommend when that "counterpart" might be targeted for capture.

The center had dozens, if not hundreds, of dossiers on alleged VCI cadre. They ranged from the VC Châu Thành District chief and village chiefs to commo-liaison couriers, recruitment cadre (kidnappers of teenage males) and security cadre—the nastiest, responsible for eliminating government officers, teachers, and anyone suspected of pro-government activity. I went through a lot of those dossiers. The documents reported suspected activities but notably lacked actionable information on location and movement patterns—information vital to actually finding a VCI. Directions from the national PH leadership were very specific: before a VCI cadre could be apprehended or neutralized, there must be multiple pieces of evidence from different sources. Designed to counter arguments that the PH operations were rogue assassination missions, the restrictions made it difficult to accumulate the multisource information required for neutralization operations. This was a major reason why there were few targeted PH anti–VCI operations in Hàm Long.

Sergeant Tag was very helpful in orienting me on the DIOCC's personnel, activities, and methods of operations. However, after a couple weeks, it was apparent that I was wasting my time in the DIOCC. Because of the steady withdrawal of U.S. military units and personnel from Vietnam, district advisory teams were considerably smaller in mid–1971 than they had been just a few months earlier. The Hàm Long District advisory team went from five American personnel when I arrived to three personnel two weeks later. I relied on Mr. Toi to keep me abreast of DIOCC activities. My main contribution was to participate in the weekly DIOCC reporting and analysis meetings and to attend the monthly PH program meetings in Bến Tre.

First Priority in Field Operations: Learn the District

Because of the reduced size of district advisory teams, the PSA had the option of reassigning the district PH coordinator to the deputy district senior advisor (DDSA) slot or not. That determination involved many factors, including the effectiveness of the DIOCC and the individual officer's capability and readiness to take on the duties and responsibilities of a tactical DDSA. The DSA made the recommendation to the PSA depending on his evaluation of the officer's ability to take on active tactical responsibilities. I told Major Kretschmar that I was wasting time in the DIOCC and preferred instead to go out on operations, whether tactical forays or administrative visits. I wanted to be considered his DDSA rather than his PH coordinator. I felt it was very important to share field operations with him rather than sitting in the DIOCC all day. He agreed and suggested I begin by going on operations with the S-2, so immediately I did just that.

I told Trung-úy Hương that I wanted to go to the field with him if he approved. I told him that he had far more experience fighting the VC than I did, and I would rather learn from him than attempt to advise him. Besides, I said, "I'm a pretty good shot if we get into trouble." That might have been a key factor. Lieutenant Hương was more than the S-2— he was the district chief's right-hand man, more so than was the deputy district chief. Most of the operations that Trung-úy Hương led were intelligence-gathering efforts in the hamlets and villages we went through and inspections of outposts rather than operations targeted at specific VCI cadre. He also regularly commanded standard combat operations against the enemy's tactical units.

He immediately agreed for me to go on his operations and seemed pleased that I had raised the suggestion. In retrospect, he certainly selected reasonably secure areas for the first couple of times we went on operations together. He wanted to know what kind of physical condition I was in, how well I adapted to the hot and humid weather, whether I knew how to prepare adequately for an operation in terms of weapon, dress, equipment, and attitude. The interpreters were my best source of information on the status of the developing relationship between Trung-úy Hương and me. I told them that I wanted their honest opinion and advice about my operational activity, and they were more than happy to give it.

My first operation with Trung-úy Hương in mid–August 1971 was the first of my "walks in the sun" that characterized many field operations in Hàm Long. The patrol route went through a nominally secure area of Tiên Thủy village between the main road and the Hàm Luông River. The area was well settled with typical rural peasant homes with neat and tidy surroundings and well-packed dirt pathways. The entire area was planted with fruit trees and coconut groves rather than rice paddies. The operational objective was to locate and capture a VCI suspect who reportedly used that area for periodic recruitment and logistics visits.

The patrol route followed local pathways past banana and coconut groves and widely spaced individual houses, some with thatched walls and roofs and some of more substantial concrete or cement block con-

struction. Trung-úy Hương led the patrol on a seemingly random zigzagged route along many heavily used wide pathways. It was an easy start for my field operations. From time to time he or one of the intelligence NCOs stopped to greet and talk with villagers along the way. Sometimes one or two NCOs dropped off and rejoined the patrol later on.

As we walked through the area, I could tell that he and his soldiers were keeping a close eye on me to see how I did. Well, I did just fine. Yes, it was hot and humid,

Starting my very first tactical patrol with First Lieutenant Hương in Tiên Thủy village.

and I quickly sweated through my jungle fatigues. I took enough water and had no trouble keeping up with the pace of the operation. Sergeant Tu stayed right with me. It was an easy introduction to this village area. We followed established, wide pathways of well-packed dirt, irrigation waterways had substantial bridges, and only the occasional muddy puddle reminded me that I was experiencing the rainy season in the easiest possible way.

Even though obviously planned as a very easy operation, I was excited. Everything was new—the vegetation, the pathways we moved along, the houses, the villagers themselves. All of the smells were new too. Whether the scent of cooking, the natural odor of wet and rotting vegetation, moist soil, or the unmistakable and distinctive odor of the many family-size *nước mắm* "stills," it was all new, sometimes unidentifiable. In short order those new sights and smells became commonplace as time passed. I was a bit nervous because there was always the threat of danger, even in such a well-settled, populated area. Nobody else seemed nervous, so I calmed down and enjoyed the experience.

After a couple of hours of walking through the target area, the patrol emerged back on the main road between the district headquarters and Bến Tre. By then I was very sure that Trung-úy Hương and his NCOs had been collecting intelligence along the seemingly random route, even though the targeted VCI cadre was not found. It was my first lesson in local intelligence collection, a pattern I was to participate in during dozens of similar operations in the coming months. That first operation was a good primer

Back on the main road after that first operation. My patrol mates pose on the road.

for the rest of my time as an advisor. It also gave the soldiers a good look at the new advisor and how I fared on what was a very easy operational patrol.

The many following operations with Hương were walks in the sun much like that first operation, with no enemy contact. Most were visits to outposts all over the district. I went out with him every two or three days, while Major Kretschmar was out with the district chief. SFC Logan kept track of both of us on the radio. I don't recall the capture or neutralization of a single VCI suspect. Nonetheless, these operations were invaluable for me because I quickly became familiar with the geography of the district— what villages were where and how to get to and from them, what personalities were important, which village chiefs and PF units were good and which were not.

Major Kretschmar was invaluable as a mentor and teacher. He had me brief him after each operation, and he briefed me on the operations he went on when accompanying Trung-tá Sơn. I learned what was required of me as an objective observer of my surroundings, got to know the leaders of the operations I accompanied and the atmosphere and description of the villages and countryside. I was fortunate that those first few weeks of operations were unremarkable in that there was no contact with the enemy. I watched, I learned, and I absorbed everything. I also lost weight from the heat and humidity, the exertion, and all that new-style exercise. I felt my body become stronger and more fit than I had ever felt before. I was slowly but surely becoming a field soldier.

Fortunately, unlike American soldiers assigned to the large combat units, I was not burdened by the weight of ammunition, food, and equipment—a load often weighing more than 80 pounds—that American grunts routinely carried on combat operations. The lighter load was a significant difference between district and province advisors' operations and those of the large combat units. The other major difference was the size and composition of the operation. In Hàm Long District only one or sometimes two Americans went to the field accompanying Vietnamese RF/PF units. There was no nearby large combat unit, either U.S. or Vietnamese, to come to the rescue if the situation turned very dire.

Tan Bắc Outpost

Major Kretschmar kept his word and continued to send me on operations that expanded my knowledge of the district and the advisory role. The Tan Bắc outpost project was the first time I went on an outpost operation, in the rainy season in August 1971 only a few weeks after I arrived in

Hàm Long. It was also one of the few times I went on an operation with the District S-4 Đại-úy Tan (not his real name). My first impression was that he was a good staff officer but not too strong as a leader. Initially I found him cool and standoffish toward me. This operation proved me wrong. He was clearly in charge, knew what needed to be done, and we got along well—walking out in the rain together helped forge a relationship that strengthened as time went along.

It was raining when we left the district compound just after 0700. Tan Bắc was in the far western part of Hàm Long. We went by jeep and truck as far as Tân Lợi and then walked the rest of the way. In no time at all we were soaked to the skin. It didn't rain really hard; it just rained really steady. The road west of Tân Lợi was mostly rock and dirt, which was a solid bed to walk on, but both muddy and rough enough to be hard on the ankles. By the time we got to the site of the new outpost, we had splashed mud above the knees of our jungle fatigues, which mixed well with the soaking wet uniform.

The PF platoons involved walked with us on the road rather than spread out on the flanks. That concerned me, but when I mentioned it to Đại-úy Tan, he told me that a succession of PF outposts was providing security out of sight from the road. It took a couple hours to get to the outpost location. It was an open area with good fields of fire all around. Any attacking enemy would find it difficult to sneak up on the outpost, but it probably would be easy for the enemy to mortar it from the coconut trees to the north and northeast.

We spent much of the day at Tan Bắc, and the rain stopped around lunchtime. Local villagers set out lunch for us in the school building—including the potent *ba si đế* rice wine. I fell off a monkey bridge afterwards on the way back to the outpost, much to everyone's amusement. Đại-úy Tan supervised all aspects of the first day of the outpost construction. There was little for me to do except note everything that was going on, how the soldiers and civilians worked together, and see how an outpost began to grow. There was enough time to talk and get better acquainted. His excellent English made it an easy conversation. In the late afternoon he, Sergeant Hung and I walked back to Tân Lợi with a small security force, leaving most of the soldiers at the outpost until it was completed.

It was seemingly small events like this that, together, forged the ever-important relationship with my Vietnamese counterparts.

For context, this next segment is out of chronological order time-wise but provides an important connection that shows how events at one time could have an important impact at a later time. I always kept a spot in my heart for the Tan Bắc outpost—my first outpost operation. It was in an

By afternoon, Đại-úy Tan and I are a bit drier but still muddy.

important location and came under heavy pressure months later when the NVA invaded Hàm Long. Trung-tá Sơn made the decision to pull the outpost soldiers back into Tân Lợi (which helped during the Battle of Tân Lợi told later).

Shortly after I returned to Hàm Long as DSA in August 1972, Tan Bắc was one of the first outposts to be re-established as security improved. Just a few weeks after it was rebuilt and manned with a larger PF platoon, the VC attacked it again, in broad daylight. The defenders fought well but needed help. I requested that Province get a FAC and planned with Trung-tá Sơn for tac air support. When the Covey FAC arrived, he quickly identified the Tan Bắc outpost. I was able to describe the exact location where the heaviest attacking enemy force was, thanks to that rainy day operation with Đại-úy Tan almost a year before. The outpost commander provided good information on the enemy attacking forces to Trung-tá Sơn by radio from the outpost, which I relayed to the FAC. The FAC soon had tactical aircraft inbound, directed several air strikes against the enemy attacking the outpost, and drove them away.

A day or so later Province gave Hàm Long the swing ship for VR. Trung-tá Sơn and I flew out to Tan Bắc and spent about an hour on the ground getting briefed on the details of the attack. He awarded medals for valor to the defenders, and he asked whether the air strikes had helped in their defense. The outpost soldiers said they could not have held off the larger enemy force without the air strikes. When Trung-tá Sơn told them that I had been the one directing the air strikes, I was quickly surrounded by a happy crowd of soldiers, all of whom wanted to pat me on the back. I was very proud of them.

... Walking 8 klicks in the rain with Đại-úy Tan to build Tan Bắc outpost, and laughing. Excitement when a coconut fox is caught and eaten for lunch, and really tastes good. Getting a few too many cups of ba si đế at lunch and falling off a monkey bridge on the way back to the outpost. Sharing my poncho liner with a PF whose gear got soaked in the rain...

This picture shows most of the area west of Tân Lợi village. The point, center top, is where the Mekong River, flowing toward us, splits into the Mỹ Tho River (right) and Hàm Luông River (left). "Hàm Long" means "Mouth of the Dragon," and the "dragon" is about to devour us. Part of Tan Bắc outpost is visible at the extreme lower right.

and helping these men out with four air strikes the sharply sunny after-noon when the enemy decided their outpost would be next, and driving the enemy away … visiting a few days later by swing ship with Trung-tá Sơn and getting mobbed by the happy soldiers when he tells them I had called the airplanes.

Those operations with Trung-úy Hương and Đại-úy Tan, examples of many operations to come, served to get me settled into my advisory duties. I was becoming fully accepted by my counterparts and the soldiers.

4

New Geography,
New Terrain, New Soldiers

The many operations during August and early September went much the same. Major Kretschmar and I traded off on accompanying our counterparts into the field. Sometimes we both went together on the same operation. Other times we were each in the field on separate operations. SFC Logan usually remained at the team house on radio watch, but from time to time he went with one or the other of us as well.

Rain, More Rain and Water, More Water

It was still the rainy season, and although it did not rain all day, it did rain every day, mostly in the afternoon and evening. It was always hot and humid. By now I was more or less used to the weather, but for sure the combination of heat, humidity, and rain made for an uncomfortable environment.

Everything on the ground was new to me. Although I had spent almost a year across the Mekong River in Dong Tam and Mỹ Tho, I had rarely gone on ground operations. I had been up to my waist in water on the Plain of Reeds and had experienced the dense growth in the villages around Dong Tam. On those few field operations from Dong Tam I had always been with American troops, either reacting to intelligence information on weapons caches, or MEDCAPs to nearby villages. Now I was going on tactical operations on a regular basis, and I had a lot to learn about the environment I was to live in. I also had a lot to learn about the soldiers I would fight with and how to establish a good relationship with them. Slowly but surely I could feel that essential sense of trust forming between the Vietnamese officers and soldiers and me. Most importantly, eventually, I would also learn how they—and I—would fight the enemy.

Hàm Long—and all of Kiến Hòa Province—was flat as a tabletop. There were no hills. None. The entire district was barely above sea level; perhaps the highest point was about two meters above high-tide level. Unlike the terrain further north in the other three military regions of Vietnam, there were no high points. We had no vantage points to see out over our area of operations. The headquarters compound watchtower was the highest "ground" in the entire district.

The most significant aspect of the environment was water. Kiến Hòa Province, like all of the Mekong Delta, was honeycombed with rivers, canals, and streams. The smallest streams and canals were for local irrigation, drainage, or were "just there." The district was surrounded on three sides by major branches of the Mekong River. Smaller rivers and canals crisscrossed the district, ranging from wide and navigable for large water taxis and cargo boats to tiny rivulets used only for irrigation of crops. Some of these waterways had real bridges, but most did not. Streams and canals were crossed by the ubiquitous "monkey bridge" of bamboo or coconut logs. If no bridge, we waded across. Rivers and streams narrow enough to ford required laborious movement through deep mud. I routinely sank in over my boot tops, and occasionally the mud was almost knee-deep. We had to help each other move across the mud to the other side. For the larger rivers the operation chief routinely commandeered sampans and water taxis to cross or traverse the waterways. Any operation was most vulnerable to attack when crossing waterways, whether wading, using a bridge of any kind, or using boats.

We either waded across the smaller streams and canals or crossed them by a devilish bridge that somehow became known to Americans as a "monkey bridge." In Hàm Long all monkey bridges featured a rounded walking surface that was either a coconut log or else several long pieces of bamboo tied together. The best monkey bridges had handrails, and some of them were quite elaborate and well-constructed. I could usually get across those, slowly but surely, remembering the foot space was only a few inches wide, and round, and I was twice as heavy as the Vietnamese soldiers. The worst ones were a single coconut log with no handrails at all. Those posed no obstacle to Vietnamese soldiers, who nimbly trotted across without slowing down. I, on the other hand, was not nearly so nimble. I usually took the tactic that said, "Go fast, don't look down, and your momentum will carry you across." Sometimes.

Whenever an advisor did not negotiate the monkey bridge and fell into the water, it was a source of great hilarity to the Vietnamese. They invariably watched as the large, ungainly American *cố vấn*[1] attempted to duplicate the abilities of the smaller, fitter, nimbler Vietnamese. The soldiers NEVER fell off a monkey bridge. If I got across safely (meaning dry),

A local farmer leads the command group across a muddy stream. Lieutenant Hương is third from the right. I'm glad it was low tide.

that was good. If not, well … like I said, great hilarity. Usually a soldier or an interpreter offered to carry the PRC-25 radio and/or my rifle when we encountered a monkey bridge. I always let them do so because I knew the radio and rifle would stay dry.

The operation shown here took place in early September 1971, with the mission to inspect an outpost in Thành Triệu village, northeast of the district headquarters. Trung-tá Sơn led the operation, and both Major Kretschmar and I went along. The Thành Triệu village office was right on the highway to Bến Tre. About half of the village population lived between the highway and the Hàm Luông River, where prosperous homes and orchards were connected by neatly packed mud pathways. The other half lived in a strip of combined rice paddies and thinly planted coconut and other fruit groves on the north side of the highway. The outpost objective was located at the former village center, situated where the rice paddies and fruit orchards began to merge into the larger, darker, and more dangerous solid jungle of coconut trees. All of the villagers had fled VC control years ago, and not much remained to show it was once a prosperous rural agricultural hamlet. There was no anticipated enemy threat for this operation, but like Trung-tá Sơn, the major and I both carried our .45 pistols; the soldiers had either M-16 rifles or smaller carbines.

This was a "perfect" operation—the objective was considered a secure area; visibility all the way to the outpost was clear rice paddies and small groves of fruit trees. The pungent odor of home-style *nước mắm* fermenting outside the occasional house or hooch was strong, so was the warm smell of fertile rice paddies. Most of the rice was ripening and shone brightly in the sunlight. As it turned out, this pleasant "walk in the sun" was uneventful—except for the two monkey bridges I needed to cross. The first one crossed a slough, almost bank-full. The bridge was one long, thick bamboo "log," and on one side there was a knee-high bamboo rail as a handhold. The second bridge was much better, maybe the best monkey bridge I can remember. The bridge was several long pieces of bamboo tied together with sturdy (but still low) bamboo railings on both sides. The two ungainly *cố vấns* made it across both bridges.

Having successfully negotiated both monkey bridges, I was feeling smug and a bit proud of myself. However, I was not prepared for the narrow defense canal just before the destination outpost. This "bridge" was a single coconut log over the moat, no hand rails. I knew immediately that I was in trouble. I gave the radio and camera to Sergeant Bé, and he and the soldiers trotted right across. Not me! I fell off, but the water was only waist-deep. Several solders helped me clamber out of the mud and water.

Sergeant Bé and the PF soldiers (and even me) had no trouble with this one, probably the best monkey bridge I have ever seen. Note that none of the soldiers are holding on to the handrails. They didn't need them!

They managed not to laugh out loud. But several civilians working on the outpost howled loudly with laughter. Not to mind, I survived, dried out at the outpost, wiped and cleaned the pistol. We took a different route for the return patrol, no monkey bridges.

Hàm Long District was fertile and had a bountiful agricultural economy. The most important crops were rice, for which a gorgeous mosaic of paddies stretched north and south of the only road through the district, and coconut products. There were a lot of things to consider for movement in and around rice paddies during field operations. This area of the Mekong Delta enabled farmers to raise three crops of rice per year. Therefore, every area of rice production had some paddies deep with water and mud for most of the year, while other paddies would be hard, awaiting the start of a new cycle of rice. District soldiers were reluctant to cross through the wet paddies and perhaps damage or destroy a valuable crop and antagonize the populace. The alternative was to walk on the mud dikes between rice paddies. That required everyone to be constantly alert for booby traps and mines. Dikes were of different size and firmness. Many of them were hard, well-packed, wide main pathways between hamlets and roads. Some were merely soft mud that delineated paddies but were not strong enough to walk on.

Rice and coconuts were not the only things Hàm Long farmers produced. They also cared for a variety of other fruit trees as well as animals both large and small. Hàm Long, in particular, was well known for its homemade fish sauce, called *nước mắm,* used to flavor most Vietnamese dishes. *Nước mắm* smells MUCH worse while it is fermenting in the heat than it does when it turns delicious when added to many Vietnamese dishes. We always knew when we were patrolling near the many home-style *nước mắm* "factories."

The water buffalo was the most important, and the largest, of the village animals, and lots of families raised ducks and chickens. Like small boys controlling buffalo, small boys also herded ducks. You would think it would be harder than herding cats, right? Wrong! Ducks follow a fluttering bit of cloth (call it a flag), so the kid only had to plant the stick with the flag into a harvested rice paddy, and the ducks flocked to it and then found all sorts of critters to eat in the dry rice paddy. When the boy wanted to take the ducks home, he just picked up the flag and walked off, and the ducks followed in a compact bundle of quacking feathers.

Besides farming and animal husbandry, the people also fished for themselves, but commercial fishing was not yet a big industry in Kiến Hòa Province. We often saw people out fishing during our operations. They were good luck signs—if they felt it was secure enough to go fishing on a river or canal, it probably meant there were no VC forces nearby. The sights of the local people living their lives as best they could in the midst of a war were a huge part of my continuing education as an advisor.

Hàm Long's Regional Force and Popular Force Soldiers

Hàm Long's soldiers were all RF and PF, organized in RF companies and PF platoons. The size of these units varied considerably depending on their location in the district. They were almost entirely composed of men from the district and province who were thus defending their homes and families. They were much less likely to rape and pillage, as some American and ARVN units were infamous for. But they had less training and less formidable supporting armament than the large ARVN units. Personnel in large American units tended to have negative opinions about the abilities and eagerness of RF/PF units to fight. There were certainly examples of relaxed rural units—why risk too much of life and limb when those big American soldiers with bigger, stronger, better weaponry and equipment were there to do the fighting. I never felt that attitude. "Our" RF/PF soldiers did not hesitate to fight the enemy.

Most of Hàm Long's RF and PF soldiers had undergone basic training at the ARVN National Training Center at Chi Lang, far up the Mekong River almost at the Cambodian border.

However, many of the PF platoons and RF companies also underwent refresher unit training at the Con Ho Training Center in Kiến Hòa's Ba Tri District. From time to time the district chief moved a PF platoon from its outpost and replaced it with another unit so the PF platoon could deploy as a unit for refresher training at Con Ho. Unit training lasted from two to three weeks, shorter for PF units and longer for the RF platoons and companies.

I had never operated with RF/PF units until now. Almost instantly I came to respect them for their operational prowess and courage. They had paid attention during their individual and unit training. Sometimes their leadership was less than sterling, but I never doubted the soldiers' bravery and ability in combat. The PF and RF soldiers were fun to be with in the field. During rest stops or on outpost construction, they were very curious about us advisors. I was always approached by small groups of men, usually two or three at a time, who wanted to say hello, to "smell" and sound out the new American.

They were curious about everything concerning American advisors: our home, our family, our equipment and—yes—the size of our "personal equipment." Sergeant Bé practically collapsed with hysterical laughter when one of them asked me exactly that. He could barely get his words out to me; he thought it was so funny. No, I did not show them the prize they sought, and they clearly did not believe my serious (!) response that it was "just average." Most spoke no English, but between my limited Vietnamese language ability and hesitant English on their part, we were able to communicate. One of our interpreters was always with me in the field and could make conversation easier and better understood. I felt that it was very important for me to establish good rapport with the soldiers—after all they were also "my" soldiers. If and when we found ourselves under enemy fire and maneuvering in combat, I wanted to be able to anticipate their actions and movement, understand them, and hope they understood me.

... Happiness Is Going on an Operation and Not Getting Shot.

Hàm Long was the second-most secure district in Kiến Hòa Province. Even so there were several very bad areas. Phú Túc village on the north side, stretching along the Mỹ Tho River, was the worst. For most of my time there was no village office there, and VC/NVA units habitually stayed there in well-concealed and well-fortified small base camps. Phú Đức village, in the northwest part of the district, was almost as bad. Those two villages were across the Mỹ Tho River from Dong Tam and had frequently been the target of 9th Infantry Division operations. Several swaths of vegetation had been defoliated by Agent Orange flights, but those two areas were still the more-or-less permanent home for VC regional force units. Other villages had both good and bad areas. Small, well-kept hamlets and rice paddies were reasonably safe, but particularly north of the main road the terrain switched from well-tended rice paddies to heavy coconut "jungle," and those areas were periodically the location of small guerrilla units.

How We Operated

Because Hàm Long operations were short and never lasted more than two days, advisors did not have to carry the large and weighty backbreaking loads that soldiers in American combat units carried. I wore jungle fatigues, a T-shirt but no undershorts (to prevent crotch rot from the constant wet rubbing), jungle boots, and on most operations I wore a steel helmet during all but rest periods. I carried two large canteens of water and plenty of halazone or iodine tablets to purify water collected along the route of the march. I rarely carried a combat pack, although we were issued one.

The jungle fatigues had lots of pockets into which a lot of smaller items went, including my waterproofed acetate-covered 1:50,000 maps, usually folded and carried in the large pocket on my trouser leg. I stuffed in a comfortable bush hat for rest periods. I carried my M-16 rifle everywhere, even to village offices. In addition I often wore a caliber .45 M-1911 pistol on the pistol belt. The pistol belt also carried several pouches into which went ammunition magazines, two or three fragmentation grenades, a smoke grenade, insect repellant, and my super-lightweight hammock. I usually wore the combat suspenders, which provided support for the heavy pistol belt as well as more space to carry stuff.

Operations rarely lasted more than a day, and we seldom were out overnight, so there was no need to carry extra clothing. We didn't carry food because the villages or outposts along the way provided it; we ate what the troops ate. I did not carry an air mattress or poncho, but I often rolled up the poncho liner and carried it along. During the few overnight operations, the Vietnamese provided a secure place to sleep, either in an outpost bunker or fortified village office.

I carried the team's PRC-25 radio on almost every operation, with both the short whip antenna and the longer antenna folded up and tied to the back of the radio. The operation commander always offered to have a soldier carry the radio, and the interpreter also offered to carry it, but I always insisted on carrying it myself. For one reason, if there was enemy contact, I did not want to wonder where the radio went if someone else carried it. I did not want to expose somebody else to enemy fire—the VC always shot at the radio antennas. I figured that, at 6'2" and towering over all the Vietnamese soldiers, the enemy could easily pick me out.

The Vietnamese officers had a choice of equipment and small arms. Trung-tá Sơn and Trung-úy Hương always wore a pistol belt with a holstered .45 pistol. Hương's pistol hung low on his leg, he must have watched American cowboy movies. Trung-úy Liêm always carried an M-16 instead of a pistol. The RF and PF soldiers all carried M-16 rifles. None of the Vietnamese officers carried a radio—they all had RTOs. Everyone carried extra ammunition and some combination of hand grenades and smoke grenades.

We were fortunate in Hàm Long to have a third American on our team. SFC Logan, the operations NCO, was a large, friendly, gregarious Black NCO with a gentle personality and a great sense of humor. He was so much bigger than the Vietnamese—they loved him, and he got along famously with them. Major Kretschmar assigned him to the primary training missions we had, principally training PF platoons and PSDF units in how to use and maintain the M-16 rifle, which by 1971 were finally being issued to this lowest level of organized Vietnamese military personnel. He was also in charge of the maintenance of our Boston Whaler motor, the generator, and supervising the team house. Most importantly for us, he was the base radio operator and relay. When both Major Kretschmar and I were in the field on the same day, SFC Logan remained on radio watch to relay our transmissions to Bến Tre when we were out of direct commo with the TOC because of distance or atmospheric conditions.

At some point during those first several weeks, Major Kretschmar recommended to the PSA that I be moved from the PH coordinator slot to the DDSA slot. I did not know he had made the recommendation until one day he told me that I was now officially the DDSA. This was a big deal personally for me because it meant I had demonstrated the ability to be a combat arms officer regardless of the brass on my collar. I was proud that he and the PSA had both evaluated me as qualified to fill the combat arms position. I never asked, but I suspected that he had talked with Trung-tá Sơn and Trung-úy Hương for their opinions on my suitability to be DDSA. The big chip I had carried on my shoulder was gone.

Field operations almost always followed the same general pattern. The district chief briefed the DSA or DDSA the evening before the mission on the route march, the objective, and the timing of the operation. The mission could be a reaction to intelligence about an enemy unit, movement of VCI cadre (such as tax collectors, political leaders, or recruitment teams), outpost inspection or construction, and the enemy situation where the operation would go. We took that information back to the team house, prepared our own plan, and marked possible enemy troop locations on our maps for tactical air support should there be enemy contact.

There were usually three elements to operations, regardless of the mission. There was a forward screening force, the headquarters group, and combat and security forces on both flanks. Flank security came either from PF platoons stationed in outposts along the route march or for larger operations from RF company elements that deployed with the headquarters group and then moved on the flanks. The headquarters element included the operation commander, RTO, and a security element from headquarters troops or a designated PF platoon. Advisors and interpreters always moved with the operation commander.

I was pleased to see that the RF/PF soldiers were well trained in the basics of operational movement. They practiced good spacing discipline and avoided bunching up at choke points like water crossings. Movement was steady but slow, especially when walking on rice paddy dikes. Some of those were solidly compacted and were village access trails, wide enough for bicycles and motorcycles, broader and stronger than dikes used only for paddy borders. The ordinary paddy dikes were much more loosely compacted and quickly deteriorated from the passage of dozens of soldiers and extra-large advisors. Packed or loose, paddy dikes were frequently booby-trapped, so soldiers were very observant as they moved.

Almost all operations began by truck movement from the district compound to a selected deployment point. Once dropped off, the soldiers moved on foot or boat toward the objective. When any of the force made contact with the enemy, the operation commander was responsible for deploying all of his forces against the enemy but always maintaining an effective security force around the command group. When the command group was attacked, at least one element of flank security would maneuver against the enemy while the other consolidated with the command group. The advisor's mission was to maintain close contact with the operation commander, determine if tactical air support was needed, and if so, to work with the province TOC to obtain a FAC, armed helicopter or tactical air support and fight the enemy.

Most operations were incident-free. In those cases we did what the mission called for, whether outpost construction, sweep with no contact, or administrative village visit, and returned to the nearest secure road. The RTO called for the trucks to take us back to the compound. The return march to the trucks was always over a different route than the outbound march. We never wanted to be ambushed by the enemy waiting for us along the route we had started on. Because of the great expanse of rice paddies along the main road, operational movement there was very relaxed because there was excellent visibility for a long distance, unobstructed by trees. Vigilance was much more strict when inside the coconut groves and scraggly jungle.

Those early operations were a good experience for me, as I learned about the geography and terrain of the district and became familiar with the village office locations and the many outposts that we visited. Those outpost operations were usually a combination of resupply and inspection. The operation commander needed to check on the condition of the outpost itself—bunkers, fortifications, cleared ground on all sides, functional fire arrow, and a neat appearance. The outposts were triangular in shape, with large bunkers at the points and a thick-packed mud surrounding barrier at least waist high. The ground all around was clear-cut and full of barbed wire barricades and tanglefoot. We spent a lot of time on outpost operations as the soldiers and officers went about inspecting, upgrading, and repairing outpost facilities.

The fire arrow was an important part of an outpost. Usually in the center of the outpost, the fire arrow was a board a couple meters long and narrow, with a point or arrowhead at one end, mounted on a swivel atop a short post. The arrow was large enough for a lot of attached clay pots filled with gasoline or kerosene and a wick. In case of a night attack, when tactical air support was available, a soldier lit the fire arrow and pointed it at the enemy strongpoint. It was big enough for the FAC to see it and know

This large outpost in Phú Túc village was manned by a reinforced RF platoon. It was the most difficult of all the outposts to access. Much of the adjacent canal was elsewhere subject to VC ambush; the overland patrol was long and difficult. It was frequently attacked—note the bomb scars from tac air directed against enemy forces attacking the outpost.

where to direct air attack assets. The fire arrow was also pointed to the LZ near the outpost in the case of night medevac flights.

The Risks We Worried About Most

There was plenty of risk, no matter where we were. The district compound was mortared, which required instantly sprinting to a bunker or other cover. Operations usually were uneventful, without firefights with the enemy. But when there was a firefight, it was quickly intense, and I had to know how to react and what to do next. I was never shot, although I certainly heard a lot of bullets flying around. More insidious was the threat of mines and booby traps. A command-detonated mine killed Major Kretschmar's predecessor as DSA on the main road to Bến Tre. Booby traps and mines caused the majority of troop and advisor casualties.

Each district advisory team prepared an emergency escape and evasion plan to be used in the event that the district compound was attacked and overrun. That almost happened in next-door Trúc Giang District. The

Hàm Long escape plan called for us to leave the compound in any direction away from the enemy's strongest attack and surreptitiously make our way south to, or adjacent to, the Tiên Thủy market, where we could commandeer some sort of boat with which to escape on the Soc Sai River. Luckily, we never had to use that plan.

... Feeling bad about writing a classified escape and evasion plan for the advisors, without telling our counterparts, but knowing that it was necessary.

Speaking for myself, but reflecting on what many of my colleagues thought, the risk we worried about most was not being wounded or killed during an operation. The biggest worry was finding ourselves suddenly left behind during a firefight and being captured by the enemy. That happened in October 1963 to First Lieutenant Nick Rowe[2] and Captain Rocky Versace, who were on an advisory team down in An Xuyên Province near the infamous U Minh Forest, and to a number of other advisors up and down the length of Vietnam, particularly during the 1972 NVA offensive. We worried that RF or PF soldiers would simply evaporate during a major enemy contact without telling us. So we spent a lot of time on operations, keeping our eyes on the operation commander, whoever it was, and keeping an eye on soldiers around us. We went where they went, and I always felt I was not going to be left behind if something bad happened.

Lots of Things Kept Us Busy

There was always plenty for the advisors in Hàm Long to do. First priority was operational support. There were two RF companies in Hàm Long and dozens of PF platoons. Other lightly armed elements included PSDF, who lived in the hamlets and were composed of men and women too old or too young to be in the other military elements, and RD Cadre, who were often important intelligence sources. District advisors were charged with evaluating all of these forces with a standard monthly report called the Territorial Forces Evaluation System (TFES).

Earlier in the war effort, when the number of American advisors was much higher, small five-man MAT Teams augmented the district advisory teams. The MAT Team mission was to live in the villages and hamlets on a rotational basis and train the local PF platoons and PSDF forces. When I arrived in Hàm Long, there was still one active MAT Team, at An Hiệp village. Over history MAT Team IV-5 lived in and trained the PF and PSDF in several other villages and suffered heavy casualties from a more-dominant enemy force. Major Kretschmar assigned me to supervise the MAT Team. They did not need supervision; they were very professional. However, the MAT Team ended its mission only a few weeks after I arrived, as part of the ongoing reduction in the advisory effort.

"Advisor" was a misnomer. By this stage in the Vietnam War, there was little advice we could give to our counterparts. As one-year or 18-month advisors, we were just the latest in a long string of advisors that our counterparts had experienced. Advisors were barely tolerated (worst), or valued as equal warriors (best!). Our main contribution was to act as the point of contact for American air support—helicopters for visual reconnaissance, medevac, and fire support, and to coordinate with a FAC to manage tactical air and armed helicopter support. I advised the Vietnamese on what type of bombs, rockets, or other armament might be available for air strikes and how to use them with safety for friendly troops and civilians. But I can recall no time in which I actually *advised* any of the Vietnamese officers on tactical operations. We were there to support them with air support and sometimes with financial support for development projects (we had Assistance In Kind—AIK—funds for that) and—perhaps most valuable—to be a bucker-upper, morale-boosting friend.

If there was no operation on any given day, there were many other things to do. The DSA was always in touch with the district chief, planning future operations, planning outpost construction, and discussing development projects, especially those in which some financial support from the advisors was expected. I spent a lot of time talking with Trung-úy Hương and Trung-úy Liêm, sometimes discussing upcoming operations and sometimes having long chats about almost anything. We also had administrative requirements, such as keeping our briefing charts current, catching up on report writing, changing the communication code every day, or visiting development projects near the district compound. There were personal things—writing letters home, reading, sorting through clothes that needed washing or repair, and catching up on sleep.

We tried to keep out of the way of the district staff. They were always on duty, working like soldiers do everywhere. We would occasionally go to the TOC to see what was going on in the field, and whenever we heard a big noise, whether outgoing artillery or something more worrisome, a mortar attack or mine exploding, we went quickly to the TOC to find out what was going on and what support might be needed from us. Evenings were usually free time for us, after a fine meal from Cô Bai or a function hosted by the district chief. We did not go off the compound alone after dark unless there was an emergency. We were in a reasonably secure location but not at night! That's when the VC did most of their activity. Letter writing, reading, and report writing tended to get done in the evening.

Someone from the team went to Bến Tre at least once a week. We needed those trips to get mail, confer with our bosses and province staff officers to discuss problems, coordinate programs, get help with maintenance of the jeep, the Boston Whaler motor, the generator; draw supplies, replenish ammunition, shop in the compound store (film, snacks, cases of beer and soft drinks, bottles of harder stuff), and have a half day to

RF soldier Phi (Fee) was assigned by the district chief as our jeep driver and mechanic. Phi was killed in action in 1974.

relax with friends. It was fortunate that the road to Bến Tre was secure—we could make that trip without a security force. Since we had an official driver provided by the district chief, there were always at least two armed men in the jeep and usually three since the interpreters were authorized to make those trips too.

We spent a lot of time analyzing the situation in our district, by ourselves and also with our counterparts on the district staff. It was important that we had a very good idea of the situation in every part of the district. This was critical in planning operations and for the constant flow of reports we had to prepare and for our own security.

We slept in a heavily fortified bunker adjacent to the team house, but we rarely were able to sleep through the night uninterrupted. The district artillery fired occasional harassment and interdiction (H & I) fire at random times and to random locations, hoping to catch enemy units and personnel out of their bunkers, perhaps moving to another location or massing for an attack on an outpost. We were accustomed to the sound of outgoing artillery, but when the firing was steady, we knew that they were providing supporting fires when an outpost was under attack or an ambush patrol had made contact. At least one of us would go over to the TOC to see what was happening, and where, and if there was a requirement for either attack helicopter support or a medevac helicopter. Because of interrupted sleep patterns every night, we tended to sleep in on mornings where there was no operation planned. And, of course, we looked forward to "nothing at all"—time to rest, think, and recover from a tough operation.

Winston Churchill once observed that there is nothing more exhilarating than being shot at and not being hit. I agree completely. Many of our operations were uneventful walks in the sun (or monsoon rains) during which no enemy was found and nothing bad happened. In those cases the worst thing that happened to me was to fall off a monkey bridge. However, some operations were more eventful, during which anything happened, from a sniper shooting at the soldiers—or me—to mortar attacks on an outpost, or an attack or ambush or someone setting off a mine or booby trap. I adhered to Churchill's commentary in such events. I can tell you that bullets make a strange sound going through banana leaves just above your head, and once you are the target of an enemy mortar, you never forget it.

5

Villages, Hamlets,
Outposts, and the HES Report

The Monthly HES Report

Every province in Vietnam was divided into districts and then into villages (a geographic area with political boundaries), then to hamlets (where people lived). Security in every district in Vietnam was measured by the monthly Hamlet Evaluation System (HES) Report. It was the single most important report among the many that advisors were required to complete. We thought the most important tactical goal was to fight and defeat the enemy in combat and stay alive and unscathed in the process. The strategic goal was to improve security, so there had to be a statistical system to evaluate improvement or degradation of security throughout the country. In a way, the HES Report was the reason we went into combat.

The HES questionnaire was exhaustive. It included questions on security (how many enemy attacks against the hamlet last month?), economy (does the village have a stand-alone market facility?), health (how many medical clinics have qualified staff?), and social affairs (is there a women's organization?). The DSA and district chief both signed the report, and it went forward through Province to Saigon, and weeks later the results came back in the form of a computerized alpha rating of each village and its hamlets, rated on a scale from A (most secure) all the way through B, C, D, E, and V (which stood for Vietcong controlled), depending on the relative degree of government versus VC/NVA control. Naturally, district chiefs wanted to see progress by upgraded hamlet and village ratings and hated it when there was a downgrade. Contrary to widespread rumors, a DSA was NOT rated on whether there was or was not progress in security as reflected in the district HES Report—at least that was the case in Kiến Hòa Province. Emphasis was on the accuracy of the report.

Each month the district advisory team was required to complete the district HES Report in conjunction with our Vietnamese counterparts.

The district chief and the DSA always had endless conversations on the proposed answers to the HES Report questions. Hàm Long focused on one or two villages each month, visiting the village office and village chief, usually with the district chief or his civilian deputy for development. There was not enough time to visit every village every month just to do HES Report interviews, so a lot of our observations during other operations went into notebooks that helped us to remember "what was where" when completing the HES Report questionnaire.

Once at the village office we went through the questionnaire in interview sessions that lasted several hours, laboriously translated between English and Vietnamese as questions and answers went back and forth. HES interviews always included lunch laced with copious quantities of beer and/or "cognac"—which was supposed to make the interviewees more truthful and the advisors sleepier. The interviewees won just about every time.

The easiest interview sessions were in the village in which the district headquarters was located. In Hàm Long that was Tiên Thủy village, which had a B rating. Sơn Hòa was a good example of other "easy" villages. Sơn Hòa village was located on a paved spur off the main road to Bến Tre, just west of the boundary with Trúc Giang District. Its market area was near the Hàm Luông River, and it was a prosperous "B" rated village. We routinely drove to Sơn Hòa without a security escort.

In contrast, Phú Đức village was a difficult situation. An insecure D-rated village, visits to the fortified Phú Đức village office required at least a platoon of PF for security. It was hard to get to Phú Đức. What had once been a connector road had deteriorated to a wide path with destroyed bridges, impassible for military vehicles. There were no navigable canals either. To get to Phú Đức we went to Tân Lợi by vehicle and then walked back along the road to the path that led north to the village office and outpost. We left the vehicles at Tân Lợi for security and returned by a different route. A lot of combat occurred in Phú Đức because of its location on the south bank of the Mỹ Tho River adjacent to the really bad Phú Túc village, which was always occupied by VC units.

The villages along the road through the district ranged from B through C, and the ones accessible only by boat or on foot were rated from B though D. In all of Hàm Long District there was only one hamlet rated "A," in heavily Catholic An Hiệp village. I argued, unsuccessfully, to downgrade Phú Túc village to level E. I was told it was politically impossible to rate a village so low.

Regardless of the level of difficulty to get to villages for HES Report interviews, every session gave us a chance to meet, often for the only time, the variety of village-level officials who conducted day-to-day government affairs. Often we were surprised by the answers to some of the questions, and every session provided important information to both the district chief and the advisors.

...*Happiness Is Surviving an Outpost Operation.*

The main tool in expanding security in Hàm Long was the small outpost, usually manned by a PF platoon of eight to 20 soldiers, depending on the security situation in the area. Outposts were placed in heavily populated areas as well as in more dangerous areas as the security net expanded. There were some successes and some failures. The security net expanded and contracted almost entirely based on the strength and activities of the enemy. Success was expanded security, cutting VC lines of communication, and denying them the use of an area for their own security. Failures were the loss of outposts, either overwhelmed by a larger enemy attack or betrayed from within by traitors, VC-forced recruitment of villagers, and the assassination of village officials and teachers.

The larger outposts in Hàm Long were manned on a rotational basis by platoons from the two Regional Force (RF) companies. Often families went with their soldiers, a Vietnamese cultural characteristic but one that sometimes resulted in women and children being killed or wounded when an outpost was attacked.

Trung-tá Sơn had an "expert" on his staff—Warrant Officer (Chuẩn-úy) Thiệu (not his real name), who was the honcho for all outpost construction operations. Long before I arrived in Hàm Long, Chuẩn-úy Thiệu had been shot in his right hand and had lost several fingers, which prevented him from firing a rifle. But he sure knew how to build outposts! He reminded me a lot of the crusty senior first sergeants in the U.S. Army—no nonsense, knew what he was doing, and he wielded an iron hand overseeing the building of outposts.

Hàm Long's soldiers were well regarded for their ability to plan and build good-quality outposts in a short time. The usual format was for the district staff to plan the location of the outpost, then design an operation that included security for the construction period and then assign the RF or PF unit to man the outpost. Whenever new outpost construction was planned, the affected village chief was responsible for rounding up manpower to help on the construction, thus investing the villagers in the success and security of the outpost. The village chief and hamlet chiefs in the area monitored and supervised their residents. Each civilian worker got a small amount of pay for the work. Soldiers provided security for the project and were a major part of the workforce.

There was a firm process to building an outpost. It began with an analysis of where an outpost was needed. The purpose could be to add security to a difficult area or to move into position to interdict known enemy communication and logistics routes. Planners got together to determine the exact location and to purchase land from villagers if necessary. The district chief, the S-4, and Chuẩn-úy Thiếu determined logistics requirements—coconut logs, sandbags, barbed wire, steel supports, etc.—and then the district chief assigned the PF platoon or RF company (for larger outposts) to man the outpost. Some outposts were close to the main road, some accessible on foot or by boat, some only by walking. Trung-tá Sơn often went out for a day to oversee outpost construction, provide leadership and command presence or to formally mark the opening and manning of the outpost. Other times he assigned one of the staff officers to oversee the operation. Advisors went on lots of operations to build, repair, or inspect Hàm Long's many outposts.

Strange Meal at Lunch

The largest outposts in the district were in the difficult northern areas in the villages of Phú Đức, Phú Túc, Quới Thành, and Tương Dạ. These were manned by one or more RF platoons that were rotated out to the field and back to the company compound across from the district headquarters. The operation described here took place in early September 1971; it was my first trip to a large RF outpost. The purpose of the operation was to rotate a platoon of RF soldiers.

It was an uneventful walk through dry rice paddies along well-packed dike paths with no booby traps. The objective was a newly upgraded and repaired mud-walled triangular outpost in northern Tương Dạ village. As we walked single file along the paddy dikes, I noticed that the soldier in front of me had a backpack with a small dog peeking out. I thought it was cute that a soldier would bring his pet out to a new outpost.

After the usual inspection of external tanglefoot wire defenses, lines of fire for the machine guns, a working fire arrow, and sturdiness of bunkers, the outpost commander invited us to stay for lunch. Sergeant Tu and I were served a ceramic bowl of soup with chopped-up hunks of meat in typical Vietnamese fashion—just hacked up with a meat cleaver with bones protruding here and there, just like they prepare chicken. There was no such thing as a "wing" or a "thigh" with Vietnamese chicken; they just hacked the bird up with a cleaver. The meat in this soup was processed the same way, but it did not taste like beef or pork. I asked Tu what it was. "I'm not sure," was his diplomatic answer.

It took me only a few moments to put two and two together. I remembered that RF soldier with the puppy dog in his backpack. Well, of course,

Everyone—including me—enjoying a gourmet outpost lunch, bowls of soup with vegetables and hunks of meat, thus chopsticks, as I enjoyed my first meal of dog meat.

This outpost is in terrible shape! Look at how high the grass is—no visibility, the enemy could sneak up very close and not be seen. The operation commander, Trung-úy Hương (second from the left in front of the RTO), quickly had all the soldiers out with machetes cutting the grass.

that soldier was not carrying his pet puppy in the backpack. It was not a pet; it was a fresh lunch! Dog meat is quite popular in some parts of Vietnam, particularly in Hanoi and the Mekong Delta. That was the first time, and assuredly not the last time, that I ate dog meat at a meal.

Hàm Long's outposts were all constructed with thick mud berms with bunkers topped with coconut logs for protection against enemy mortar attacks. A newer outpost always looked nice and fresh, but the climate and the rigors of war took a quick toll. Most outpost operations were for inspection and repair, and Chuẩn-úy Thiểu went on all of them. He and the operation commander were draconian in their demands for repair and strengthening of the mud walls and bunkers, for cutting down foliage around the outpost, and for strengthening the barbed wire concertina and tanglefoot defenses. These operations were large, with extra soldiers brought along to help with repairs as well as security; often a village chief would provide civilians to assist in the work.

Quới Thành Village and Mr. Hoa

One outpost I wish I had a few pictures of is the Quới Thành village office and outpost. It was located between the district compound and the town of Tân Lợi, but it was one or two kilometers off the road, inside a dark and forbidding area of dense coconut trees. Mr. Hoa, the Quới Thành village chief, was a real character. He had been around a long time and never found a glass of alcohol he didn't like.

Quới Thành was an important village because its borders reached very close to the district headquarters compound, and so its security was crucial to securing the district headquarters. Yet its difficult, heavy vegetation and lack of usable roads or canals made access difficult for the RF and PF soldiers but very convenient for small bands of enemy soldiers.

The Quới Thành village office was one of the places where I went on an overnight operation. We went out there to do HES Report interviews with Trung-úy Hương as commander. Like Phú Đức, the Quới Thành village center and office was north of the road to Tân Lợi and was reached only by a wide and hard-packed pathway but only by narrow plank bridges over the several small irrigation canals—good enough for bicycles and motorcycles—and soldiers—but not for four-wheeled vehicles. The main part of the office was a large open-air pavilion with a concrete floor and a sturdy roof. Stout bunkers stood outside the four corners of the pavilion. Office furnishings featured a very heavy, large, high rectangular wood table. It was so big and heavy that I was able to tie my hammock *under* the table. If we got mortared that night, the wooden table would protect me if I was under it, and if hit by a ground attack, we could upend it and the thick tabletop would stop a lot of bullets.

After a long afternoon and dinner with HES Report questions, well-fueled with beer and cognac, I went to sleep after dinner and a few brandy toasts with Mr. Hoa. Much later a soldier came to wake me up. He startled me in the darkness, and at first I thought we were under attack. But no, Mr. Hoa wanted to talk some more and propose another alcoholic toast or three with the American *cố vấn*. He had been the elected village chief of Quới Thành for so long nobody could remember his predecessor. No matter his abilities or lack thereof, or his personal connections with the enemy or not, he was a real character, and I always enjoyed the conversations whenever we got together.

Counterpart Intelligence Collection and Analysis

Despite my close relationship with Trung-úy Hương and the intelligence NCOs, he never briefed me about his intelligence operations, not even once. Even from discussions with him and his NCOs, with our interpreters, and some personal evaluations and observations, I had only a vague idea of how intelligence operations were conducted in Hàm Long. To be fair, I had the same experience later in Mỏ Cày as well.

Hương's S-2 section occupied a small office in the row of adjoining staff offices along one side of the compound facing the open parking area. His office contained several small work tables for himself and the NCOs. Trung-úy Hương and his very tough senior NCO worked there full time, and I noticed over time that several other soldiers also worked in the office and shared the other work tables. The office was not large enough for all of them to sit and work together at the same time. I figured out that those more junior NCOs were field operatives collecting information and meeting with confidential sources in areas secure enough that no full-scale operation was involved, and then they came into the office to write their reports. All of the staff offices were open to view from outside, so there was no situation map or any wall charts with enemy locations and activities marked. Those details were noted on the joint intelligence and operations situation map on the wall inside the TOC, which I could see whenever I was in there to consult on the situation and any ongoing activity.

I assumed that Hương and his NCOs operated a network of informants and sources throughout the district which, I concluded, included VC (known to them) as well as ordinary villagers. I was never privy to the details of any of those sources. A considerable amount of the information went into the PH dossiers in the DIOCC file cabinet. When he planned an operation, Trung-úy Hương told me his assessment of the enemy situation in the area of operations but not how he had obtained that information. And as noted previously, I often observed him and other soldiers on our operations off to the side talking to civilians in the hamlets we passed through. I quickly learned not to ask questions about specific sources of information because he never gave me any details. The most he would say was something to the effect of "one of my sources told me." Obviously he believed that I had no need to know his sources and methods.

The S-2 section provided the advisors with copies of their written intelligence spot reports, but none of them identified the source of information. Each day various soldiers delivered to the team house a number of typewritten intelligence reports that our interpreters periodically translated into English for us. The quantity of reports was impressive, and they often contained interesting tidbits of information. Unfortunately, the majority of those reports were "historical" in that they provided information that had already taken place. It might be something like this: "On 5 Sep the VC Tương Dạ village secretary held a meeting with hamlet cadre at coordinates ABxxxxxx." I never saw actionable reports advising of important enemy troop locations or VCI movements that would take place in the future.

Major Kretschmar told me very early on that we would never get specific details on intelligence sources and methods. As a military intelligence officer, I was well trained in source protection, compartmentalization, methods of analysis, everything professional intelligence organizations routinely do, so I was not surprised that our counterparts did not share details with us. As my experience widened over time, it was clear that Lieutenants Hương and Liêm were fairly certain whether an operation would encounter the enemy or not. While we were often surprised, either by unforeseen booby traps or mines, ambush, or a firefight with the enemy, most of the time operations really were quiet walks in the sun.

The Province S-2 section provided information to the district, but that input dealt almost entirely with enemy unit sightings, mini-base camp locations, and known trail networks used by commo-liaison cadre as well as small unit movements. That information was put to use with artillery targeting and later, as the enemy situation worsened, with tac air strikes. I never saw any sophisticated technical intelligence collection systems, and I estimated that the majority of the intelligence "take" came from agent reports and person-to-person meetings. This "system" gave added importance to the frequent village visits and outpost operations. Both gave ample opportunity for Trung-úy Hương and other intelligence personnel to contact organized sources as well as have impromptu talks with other villagers.

The other side of the coin was VC intelligence about Hàm Long's forces and advisors. Discussion among us, as well as with other advisors, always included surmised opinions on who, or what percent, of the counterpart forces were actually VC or VC supporters. My guess was that about one-third of the friendly force had VC connections, but I never guessed who was in that one-third. VC assets among the Hàm Long headquarters personnel were able to provide intelligence to the enemy, apparently very quickly and probably very accurately. I also had no doubt that there was some level of accommodation between PF soldiers in outposts and their enemy counterparts. That accommodation might take the form, for example, of instances of PF outpost patrols that went "that way" while the VC went "this way." But collaboration or not, the level of combat was so high that our counterparts were actively seeking to find and neutralize the enemy.

ARVN counterintelligence was conducted by the ARVN Military Security Service (MSS), a tightly controlled and secretive national-level agency that was organized down to the district level. In Hàm Long the MSS element was a small section headed by Second Lieutenant Theo (not his real name), a professional intelligence officer. Both he and his subordinates wore both military uniform and civilian clothing—and I never learned the real names of most of them. One or more of them frequently went on operations or attended HES Report interview meetings. None of them, even once, hinted at who in the district headquarters or village offices were, in fact, VC.

... *Happiness Is a Drink of Fresh Coconut Water After a Tromp Through the Jungle.*

This is a bit deceptive, because Hàm Long had no real sections of "jungle"—that is, wild, heavily vegetated, double- or triple-canopy terrain. Most of Vietnam's jungle areas are in the Central Highlands and mountains. But Hàm Long District had large tracts where nobody lived, either because of VC pressure or because it was all planted in rice or coconut. Hàm Long District was reportedly the largest producer of coconut and coconut products of any district in Vietnam. Most of the productive small plantations were north of the main road, although small groves were everywhere.

Coconut trees are planted in long rows about 15 feet apart. Between the rows is a trench for water. These trenches are about two or three feet deep and five or six feet wide. They are ideal for the enemy to hide in to ambush or snipe at friendly forces. They are equally ideal for the soldiers and advisors to jump into when ambushed or sniped at. I have been in a lot of coconut grove ditches.

Coconut was the predominant vegetation in the most dangerous areas where enemy units habitually stayed. Coconut logs provided overhead cover for RF/PF outposts as well as for enemy bunkers. As productive and fertile areas were deserted by the population fleeing enemy control, a rough and scraggly secondary growth covered the area as well, which provided additional cover and concealment for enemy activity.

The coconut groves, in addition to the trenches between rows of trees, were also characterized by a variety of maintenance. Some owners trimmed the grass, vines, and shrubbery between trees, and others did not. The degree of neatness was directly proportional to the degree of security in any particular area. Universally, the coconut groves in the least secure villages were unkempt, with lots of high grass and shrubs on the tree lines. This gave concealment to enemy forces but did not provide cover from attacks. Tactical operations involved a lot of coconut plantations. Those were easy if you were going "with the trees" but very tiring and difficult if going "against the trees" because we had to cross all those ditches, climb up to the next row of trees, back into the ditches, back up with the trees—you get the idea.

The best reward of operating in the coconuts was the supply of coconut water. After three or four hours of humping through those trees, rough grass and shrubbery and in and out of ditches, I always welcomed the short rest break when soldiers climbed up the trees, hacked off coconuts, and then cut off the top so we could drink the fresh coconut water inside.

Coconut shells are hard and difficult to open, and it is necessary to know which ones are still young enough to have water inside instead of just hardened coconut. There were always experts among the soldiers—they lived in these surroundings—who could quickly find the right young coconuts with lots of water and immature flesh and knew how to hack them open with a few whacks of a machete. They always made the hole large enough so, after you drank the coconut water, you could scoop out the young flesh inside using a small, sharp piece of coconut hull as a spoon. Coconut water is fresh, flavorful, and immaculately clean and is a wonderful refreshing drink after a long, hot muddy tromp.

The 9th Infantry Division defoliated a lot of the northern part of Hàm Long's coconut areas during their short tenure in Vietnam because that area is directly across the Mỹ Tho River from the Dong Tam base camp. In subsequent years villagers built their houses in defoliated areas anyway because the relatively open space enabled them to grow crops easier. Several outposts were also built in defoliated areas for the same reason—easier to maintain an open area for security around the outpost. Back then none of us understood the insidious, dangerous effects that Agent Orange would have on our health. As a cancer survivor myself, I know well how both American soldiers and Vietnamese civilians suffer to this day from the effects of Agent Orange and other defoliants.

Villagers with a large complex of vegetable gardens located in the midst of defoliated coconut trees.

... *Happiness Is Being Served Duck's Blood Soup and Keeping It Down.*

If I had to guess, the most infamous food "test" given to American advisors by Vietnamese counterparts was not serving a chicken foot or a fish eye. (I had both of those delicacies at least once.) Rather, it was offering them duck's blood soup for lunch or dinner. It looks yucky, it has a nasty texture, and the idea is revolting to many. But especially when visiting villages or outposts where food availability is scarce, with little variety, we ate what the Vietnamese ate—and everything that is edible is eaten.

Duck's blood soup is considered a manly food that gives virility and strength to the consumer. Being offered duck's blood soup by soldiers in an outpost was a compliment. Sometimes they just handed me a small bowl (never a glass) filled with the duck's blood. Most of the time it was made into a soup, thinned with water or other broth, with vegetables and pieces of duck meat added. The copious quantity of beer or whisky served with duck's blood soup was also helpful in digesting this treat.

Cultural and Religious Diversity

No matter what was going on, whether operations, administrative village visits, or reactions to enemy activity, I was always aware that the ordinary lives of the people went on normally, all around us. Life in the midst of a dangerous wartime environment impacted everyone, but seeing "normal" activity kept my mind on an even keel, such as coming back from an operation in northern Tiên Thủy village and seeing a Lambretta on the way to Bến Tre, filled with dozens of bags of rice. Farming and commerce kept on, with the people taking the best possible courses of action in a world of abnormal events.

There was extensive religious diversity in Kiến Hòa Province that I saw and learned about on all those operations. The largest Buddhist temple in the province was the Cao Đài complex in Hàm Long. Catholicism was the primary Christian religion in Kiến Hòa Province, based largely on refugee families who had moved south from North Vietnam in the 1954 partition of the country. Small Catholic communities formed in An Hiệp and Thành Triệu villages in Hàm Long and Rạch Dầu in Mỏ Cày. The largest Catholic congregation was in Bến Tre, where the large, modern Catholic church was built after the 1968 Tết Offensive, after the original church was destroyed.

Several of the districts had a *đình,* which combined Buddhism with ancestor worship. But there were many other temples and churches all over the province, some in good condition and others badly deteriorated. I managed to see several of them during my 18 months in the province. Elsewhere in this book there is a bit more detail on some of the interesting aspects of local traditions, history, and religion. It all fit into the tapestry of experiencing a new culture that was always all around me no matter what the immediate circumstances might be. It was a hugely important aspect of life as an advisor in the countryside, and I thoroughly enjoyed it.

The Coconut Monk

No religious lifestyle was stranger than that of the "Coconut Monk" and his community of about 4,000 adherents. It was located on the eastern tip of Phoenix Island, between Thới Sơn Island and the Tân Thạch ferry landing, in the Mỹ Tho River. Claiming to be a unique sect of Buddhism, the sect included both Buddhist and Christian precepts as well as the pacifist beliefs of its leader. The Coconut Monk and his followers dressed all in brown and claimed to eat only coconuts and coconut products, of which there was an ample supply growing on the island.

The Coconut Monk's movement called for peaceful reunification of Vietnam, an end to combat between north and south, and was therefore disliked by the South Vietnam government, but it was left alone. I went out with, a few other advisors only one time, out of curiosity to see what was there. The first thing we were told when we got off the boat was not to talk with the Coconut Monk himself because he had taken a vow of silence until the end of the fighting and reunification of Vietnam. We were free to walk around and talk with any others in the community. We discovered that many of the male members of the commune were of draft age, and we speculated that they had become disciples to avoid being conscripted into the ARVN, RF, PF—or the VC. Nonetheless, neither the Kiến Hòa provincial government nor the Trúc Giang District government ever detained any of the "monks." Apparently, the commune did not provide shelter for VC/VCI personnel, for if that was the case surely the Trúc Giang District forces would have become involved in combat with the commune members.

The commune grounds were partly on land and partly on a platform over the water supported by large coconut log pilings. The grounds featured garishly painted towers and decor, much of which consisted of repurposed and repainted steel 55-gallon barrels and a plethora of unusually shaped towers. The easternmost tip of the island featured a huge flat map of the outline of Vietnam with one of the supporting pillars placed at the location of Hanoi. A platform above and facing the map held the seat for the Coconut Monk—a U.S. PX-style folding chair backed by stylized outlines of green mountains.

In contrast, the housing for the commune residents was almost identical to the very rustic rural housing, constructed of woven leaves and reeds, bamboo, and big leaved roofing (not tin or zinc metal). Although tolerated by both provincial and national authority during the war, in 1975 the victorious communist government banned the sect, although for some years the commune residents and their leader were allowed to continue living on the island.

6

First Contact

My first two months in Hàm Long were very busy but relatively uneventful. I spent the time learning my job, getting to know my team and counterparts, and getting used to life as an advisor. I went to the field often, probably twice a week, but nothing dramatic happened. There was plenty of enemy activity in the district, with attacks on outposts and ambushes of patrols, but no enemy encounters for me—yet. It was the monsoon season, and both sides in the war slowed down a bit because of the weather. This was a good introduction for me as I literally got my feet on the ground and became familiar with my new territory. I had gotten to most of the village offices, many of the outposts, and had accompanied the district chief, the S-2, the S-3, and the S-4 on a variety of operations. It was a good introduction to Hàm Long and the types of operations I could expect in the many coming months.

That quiet all ended in September 1971 when what seemed like an uneventful operation turned out to be anything but. Everyone who has written about their Vietnam combat experiences have said essentially the same thing: life in Vietnam consisted of days and weeks of total boredom and a few moments of sheer terror. However, there was a big difference between serving in a huge American tactical unit and being a district-level advisor. For advisors, the slack time was never boring. There was always something to do. Besides operations, there were meetings, intelligence briefings, building relationships with counterparts, report writing, house maintenance, shopping or paying for food, supervising the staff, repairing the generator, and on and on and on. But there were also those moments of sheer terror.

My baptism of fire happened during an operation in Hàm Long District's Tương Dạ village. This village had a troublesome history. Major Kretschmar's predecessor as Hàm Long DSA, Major James Coddington, was killed in action in November 1970 in Tương Dạ. The VC exploded a command-detonated mine while his jeep was waiting for an oncoming vehicle at a one-lane bridge over a canal on the main road between Hàm

Long and Bến Tre.[1] There were houses and people in the immediate area, and the village office was only 100 meters away, but there was no warning of the explosion. The district chief ordered an outpost built on the edge of the road next to the bridge, which may or may not have improved security over the intervening months. Tương Dạ was a dangerous village that as late as 1970 was rated on the HES as "V"—VC-controlled.

The operation plan was for several platoons of PF and RF soldiers to patrol north from the main road into the coconut trees. The objective was a VC guerrilla unit and a small base camp reported by intelligence to be in a specific place. Trung-úy Hương commanded the operation armed with his .45 pistol. I carried the advisory team PRC-25 radio and was armed with my M-16. My interpreter also carried an M-16, as did Hương's RTO and all of the RF and the PF soldiers.

The operation started out quietly. We dropped off the trucks near the village office and formed up on the road for the patrol across the rice paddies. The point PF platoon and the flank units were clearly visible as we left the main road and began patrolling north toward the target area. It was overcast, hot and very humid; heavy monsoon rains threatened.

The first hour or so was uneventful. Recent rains had filled the rice paddies, and the view of the wide green expanse of growing rice was gorgeous. The soldiers moved on a random zigzag route along more-or-less parallel rice paddy dikes and firmly packed paths and stayed out of the nicely growing rice and the deep mud. We had unobstructed, clear views for several hundred meters in every direction. The soldiers showed good discipline as they moved in single file along the several zigzag routes. They were well spaced and alert. There was no indication of trouble. Even so, everyone became more cautious as we passed the last of the rice paddies and approached an area of small overgrown orchards of fruit trees, coconut groves, bananas, and scrub brush. Two unoccupied hooches made of dry straw and reeds stood right at the edge of the dark, forbidding-looking forest of coconut trees. Everyone became more alert as we moved into the scrub vegetation, but there was still no discernable enemy threat.

All of a sudden all hell broke loose! The craaackkk craaackkk of AK-47 fire was unmistakable. The command group came under fire from an unknown-size enemy ambush force hidden in the scrub at the edge of the coconut trees. They had spotted Hương's RTO and me by the radio antennas, and my height marked me as an American advisor. We all quickly hit the ground—me with a loud "uuffff" with the weight of the radio on my back. Everyone returned fire in the direction of the noise of the enemy's incoming fire. I could not see any enemy and could not tell how many enemy had ambushed us, and I was not about to stand up to see better.

Trung-úy Hương on the radio with RTO Tinh. Soldiers on point are now headed toward the coconut trees at top left. There is no discernable threat.

The point element quickly moved back toward us, and the PF platoon providing security for the command group moved close and hit the ground next to us. I paid close attention to Trung-úy Hương's radio transmissions to the other PF and RF platoons: "I send one platoon behind houses!" He ordered one RF platoon to move around behind the empty hooches on our right and into the coconut trees to our right front in order to flank the enemy before the enemy could flank us. Enemy fire was heavy, but there was no indication that the ambush force was moving either toward us or to the flank.

Though I could not see the enemy, we could all sure hear incoming fire and the explosions from grenades—the enemy had lots of those. Scrub brush and the dense banana tree grove gave us concealment from the enemy, but we lacked covered protection from the incoming fire. Bullets whispered through the banana leaves over our heads—a very strange sound. Fortunately, the enemy fire was high and had not hit anyone. But they sure would have gotten us if we had moved less quickly.

RF soldiers maneuvered around on our right flank, as ordered by Trung-úy Hương, screened behind one of the empty hooches. They moved quickly, planning to attack the enemy ambush force from their flank before the enemy could move toward us or retreat deeper into the coconut trees. Adrenaline pumping, I kept firing, pleased to see the PF soldiers

around us were firing steadily. We all were trying to suppress the enemy's
fire, prevent them from attacking toward us, and keep them from notic-
ing the RF platoon's flanking maneuver—and maybe to kill some of them.
They had us pinned down, and wisdom was to stay down and distract the
enemy with return fire.

The flanking RF soldiers surprised the VC and took them under fire
from our right front, and soon the enemy fire stopped as they withdrew
away into the jungle. I had no detailed memory of firing my M-16, but I
know I did because I had fired off not only the magazine in the rifle but
also several magazines from my ammo pouches.

Hương and the RF platoon leader gave loud cease-fire orders when
the enemy fire stopped. We all cautiously stood up. "Good shooting,
Đại-úy," Hương said after things quieted down. "I think you got some."
He insisted that I had hit several of the enemy soldiers. Who would know?
We all were firing M-16s. Well, somebody did very well. When we moved
forward to join up with the repositioned RF platoon, we found a small but
well-constructed mud and coconut log bunker that was not large enough
to hold the number of enemy soldiers who had ambushed us. That might
explain the four dead VC lying on both ends of the bunker but not inside.
There were no enemy weapons; they had been policed up by the retreating
enemy. Best of all, there were no friendly casualties. The entire action from
the enemy opening fire until we regrouped at the bunker lasted about 30
minutes.

Hương and I both got on our radios, he to report to the district chief
and I to report to the American side at the province TOC. At my request a
nearby USAF spotter plane flew over our location, and the pilot searched
over the coconut trees to see if he could spot the retreating enemy soldiers,
without success.

Kiến Hòa Province advisors were required to submit a standard-format
written report "Advisor Under Hostile Fire" whenever we were in any contact with the enemy. Here is part of the report I submitted:

On 16 September 1971, CPT Haseman accompanied a Cửu Long[2] operation to
the field in An Hiệp and Tương Dạ villages, Hàm Long District. Taking part
in the operation were the 301st Regional Force Company and the 060, 061, and
339 Popular Force Platoons. The operation was under the command of 1LT
Phùng Hữu Hương, the S-2 officer of Hàm Long District, who was Acting Deputy District Chief for Military Affairs. CPT Haseman accompanied the operation as senior U.S. tactical advisor. He moved with the command group,
located with the 061 PF Platoon.

At 1330 hours 16 September 1971, the friendly forces encountered a mud
bunker located at XS 408383. Enemy troops estimated at one squad in strength
took the command group, 060, and 061 Popular Force Platoons under fire from

the bunker with small arms and M-79 grenades. CPT Haseman assisted 1LT Hương in maneuvering friendly troops against the enemy and requested U.S. surveillance aircraft. A U.S. L-19 aircraft (call sign Shotgun) arrived over the contact and was controlled by CPT Haseman in an aerial search for the enemy's withdrawal. Friendly forces maneuvered against the enemy and captured the bunker, silencing enemy fire.Results of the operation were four VC KIA, the remaining enemy withdrew with the weapons of the dead. There were no friendly casualties. The contact lasted for approximately 35 minutes, from 161330 to 161405 hours. CPT Haseman was physically under fire by enemy small arms and grenades for this entire period.[3]

So now I had experienced my first moments of sheer terror. There would be many more, but that first time under enemy fire has stayed with me ever since. No matter how many times something bad happens, instinct and experience quickly teach how to react intuitively, how to fight back, how to survive, how to take care of those around you. But you are still scared, and anyone who says they were never scared is plain crazy. And the first time under enemy fire—even if just for a few minutes and

The enemy ambushed us from the coconut trees behind the abandoned hooch on the left. The command group was lying in the banana grove in the center. Two RF squads maneuvered around the abandoned hooches to our right to assault the enemy bunker. I took this picture after everything had calmed down.

even if there are no friendly casualties—becomes one of life's defining moments.

Here's how I remembered it afterwards:

.... the cold flash of danger lying with PF soldiers in the grass of a banana grove, the bullets of the enemy ambush force rustling quietly through the banana leaves over our heads. Looking frantically for the enemy, knowing that somebody out there is trying to kill me. Cordite from my M-16, fired in anger for the first time at an enemy I can hear but cannot see. Relief when the firing stops and the wonderful, sensual feeling of adrenaline still pumping. And the feeling of savage delight at learning we killed four VC and suffered no friendly casualties. The looks of respect from the PF soldiers at me, for sharing their danger and doing well. And walking out of the Tường Dạ jungle, alive.

This sketch shows the layout of the ambush. It was my first time under direct enemy fire. I remember the details like it was just yesterday.

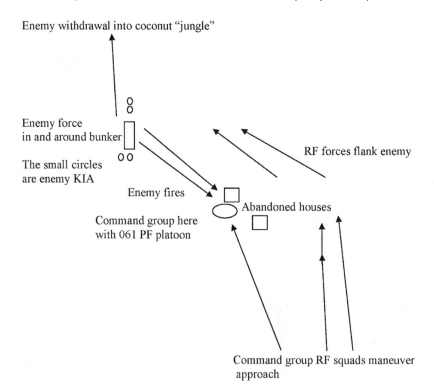

Enemy withdrawal into coconut "jungle"

Enemy force
in and around bunker

The small circles
are enemy KIA

Enemy fires

Command group here
with 061 PF platoon

RF forces flank enemy

Abandoned houses

Command group RF squads maneuver
approach

7

Dry Season Operations
in Hàm Long District

Change in Seasons, Change in Operations Tempo

I arrived in Kiến Hòa Province in July 1971, right in the middle of the rainy southwest monsoon season in the Mekong Delta. It did not rain all day, every day. However, it rained hard when it did rain. Usually the mornings were clear and hot, with clouds quickly gathering around noon and then heavy rain falling in the afternoon and evening. By October, the weather began to change, and soon we were in the dry season—hotter and drier, which meant increased operational tempo. Ground was more firm, and after rice was cut and threshed, soldiers could walk on the dried-out rice paddies instead of sticking to the dikes. There was no difference in the water obstacles—tidal flow from the main rivers kept rivers, canals, and streams full of water and soft mud.

The change of seasons brought visible changes to the countryside. Rice paddies were filled with rice changing from green to golden tan. As harvest neared, the paddies dried out to become firm, dry mud. Just as the planting of rice fascinated me, so did the harvest. Farmers built sturdy threshing enclosures of dry reeds and bamboo that provided an enclosed platform of bamboo slats where they pounded the dry rice stalks. Rice grains fell through the slats into a basket below; the dry rice stalks were laid on the ground, either gathered for future use (fronds for brooms, for example) or burned off and plowed under during the next monsoon season. The rice was moved to a flat, dry platform to dry in the sun. That platform could be hard tamped-down mud, it could be a paved cement outdoor patio near homes, or even could be spread out on the road where passing vehicles would crack the outer shell and make it easier to mill the rice later on.

It was normal to see PF and RF soldiers out in the paddies helping their families with the rice harvest. It brought home to me that the soldiers

Just outside the district compound the rice harvest is well underway. The threshing contraption—and hardworking women—combined to be surprisingly efficient in separating rice grains from the chaff.

were almost all local men, recruited from their home villages and hamlets, out taking care of their family or their hamlet's rice harvest.

The change in the weather also meant that our small advisory team would take on more tactical responsibilities. To be more effective I needed additional training.

"Back Seat School"

"Back Seat School" was a program to provide on-the-job training to CORDS and tactical unit advisors on how to coordinate tactical air strikes with a USAF FAC, how to assist in directing and coordinating ground tactical operations by command and control use of the helicopter, maximizing time for visual reconnaissance (VR) flights, and other aspects of air support. Major Kretschmar asked Province to arrange back seat training for me.

I flew to Cần Thơ in a Porter aircraft early on 15 November 1971. After finding the 164th Combat Aviation Group (CAG) Headquarters, I settled in for several hours of ground school. The classroom briefings covered ground control operations and the organization and methods of operation of the 164th CAG and the organization and mission of the various subordinate aviation units I would likely work with. Then they flew me up to Vĩnh Long Air Base by helicopter later that afternoon, and I began flying the next day. The CAG conducted on-the-job training by placing the back seat school trainees on already-scheduled missions flying in support of tactical operations.

I flew all day for three consecutive days, each day in support of a different type of combat element. On 16 November I flew all day on an air assault package with the 162nd Assault Helicopter Company, 13th Combat Assault Battalion, across the river from Kiến Hòa Province. In the morning we flew in support of Định Tường province-level operations and in the afternoon in support of the 11th Regiment, 7th ARVN Division. The next day I flew with the 114th Assault Helicopter Company, 214th Combat Aviation Battalion, in support of Vĩnh Bình Province operations and then the 12th Regiment, 7th ARVN Division. On 18 November I flew with B Company, 7/1st Air Cavalry Troop in support of the 44th Special Zone over the Plain of Reeds in Kiến Phong Province.

There was one "oh shit" moment. The helicopter I was riding in was covering a tactical operation by, as I recall, the 7th ARVN Division. Two of the advisors were in contact with their ground command element, while I was listening, watching, and learning. The advisors' unit was in contact with the enemy, and they were directing air strikes to support the ARVN units. Good training for me! The Oh Shit moment came when the command pilot said we were going to have to make an emergency landing because of some warning lights on the control panel. Oh shit!

The pilot was highly skilled, and we landed quickly. Fortunately, we landed behind the friendly forces, not among the enemy. Although there was plenty of shooting going on near us, nobody was shooting *at* us. Another helicopter from the CAG quickly came to our assistance and flew cover in case we had to abandon the helicopter. Quick checks by the pilot and crew chief revealed no major problems, and after only about ten minutes on the ground, we took off again and successfully completed the mission.

Each of these flights was conducted to support experienced advisors and their counterparts. I was fortunate to fly with two regiment senior advisors and their Vietnamese counterparts, all of whom were very helpful at explaining to me what was happening and how they coordinated with their counterparts. I got to fly with three different combat aviation units, which in itself was good information that would be very useful in later months. The entire experience was fantastic OJT that taught me how the advisor-counterpart-FAC-tactical air support team worked together on tactical air support missions. At the end of that final operation, they were kind enough to drop me off back on the Hàm Long District helicopter pad.

The four-day back seat school was a very valuable experience for me from an important practical standpoint, and it also resulted in a formal "eligible to control tactical air assets" certification. From then on I could coordinate with FACs, direct air strikes, conduct VR flights, and train my counterparts so they could do it after all U.S. advisors had left Vietnam. The short training session at Vĩnh Long was invaluable for the rest of my tenure in Kiến Hòa Province. In both Hàm Long and Mỏ Cày Districts I frequently coordinated with FACs, managed air strikes, and coordinated reconnaissance flights with my counterparts.

... Happiness Is Being First on the List for a VR.

The only way to see the big picture in the district was by going on a VR flight. Allocation of aircraft was from the supporting aviation command to the province, which then allocated flight hours to the districts by priority of operational requirements. Each day Kiến Hòa Province was allocated at least one helicopter for administrative support. We called it the "swing ship," the aviation unit called it "an ash and trash mission." Depending on operational priorities, the swing ship attempted to visit each district to deliver mail, movies, visitors, province senior staff, and press reporters.

The primary mission for the swing ship was to support tactical operations, again allocated by Province based on priority if more than one district was conducting large operations. First priority always went to support of troops in contact, in which case the helicopter was diverted from its administrative duties to the DSA and counterparts with troops in contact. If more than one district's operation developed contact, Province could request additional aviation support and hope that additional helicopters were available. Priority for use of any helicopter was first command and control for troops in contact, then to assist in spotting for air strikes, next was "to go looking." If no separate medevac helicopter was available, those wonderful U.S. Army pilots prioritized medevac missions in support of advisors, no matter if the casualty was Vietnamese or American. They ALWAYS came if needed.

Hàm Long was usually far down the list for VR allocation because of the relatively better security situation, but from time to time we got to use the ship to support operations, and we made full use of it when it was our turn. Better weather meant better flying conditions as well as more operations to support. The swing ship was a Huey (UH-1) "slick" with a machine gun on each side, with a gunner and the crew chief manning them but no other armament. The dry season and the increased operations tempo increased the priority for VR usage in Hàm Long.

When we received a helicopter for VR, priority for passengers went to the district chief and his radio operator, and one advisor with a radio and interpreter. That way if we spotted a good target or were supporting troops in contact, both the Vietnamese commander and the advisor could talk to operations staff in the province TOC for air strikes or whatever else needed to be passed along. I always briefed the command pilot on the type of operation to be supported or locations for VR using the 1:50,000 tactical maps we all used. The helicopter crew always gave the advisor a flight helmet with earphones and a microphone for communication with the two pilots. I would tell them where to go, guide them by map coordinates and ground landmarks, and relay support requests from Trung-tá Sơn, who would be talking to the forces on the ground using his own tactical radio. I used our PRC-25 radio to talk to the FAC, to our team house, and to the province TOC. I was proud, and excited, to use the knowledge I had gained in back seat school to support our counterparts and troops in the field.

The system worked well. Directions to the pilot usually began with something like "See the tree mass by the squiggle in the river at such-and-such coordinates." Depending on what we saw down there, we would either call for a FAC and air strikes or would move on to another area of reported enemy activity.

Learning More About the Culture Around Me

Not all of the time was spent on operations. Easier movement through the district allowed me to get more familiar with places around the headquarters compound and Tiên Thủy market. In my eagerness to learn more about the Vietnamese culture I was living with, I became very interested in the visible manifestations of the several religious "sects" in the Mekong Delta region of South Vietnam. In the process I got a much better feeling for religious diversity in what I had at first thought was a homogenous Buddhist religious culture. There were a couple of opportunities to learn more within just a few hundred meters of home base.

Cao Đài Temple. The largest and prettiest temple in Hàm Long was the Cao Đài temple complex, located just a few hundred meters from the district compound on the road to Bến Tre. Hàm Long was a major subset of the religious organization. The complex included both men's and women's temples and two monasteries for male and female monks. At the time I did not know much about the Cao Đài sect of Buddhism except that they worshiped a variety of deities including Jesus, the Buddha, and Victor Hugo. The religion has aspects of Buddhism, Christianity, Taoism, Confucianism, and Islam. The Cao Đài mother temple is in the city of Tây Ninh, northwest of Sàigòn, where the religion was founded in the 1920s. Cao Đài expanded from a religious sect into an anti-colonialist political movement against the French, later against the first South Vietnamese government of Ngô Đình Diệm, and against the communist Việt Minh and VC.

Because of the strangeness of the complex, I was initially reluctant to visit, not sure if a Westerner would be welcome. To my pleasant surprise, between Christmas and Tết in January 1972 Trung-tá Sơn invited me to go with him for one of his periodic visits to the temple complex. We were warmly welcomed by the monks and shown inside and outside both the men's and women's temples. Part of his visits were for congenial talks with the senior monks, but he was also obtaining intelligence and looking for draft-age males among the large cohort of Cao Đài monks.

The Hòa Hảo. My first contact with the Hòa Hảo religion came through Sergeant Bé, who was Hòa Hảo himself. His family lived in Thốt Nốt District of An Giang Province, where the Hòa Hảo movement was born. The founder of the Hòa Hảo was Huynh Phu So; he took the name of the sect from his home village of Hòa Hảo. He organized this sect in 1930, declared himself a prophet, and began to preach a doctrine based on simplicity and faith. Within a year, he had gathered a following of over 100,000 converts.

The religious precepts of Hòa Hảo are essentially Buddhist. Hòa Hảo shuns elaborate rituals, and its temples are extremely simple. Sergeant Bé invited me to visit the small Hòa Hảo temple in Tiên Thủy village where he went to pray. It was very austere, without the elaborate interior decoration that characterizes most Buddhist and Cao Đài temples.

As the religion expanded its reach, Huynh Phu So also became a popular political leader, and during the 1940s and early 1950s, Hòa Hảo developed into an important anti-colonialist nationalist force in the Delta. Other anti–French organizations also took shape, including the Việt Minh. The French, distrustful of the Việt Minh, eventually provided arms for some 20,000 Hòa Hảo troops as a counter to the military strength of the Việt Minh. Hòa Hảo had developed from a minor religious sect into a powerful political force complete with its own army, just like the Cao Đài.

Hòa Hảo's struggle with the Việt Minh became a fanatical religious war. The communists reacted. Huynh Phu So was invited to a unity conference at a Việt Minh stronghold in the Plain of Reeds. He was led into a trap, and he and his escort were assassinated. The Việt Minh quartered his body and scattered it to prevent the Hòa Hảo from recovering his remains and building a martyr's shrine. This barbarous act resulted in a rupture incapable of subsequent reconciliation. The Hòa Hảo vowed to wage eternal war against the communists. That fervor was reflected in Sergeant Bé as well and led to his earlier nickname of "Tiger."

The Cao Đài temple complex just before Tết 1972, with fresh whitewash and paint, banners, and flags.

Throughout the war, An Giang Province was a haven of peace and quiet amidst the violence that engulfed the remainder of the Delta. No ARVN division was ever required to conduct full-time combat operations in the province. Sergeant Bé told me, "In my home, there is no need for a guard. My parents never have to pay taxes to the Viet Cong. Anytime I want, I can walk to the next hamlet and not be afraid. I want my son to grow up like that. Here, there is too much war. It is all the fault of the Viet Cong. In my home area there are no VC."[1]

Increased Operations Tempo

Small-scale firefights increased in number with the increase in operations tempo. Major Kretschmar and I both had our share of them, but our luck continued—neither of us was so much as scratched. One of those operations took place in March 1972. The operation involved a *hồi chánh* (a VC who rallied to the GVN side through the *Chiêu Hồi* program). The *hồi chánh,* from the Tương Dạ village guerrilla unit, had surrendered at the nearby Cay Dạ outpost, reportedly convinced to change sides by a long-time friend who was a PF soldier stationed at Cay Dạ. The *hồi chánh* said he would take soldiers to where he had hidden his weapon—ralliers were paid for turning in their weapons.

At the same time, a corollary operation was organized nearby, with the 10th Regiment, 7th ARVN Division planning an air assault into an open area along the boundary between Hàm Long and Trúc Giang districts. Several Hàm Long PF platoons were tasked to secure landing zones for the ARVN airmobile assaults. Trung-tá Sơn was in command of our smaller operation, while he also directed the Hàm Long PF platoons supporting the 7th ARVN air assault. We hoped that enemy forces would be distracted by the 7th ARVN operation, and our simple operation would be easy. Trung-tá Sơn and I were each in contact by radio with our colleagues in the 10th ARVN Regiment.

We went by truck and jeep to the Tương Dạ village office, where the *hồi chánh* joined us. We waited while the 7th ARVN airmobile assault inserted to our northeast, then began our walk north along rice paddy dikes. I was a bit concerned because the operation was not far from where I was first in contact back in September 1971—Tương Dạ was still a nasty village. The *hồi chánh* was up front on point, leading the forward security element to the site of the weapons cache where he had hidden his rifle. Only one PF platoon—the 063rd—was involved with this operation because we did not expect enemy contact with the much larger 7th ARVN Division operation screening our flank.

About an hour after starting off, while we were still in the rice paddies area and closing in on the tree line where the *hồi chánh* said he had hidden his rifle, our small force came under enemy rifle fire from the tree line to our front. We all dropped flat in the rice paddy, where a high mud dike provided cover from the enemy fire. I radioed the ARVN regiment senior advisor to report our location and situation while the PF platoon returned fire against the enemy. The adjacent ARVN assault units drew closer and forced the VC shooting at us to retreat. Our small group quickly crossed the final rice paddies. It was a "win-win" situation—we had flushed an enemy force for the ARVN soldiers to engage, and we hoped that now we would find the *hồi chánh's* rifle. The S-2 NCO grabbed the *hồi chánh* and told him—forcefully—that his rifle had damned well better be where he said he had hidden it.

A short time later he led us right to the cache, and we recovered the AK-47. It was a small victory, no friendly casualties, just one of many—in this case a bit different because of the ARVN Division operation on our flank and having a *hồi chánh* lead our small district force to recover his weapon.

Just a few days later, 25 March 1972, I went to the field with Trung-úy Hương. He was acting Deputy District Chief for Military Operations, another example of the high regard in which he was held by the district chief. It was a considerably larger force—the 890th RF Company and the 053, 054, and 055 PF platoons. We were in mixed terrain of scrub brush and high grass in an abandoned rice paddy in midmorning when our large force came under sniper fire from an estimated VC squad. One of the PF platoons provided security for the command group while the 890th RF Company moved aggressively against the small enemy force. The enemy quickly withdrew into denser growth, with unknown casualties. One RF soldier was wounded. Our "second most secure" district was generating a large number of stinging hornets.

Carnage at Quán Mèo

We valued any victory, no matter how small, because not all of Hàm Long's operations ended well. One of the worst days was the loss of the Quán Mèo outpost in April 1972, toward the end of the dry season. The Quán Mèo outpost was very close to the main road in Thành Triệu village, and I had visited it several times because it was easy to get to and its location was considered relatively secure. As it turned out, it was not at all secure.

About 0200 one dark morning a soldier banged on the team house door to wake us up and tell us to get over to the TOC. Major Kretschmar and I could hear the thump of enemy mortars hitting not too far away. At the TOC we learned that Quán Mèo outpost was under attack but still in radio contact. Hàm Long artillery was firing both tubes, attempting to get their fires close enough to the outpost without causing friendly casualties.

Then the outpost radio went silent. Faces fell in despair. We knew the

98
In the Mouth of the Dragon

outpost had been overrun. Trung-tá Sơn had dispatched the quick-reaction platoon from the RF company, but they did not get there in time. After arrival at the outpost, the platoon leader's report was grim—VC gone, no survivors among the PF soldiers manning the outpost.

This was not the first time this sort of thing happened. The first time I went on an operation to an overrun outpost I was not emotionally or mentally prepared for what I saw. Other soldiers had gone ahead of us and did what they could to respect the remains of the dead soldiers. Nonetheless, the sight of their bodies unnerved me, and I had to turn away. It never got any better. I just did not ever get used to seeing the bodies of "my" soldiers killed by a dangerous enemy. Quán Mèo was one of the worst.

At first light, Trung-tá Sơn, Major Kretschmar, and I went to Quán Mèo with a platoon from the RF company. It was a grim and unsettling sight. There were no survivors to tell what had happened, but the late-night communications and the situation we found at the outpost made it clear what had transpired in the dark of night. The outpost had been trashed, and the dead PF soldiers were left lying where they had died. There were "only" seven dead PF soldiers in the ruins of the outpost, whereas there were 11 men on the outpost roster. The four missing PF soldiers were turncoat VC who had apparently burst into the bunker where the radio operator was, killed the two men in the bunker and three more nearby, and that was when the outpost radio went dead. Then the traitors signaled the VC into the outpost and executed two more PF soldiers who had surrendered to their "friends." The VC policed up all of the M-16s, ammo, and the radio and then vanished into the night.

We were all upset, angry, and saddened by what had happened in a "secure area" outpost. I was shaken by the sight of the dead soldiers in another of many outposts overrun with the help of traitors. Recovery of the remains of the dead, dealing with wailing family members, and maintaining a professional demeanor as we did our best to help the district chief with these difficult tasks was one of the most desperately hard times I ever experienced. I had known the men assigned to this outpost. I had talked with them on previous visits and encouraged them to do well. But sadly, the good guys lost this battle. Trung-tá Sơn ordered the soldiers to recover as much equipment and as many belongings as possible, and then what remained of the outpost was destroyed and burned. In the weeks afterward the district built and manned a new and stronger outpost nearby.

These words do not adequately describe the desperately sad sights at Quán Mèo.

... The crump of mortars falling into nearby Quán Mèo outpost, frantic calls for help over the radio from the small force of defenders.... Then silence, and the look of helplessness on the faces of the district chief and

TOC personnel when they realize the relief force will never get there in time. Gall and bitterness in my throat when we arrive at Quán Mèo in the morning, overrun with the help of traitors; seeing the slaughter of seven young PF soldiers who thought they were all on the same side; bile in my stomach as I contemplate their final moments of horror when they are killed by traitors they thought were their friends.

Quán Mèo was not the only loss of outposts and PF soldiers. Bad, maybe the worst single incident I remember. But other setbacks happened elsewhere at different times but with the same sad ending. Here are a few other incidents I recall with sadness but for which the details are elusive so many years later. These "at the time" remembrances tell at least part of the tragedy that struck all too often.

… Standing in the smoking wreckage of the Thời Đức outpost and wondering how many more there would be. Wishing, terribly, for ten minutes alone with the traitors if they are ever caught.

… Visiting with two 17-year-old PF soldiers at Phước Thành I outpost one beautiful day in October, learning their names and their hopes; and helping carry out their bodies on another beautiful day in January, victims of still another traitor.

Bỏ Xoài—The Good Guys Win This One

Bỏ Xoài watchtower was just a few klicks east of the headquarters compound. It was a towering wooden watchtower, at least as tall as the compound watchtower. It was usually manned by only three or four PF soldiers who rotated in for overnight duty from other nearby outposts. There was a low mud wall around the base of the watchtower, and a mud bunker. The top platform also had heavy timbers built in a tight square to provide protection from small arms fire but not much else. Because it was built so close to the main road, it was not considered to be threatened. Its primary mission was to monitor a long, visible, straight section of the main road to Bến Tre in order to discourage VC efforts to place mines on the road. One night the VC decided to eliminate the observation tower, thinking that its small complement of soldiers would make it an easy takeover. Wrong! Major Kretschmar and I were proud to be with Trung-tá Sơn the next morning when he led a small force of headquarters soldiers to the scene.

Here's how I remembered it:

… Bỏ Xoài watchtower attacked by a platoon of VC only three klicks down the road. PF soldiers holding off the enemy by throwing grenades from their bunker. Hàm Long artillery right on target, driving off the enemy force.

PSA Mr. Kotzebue awarding U.S. Army medals for valor to the defenders of Bỏ Xoài watchtower and the 890 RF Company commander, who found and successfully ambushed the retreating VC force.

The 890th RF Company ambushing the retreating VC and scoring well. Then visiting in the morning and the surprise on the faces of the defenders when they are called "hero." .... Two weeks later a feeling of quiet pride as the Province Senior Advisor and District Chief award them medals for valor.

Advisors were encouraged to recommend counterparts and soldiers for U.S. valor awards. The Bỏ Xoài watchtower battle was a perfect opportunity to do so. Major Kretschmar asked LTC Sơn to single out which soldiers were most deserving. He selected the 890th RF Company commander and the three soldiers at the watchtower that night. We wrote up the award citations, and Mr. Kotzebue came out to present the U.S. Bronze Star with "V" device to the 890th RF Company commander and the U.S. Army Commendation Medal with "V" device to the PF soldiers.

VR and Tac Air Support for Troops in Contact

On another day in April 1972 the district chief planned a large (for Hàm Long) operation in Phú Túc village involving both Hàm Long RF companies. Trung-tá Sơn requested a helicopter for command and control of this major operation. Province approved the request, so Trung-tá Sơn, an interpreter, and I were able to supervise the operation from the air. The terrain varied, with heavy, overgrown coconut tree groves with large but unkempt unused rice paddies in between the facing tree lines. The RF companies began to leave the trees and advanced into the large open area and quickly began taking heavy fire from a tree mass on the other side of the derelict rice paddy. Trung-tá Sơn asked me to see if tactical air support was available to suppress the enemy fire. Yes, it was!

The transmissions got somewhat confusing because communication with the ground force was in Vietnamese—translated to me by the interpreter or Trung-tá Sơn—and I talked with the FAC in English. And as well, the pilots were also in direct contact with the FAC. The teamwork was flawless. The ground commander had the two companies pop smoke to show their front lines and tell us where the tac air should fire from the smoke. The FAC directed air strikes into the tree line from where the enemy was firing on the advancing RF units. The RF commander reported "perfect" targeting by the air force fighter-bombers and requested spreading the fire north and south for 200 meters in each direction.

We remained over the contact while the two RF companies moved across the dry, derelict rice paddies into the large tree mass. Trung-tá Sơn stayed in continuous radio contact with the ground forces as they moved slowly forward. The enemy forces had withdrawn during or after the air strikes. The ground commander eventually reported to LTC Sơn that they found 20 enemy KIA and some damaged AK-47 rifles "but enemy gone now, over."

I passed the BDA to the FAC, who was still over Kiến Hòa Province but working for a different district. FACs and the supporting USAF tac air crews were always anxious for, and appreciative of, BDA after their missions for us. We tried very hard to get prompt and accurate information to pass along to them.

Staying Healthy as Important as Staying Whole

The local agricultural economy provided both ordinary and unusual foodstuffs for the advisory team. Our cook, Cô Bai, prepared delicious western food that she learned to cook from the many advisory teams she had worked for. She also added her own very tasty Vietnamese dishes that we all came to enjoy at least as much. All sorts of interesting things came from the market into the team house. My 18 months as an advisor in Kiến

Hòa Province introduced me to a welter of interesting cuisine, as mentioned throughout this book.

Field operations of every kind always included a stop for food, whether in a village office, an outpost, or on the ground somewhere out of the sun or rain. Those food breaks occasionally included unusual treats. Neither Major Kretschmar nor I carried C-rations or other western military food like the packaged LRRP rations when we went to the field. We always ate what the troops ate. Most of the time the food provided was simple, easy to prepare, and remarkably tasty.

In addition to things like *măng cầu* milkshakes and Cô Bai's *chả giò*, there were plenty of other interesting things to eat. We were never hungry! The cooks kept us full of good food when we ate in the team house. Lots of fresh vegetables and greens, fresh fish and shrimp from the rivers, good pork, good (but tough) chicken. Good, basic Vietnamese and Chinese food was served at most of the social functions we attended. All of the Vietnamese foods were usually accompanied by rice and *nước mắm,* the ubiquitous thin sauce made from the liquid pressed from fermented fish and usually including specks of hot red peppers. Some advisors despised the taste and smell of *nước mắm*, but I liked it, then and now.

Then there were the "special" foods, usually served at lunches or dinners, sometimes in the district market and sometimes out in the villages. Often what we were served—and ate—was all that was available, whether in an outpost or in a village office. I cannot remember ever getting sick from anything we ate, even given the variety of things served to us. In fact, I don't remember ever being really sick from anything in Vietnam. But there were plenty of less-than-really-bad things that we had to watch out for, from which we did not escape and for which we had to be treated. The big threat was malaria. It was endemic in the Mekong Delta, with the open ponds, rice paddies, and stagnant pools ideal breeding grounds for mosquitoes. We took a weekly malaria pill, an orange thing about the size of a penny coin. I never got malaria.

We were all concerned about water because it was so important to drink lots of water to stay hydrated in the hot climate. One of the cooks' main duties was boiling water. They were constantly boiling water in their kettles then pouring it into clean glass bottles and storing them in the refrigerators. When canteens needed refilling during operations, we tried to get water that was at least clear (not muddy), and we dropped iodine or halazone tablets (awful taste) into the canteens to purify the water. My parents generously sent a few envelopes of powdered sweet flavors in every letter, which we added to our canteens to attempt to overcome the halazone taste.

We all seemed to have periodic bouts with diarrhea, not so much from the drinking water or from the food we ate in outposts and village offices during the many and varied operations. The problem was that, no matter where, food and drink were sometimes served to us on plates or in glasses that had not been properly washed. Poor hygiene was the cause of illness, not the food or drink itself. Most of the time the runs lasted only a couple days. If longer, we could get "corks" from the province team medic in Bến Tre. Whenever one of us had the runs, we did not go on operations—too much of a problem, especially if the soldiers came in contact with the enemy and an advisor suddenly had to stop and fertilize the rice paddies.

The most common ailments were ringworm (a fungus attack) that got under our skin, crotch rot caused by the constant chafing of wet jungle fatigues, and other skin infections. We used antibiotic ointments to treat these. I stopped wearing underwear after the first month in-country! We worried about immersion foot caused by prolonged walking in wet rice paddies, through canals, streams, and mud. Fortunately, the short nature of the operations meant that we did not have the immersion foot problems that plagued troops in the 9th Infantry Division and other commands during my first assignment in Vietnam. I was always able to dry my feet after an operation.

The only illnesses I remember having were fevers from some unknown malady, but they were not heavy and never lasted long enough to be disabling. Although the heat and humidity were enervating, I got used to both. I felt strong and in excellent physical condition after the first month or so of steady operations and living in the environment. It was important that we kept our strength and stamina at a high level. The usual sign that we had "caught something" was an onset of weakness and tiredness caused not by the rigors of field operations but from whatever ailed us. Between all these little things and a major change in diet, I lost about 25 pounds very quickly, and I remember coming home in 1973 weighing only 145 pounds—pretty scrawny for a guy 6'2" tall. But I felt strong and tough and in good physical condition.

... Happiness Is a Medevac Arriving on Time.

Medical evacuation helicopters (medevacs) were a way of life during the heyday of American combat units in Vietnam. Getting wounded soldiers quickly evacuated from combat saved thousands of American lives and limbs, thanks to the quick passage of time from a soldier being wounded to getting attended to by doctors and nurses in a clean hospital.

By the early 1970s, almost all American tactical units had left Vietnam. Fortunately for advisors, some of the last to leave were the army and navy helicopter units—tactical lift, gunships, and medevacs. By then, the U.S. had also trained the Vietnamese in medical evacuation procedures and turned over hundreds of helicopters—the ubiquitous Huey UH-1 workhorse—to the Vietnamese Air Force (VNAF). That was a mistake.

In U.S. forces the medevacs were flown by, and belonged to, the army, air force, and the marines. They all had a close bond with soldiers on the ground. The ties between the ARVN and the VNAF medevac units were not nearly so close. It was almost impossible to get a VNAF medevac to pick up casualties in a hot tactical situation or at night. In sharp contrast, during most of my time in Kiến Hòa, U.S. medevacs responded to calls from American advisors in the field, even under the most hazardous combat conditions, even when the casualties were Vietnamese soldiers. This was to change later during my assignment, which will be covered later.

One of the toughest things for me to deal with was helping with first aid for wounded RF/PF soldiers. The first impulse was shock and almost withdrawal at the sight of blood, nasty wounds such as multiple shrapnel gashes and even the loss of an arm or leg. I admit it: I was squeamish, but I made a great effort to control myself and get the job done. Major Kretschmar and I both had first aid training, and even our limited abilities were appreciated by our counterparts. He and I were often directly involved with bandages, medication, and compresses.

In one case four wounded PF soldiers, casualties from an outpost attack, were brought to the compound one night about 2100 hrs. They needed our help. One of the men was critically wounded; it appeared that all the skin on his face had been sheared away. A U.S. helicopter responded to our call for a medevac. Almost all of the medevac pickups were done at the district headquarters helipad located outside the compound about 100 meters down the road toward the Tiên Thủy market. The area was always secure. As the medevac flight neared the compound, we moved the four men to the helipad by vehicles and used vehicle headlights to illuminate the helicopter pad. I stood on the "H" with a strobe light to guide the pilot. He saw the LZ, turned on the landing lights, and landed without difficulty. We got the men into the helicopter and on their way to a hospital in Bến Tre. In such cases the district advisors coordinated with the province team to meet the medevac when it arrived in Bến Tre, assist the crew, and work with the Vietnamese medics to move the casualties to the hospital.

... Four wounded PF soldiers brought in from Phước Le, grievously hurt, and being able to help with first aid, waiting for the medevac helicopter to come. The look of pain on their silent faces; my hand held in an unbreakable grip; the look of gratitude on the kid's face when I lift him into the helicopter.

In the case of more serious casualties in the field, if the casualty was too isolated for land or boat movement, the procedure—if a U.S. medevac—was for the helicopter to come to the district helicopter pad, pick up an advisor with a radio and an interpreter, and then we would guide the pilot to the location of the casualty. After picking up the casualty, the medevac flew directly to Bến Tre since taking us back to the district compound wasted valuable time. It was then up to us to find our way back to the compound. We were happy to be involved in the process because we knew that the faster the time from casualty to hospital, the greater the chance the soldier would survive. If it was a daylight medevac, someone would drive from Hàm Long to Bến Tre to pick us up. We could also rely on a ride back from the province headquarters' advisors, or a jeep from the Vietnamese side would take us back as well. If a nighttime operation, we stayed in the province compound until after daylight.

American helicopter pilots were amazingly courageous and skillful. They never hesitated to come to our assistance, even knowing the casualties were Vietnamese, not Americans. I can never say enough words of praise for the skill and courage of U.S. Army helicopter pilots.

I was surprised at how quickly I became quite proficient with bandages and tape. We had a good supply of medical supplies in the team house, which we willingly used as needed, because we could get resupplied from the province senior medic. It was rewarding to know that perhaps we were saving lives by something as simple as applying clean dressings to stop bleeding.

… Calling my dozen-th medevac helicopter at 0200 one morning and wondering when it would all end… Finding out that Fort Benning's first aid courses and reality in the dust of Hàm Long are only coincidentally similar. Doing wonders with bandages and tape and realizing you're actually saving lives.

Most of the time we never saw the casualty again. Assuming he survived and was healed, since he was either an RF or PF soldier, he would return to his home village, usually near the outpost where he had been wounded. Many of the casualties did not survive, sadly. But every once in a while we would have a very pleasant surprise visitor. During the 18 months I was an advisor, maybe five or six times a recovered medevac patient came to the team house to thank us. Often they came with family members and almost always brought a small gift, such as produce or fruit from their family farm or orchard, or a small gift purchased in the market. Those were the only rewards we ever got, and we cherished them.

Recognition from Counterparts

Another short operation had a slightly different outcome and resulted in my first-and-only award for courage under fire—awarded by the Province Chief, Colonel Phạm Chi Kim.

Kiến Hòa Province Chief, Colonel Kim, pinning the Cross of Gallantry on Captain Haseman.

Phú Thành outpost was just a few hundred meters north of the district compound. When it was attacked that night, Trung-tá Sơn organized a platoon-size security force of headquarters' PF soldiers, and we went out across the Tân Lợi road toward the firing. My role was to get an aircraft with the capability to drop flares, and hope we could find a FAC available at night. We got a flare ship that helped the responding RF company to ambush the retreating VC platoon. I guided the aircraft, and Trung-tá Sơn directed the troops.

A Valorous U.S. officer well-experienced in a combat environment and always displayed an exemplary sense of service. Throughout his assignment as U.S. Coordinator to District Intelligence Operations Coordination Center in Hàm Long District, Kiến Hòa Province, Captain JOHN BALLANCE HASEMAN closely coordinated with his allied officers and contributed many invaluable suggestions in the planning of intelligence collection that obtained outstanding results and great success through his endeavor and devotion to his special duties.

Particularly in the night of 19 April 1972, the Communists attacked Phú

Thành watchtower at XS 371361, Tiên Thủy village, Hàm Long district, Kiến Hòa province, CPT JOHN BALLANCE HASEMAN timely requested artillery support and directed air assets in an excellent manner that greatly contributed in the killing of 07 Communists and the capture of one crew-served weapon, 02 individual weapons, and a large number of important documents.

AWARDED THE CROSS OF GALLANTRY WITH BRONZE STAR ATTACHED

A Pause:
From Night to Day

Even before I got back to Vietnam, I was thinking about what it would be like to be an advisor to the Vietnamese army instead of being assigned to a U.S. unit. It was impossible for me to anticipate what it might be like. I just knew it would be very different from any work environment I had ever been in. Yes, I'd been assigned to South Korea for 13 months, but I was in an American intelligence unit and had virtually no contact with the Korean people, and I had no Korean friends. Yes, I'd been in Vietnam for a year and had worked with interpreters every day and a bit with Vietnamese military personnel during my three months in Mỹ Tho. But I had not really worked with the Vietnamese.

So when I arrived in Hàm Long and settled into a small U.S. advisory team, virtually everything I experienced was new. I had no problems with the spartan living conditions; I had done that before. The food was familiar. Almost a year at Dong Tam had made me familiar with the Mekong Delta climate and environment. But now I was working every day with Vietnamese soldiers, and at the district level I was at the end of the advisory chain. Most of the Vietnamese soldiers were locally recruited RF and PF soldiers, not main force ARVN.

Not only that, but now I was being shot at by the enemy, mortared by the enemy, and shooting back at the enemy with a rifle as well as armed helicopters and tactical air. This was combat for real, admittedly at a low level, but nonetheless very serious. This was definitely a new environment. And the biggest change of all was that there were only two or three Americans; everyone else was Vietnamese. All of them had more experience in combat than I had. How was I to advise them? Could I trust them—with my life? Would they accept and trust me?

I had a huge chip on my shoulder caused by a year of snide comments during my previous Vietnam assignment with the 9th Infantry Division. The derogatory "MI Puke" comments infuriated me. That label implied lack of courage in a wartime environment only because of the branch of service insignia I wore on my collar. The lack of respect for my professionalism was galling. I was confident in my abilities, training, and experience. How to show that?

As it turned out I did not need to "show" anything, just do my job.

All of these thoughts whirled through my head for the first months I was in Hàm Long District. And then suddenly everything clicked into place. I don't remember exactly when this revelation happened, but it was like night and day. The "night" was the plethora of new feelings, concerns, and the strangeness of it all. The "day" was when it all became normal.

So what had happened? Well, a lot had happened. I had won the confidence of my bosses, who had moved me into a combat arms slot based on performance, not branch insignia. The Vietnamese district chief and his staff had accepted me as a counterpart; they did not care what branch insignia I wore. The soldiers I was with all the time had accepted me as a fellow warrior. I had won my spurs by going to the field with them, being shot at with them, fighting back at the enemy with them, laughing and crying with them. It was a huge psychological change that lasted only a few minutes, when my entire mind shifted from night to day, and from then on everything was normal.

This is hard to explain. I knew that I had been under close observation by the boss, by the Vietnamese officers, by the soldiers, and by the interpreters—all of whom had to come to terms themselves with the new American on the advisory team. And I had passed! I was never in doubt of my abilities or my circumstances after that. The chip on my shoulder was gone.

One of the biggest challenges faced by advisors was "how to advise" and how to react when your advice was either ignored or seemingly never implemented. American army officers are trained to be proactive, adaptable, action-oriented. Do something, anything! The Vietnamese did not operate that way. I quickly learned that it was very important to be careful in choosing issues to present to your counterpart, important to present them in an acceptable manner, important not to protest or argue when nothing happened. And if something you had once-upon-a-time suggested did in fact come to pass, it was important that it was ALWAYS your counterpart's idea, not yours. I had no difficulty with any of these; that's why my superiors—and I—thought I was a good advisor.

And there was the issue of trust. I trusted my counterparts and "my" soldiers. I was confident they would not leave me behind during an operation or during combat. I was confident they would not betray me to the enemy. I trusted them to protect me when protection was needed. My counterparts trusted me to be with them in the field, to fight the enemy with them, and to help them with tactical air support when it was needed.

No advisor could succeed without trust.

As I was to discover in the months to come, I felt at home working at the end of the advisory chain, only me and the boss, and sometimes only me with an entire surrounding cast of Vietnamese officers and soldiers. Although there was enough violence in my life in the 18 months I spent in Kiến Hòa Province, I feel that I survived without emotional scars. I experienced death and injury up close, frequently. I found it profoundly upsetting on the one hand but distant from myself on the other hand. I cared about "my" soldiers and felt the hurt when they were wounded or killed despite doing all I could at the time to take care of them. Somehow this separated itself in my mind, almost as if sometimes I was operating in one world, and everyone else was in another world. Sadness and emotion still spring up all these years later when some Kiến Hòa incident springs into my mind, but I do not feel that I have had any psychological damage from my Vietnam wartime experiences.

It all goes back to that one moment when night turned to day, and everything was okay from then on.

The Big Celebrations—
And One Small One

The first six months of my advisory assignment went by quickly. It was a time of adjustment, learning, exploring, education, and danger— often all at the same time. As the western holiday season approached, I added culture appreciation to my experiences. Most of the people in Hàm Long were Buddhist, and although Christmas was celebrated, it was very low key. Far more important to the people of Hàm Long were two major celebrations that were both new to me.

The Đình Ceremony

It's hard to explain what a *"đình"* is. I think the simplest explanation is that a Vietnamese *đình* is a temple that combines ancestor worship, superstition, local history, and Buddhism. The *đình* is the centerpiece of district or province cultural life. The *đình* ceremony is held once a year, on an auspicious date selected by the *đình* leadership. I was lucky to be in Hàm Long when the 1971 *đình* ceremony took place.[1]

The "superstition" part of this cultural equation is a set of ceremonial regalia and artifacts, all of which are very old and carefully cared for. In Hàm Long the *đình* regalia were stored under lock and key in the Tiên Thủy village office on the north side of the market square. The *đình* leadership was a group of village elders selected for their wisdom and knowledge of *đình* history, legend, and Buddhist rituals. On the day and night of the *đình* ceremony they dressed in formal religious clothing and were foremost in the procession to take the *đình* regalia from the village office to the *đình*. Village leaders and ceremonial guards accompanied the regalia procession to the boats for the trip down river to the *đình*.

The Tiên Thủy *đình* is located on a large riverine island between the Soc Sai and Hàm Luông rivers, downstream from the Tiên Thủy market.

To get there it was necessary to take a boat ride from the market across the Soc Sai River to the island and then walk about two kilometers or hire a boat for the trip downriver and across to the island. The *dình* leadership and regalia were transported in gaily decorated boats. Hundreds of small candles and lanterns floated down the river from the market to light the way in the dark. Smoke from lanterns and cigarettes clouded the air.

Rumor had it that the *dình* festival was a "no fire zone"—even VC attended, and only the formal *dình* security personnel carried weapons. Everyone was welcome.

Perhaps the most characteristic facet of the religious culture of the Mekong Delta region is the intermixture of the traditional Buddhist religion with aspects of animism and ancestor worship. Animism and ancestor worship center in two places: the family altar at home and the local village *dình*. The *dình*, or ceremonial hall, plays a major role in the life of rural villages, serving both as a community hall and as the religious center of the village. The annual *dình* ceremony is a major event, second only to Tet as a religious and cultural event of overriding significance.

Each *dình* has its own history, legend, and folklore. The story of the origins of the *dình* is handed down by village elders from generation to generation. There is little written documentation of a *dình's* history. The Tiên Thủy *dình* has been at its present location for over 150 years. Many stories and legends have sprung up that feature royal dignitaries, magical events, and good luck for the village. The history of the Tiên Thủy *dình*, complete with ancient beliefs, superstition, actual historical events, and judicious interpretation of propitious occurrences, is a major part of local folklore. Whatever its basis in fact, the *dình* tradition is deeply respected by the local population.

In Hàm Long the *dình* ceremonies are held in December. The specific day for beginning the three-day ceremony varies from year to year and is selected after consultation among village elders and fortune tellers. Local belief in the spirit of the Hàm Long *dình* is strongly reinforced by the documented fact that every year within living memory it has rained on the day the *dình* ceremonies begin, even though December is well into the Mekong Delta dry season.

Village elders escort the artifacts from the village office onto the boat and to the altar inside the *dình*. The ceremony was very short and simple, including a heartfelt request for the *dình* spirit to bless the village for the coming year. The simpleness of the ceremony is in contrast to the elaborate decorations inside the *dình*: beautiful carving and statuary painted bright red and yellow, the stork of fertility and the turtles of longevity, intricately carved scrollwork and antique vases, brass work, and wooden containers of all sizes.

Outside the *đình*, hundreds of people roamed the grounds, now crowded with soup vendors, small shops selling beer and more potent drink. A wide variety of gambling games had sprung up. Every evening for a brief period of three days, the *đình* grounds had become a fairyland combining all the aspects of religious festival, country picnic, and county fair. Everyone had a good time.

And yes, this year in the midst of the dry season, it rained.

... Being asked to participate in the Đình ceremony before Christmas and suddenly not having to spend the holidays alone.

... *Happiness Is a Visit from Colonel Maggie.*

As Christmas 1971 approached, Major Kretschmar went home on leave over the holidays, leaving SFC Logan and me to mind the shop.

One morning a few days before Christmas we got a radio call from Province telling us a VIP visitor was en route to Hàm Long and we should get out to the helicopter pad quickly. I asked who it was but was told to just get going. A quick call on the radio found the helicopter pilot and his arrival time, so we hopped in the jeep and headed for the helipad with a smoke grenade. Sure enough, only a few minutes later a small scout helicopter came along over the road from Bến Tre. I popped smoke; it circled once, and down it came.

Once the blades stopped turning, out hopped a female figure clad in jungle fatigues and a green beret, wearing colonel's eagles. I did the first thing that came instinctively to mind—I saluted! She returned the salute! I recognized her immediately—it was Colonel Maggie, better known to most as Martha Raye. She was famous for her close relationship with U.S. Army Special Forces, and she made frequent, unpublicized visits to troops up and down the length of South Vietnam. And here she was in Hàm Long just a few days before Christmas.

Colonel Maggie was as ordinary as can be. No aloofness, no attitude, just a big smile and holiday greetings. She hugged both of us, asked our names, and hopped in the jeep. We went back to the team house and offered her coffee. She accepted, then opened her small hand-carry and pulled out a bottle of vodka. "This makes it even better," she said.

We had coffee spiked with vodka. (It did taste better!). We had about half an hour of conversation, and then she said she had to go because she was going to visit all the advisors in the other districts. And off she went, after pictures with both of us in front of the team house.

She did indeed visit all of the other Kiến Hòa district advisors. My friend and colleague Captain Mike Delaney was on a *liên đội* operation out in the field in Giồng Trôm District and was called on his radio and ordered to report to their district team house to receive a visit from "a VIP." She did not mind his not-quite-ready-for-inspection, just-in-from-the-field appearance. Martha Raye was a wonderful person whose love and respect for American soldiers in the field, far from home, had no boundaries. We could certainly see how the Special Forces community loved her so much. She was buried at Fort Bragg with a green beret in the casket.

... Martha Raye, bless her heart, dropping in from the sky to spend some time right before Christmas. Colonel Maggie, you're a real trooper.

Enjoying the Annual Tết Celebrations

A warm Christmas hug with Martha Raye in front of the team house.

Tết is far and away the most important holiday in Vietnam. It combines elements of traditional ancestor worship with the rituals of Catholicism and Buddhism, the joys of birthdays and anniversaries, and incorporates Chinese symbols and characters as well. I was in Kiến Hòa for only one Tết celebration, in March 1972 when I was in Hàm Long.

To prepare for the holiday, soldiers cleaned, repainted, and whitewashed the entire compound. The compound never looked so good. Even the flagpole got painted! Spirits soared. The holiday lasted several days, and given the pre-holiday festivities—parades of soldiers, visits of good luck dragon teams, and lots of party-going—it was a week-long event. We advisors tried to stay out of the way and not interfere, but we certainly enjoyed watching all of the festivities.

Underlying the spirit and atmosphere of celebration, there was a lingering concern for danger, even though both sides of the war had agreed on a short cease-fire during the Tết celebration. Memories of the disastrous 1968 Tết Offensive lingered. (I was at the 9th Infantry Division base camp at Bearcat when the 1968 Tết Offensive began.) This year, however, no major incidents took place, at least in Kiến Hòa Province.

9

Little Things
That Meant a Lot

We stayed plenty busy in Hàm Long District. But we also had time to savor the small things that meant a lot to us as far as comfort, easing tension, and enjoying our very unusual surroundings. Whether relaxing in the team house, enjoying camaraderie on the compound by trying to communicate with the Vietnamese soldiers, or visiting with people in the market, a lot of little things made our lives more pleasant.

... Happiness Is a New Set of Black Pajamas.

The famous black pajamas of Vietnam are real. Everyone in the countryside wore them, both men and women. Men's were usually made of cheap cotton cloth, women's of either the same material or a shiny, silk-like cloth. Wealthy or poor, the same cloth for everyone.

The reason why black pajamas are associated with VC guerrillas is because they wore them too. They blended into the rural countryside where they lived, operated, and hid in plain sight.

Most of the Vietnamese officers I worked with wore black pajamas in their off-duty time. So naturally, Major Kretschmar and I had black pajamas too. We even sewed on our standard cloth army name tag and U.S. Army strip over the shirt pockets. They were loose and lightweight and a welcome change from the heavier jungle fatigues we wore on duty. It was a wonderful relief, coming in wet and muddy from an operation, to take off muddy boots and dirty fatigues, grab a towel and head for the shower and then put on a pair of light, airy, loose-fitting black pajamas and give the dirty fatigues to Ông Hai to wash.

Our black pajamas were made by a tailor in the market. The shop stocked the material, we got measured, and a day later the tailor brought our pj's to the compound. The material was thin, wore quickly, and tore easily if snagged on something, so we just went down to the market and ordered another set. Cô Bai and Ông Hai got a chuckle out of Americans wearing Vietnamese clothes. Ông Hai even pressed them for us after washing so they looked neat and tidy. I think our Vietnamese colleagues appreciated this small nod to their own customs.

... Happiness Is a "Well Done" from Wilbur Wilson.

The Director of CORDS for Military Region IV—the boss of all advisors in the Mekong Delta—was, for many years, the legendary John Paul Vann. His deputy was Wilbur Wilson. Both men had retired from the army as lieutenant colonels in the early 1960s in disgust with the way the war was being fought and were longtime friends and colleagues. The Kiến Hòa PSA, Mr. Kotzebue, was a colleague of both. When Mr. Vann was reassigned as commander of Military Region II in the Central Highlands, Mr. Wilson became the Chief of CORDS for MR IV.

Mr. Wilson developed a set of charts that every district advisory team in the Delta was required to maintain, accurate and current, every day. They were done on a standard-size white chart board with acetate covering them so we could easily change the information on them as needed. We had to have an easel or stand on which to place the charts during briefings. I don't remember exactly how many charts there were, but think ten and go upwards. They covered everything from a map of the district with village boundaries (hand drawn by advisors to fit on the chart), population by village, security ranking of every village with a 12-month tracking record, number of friendly troops, enemy estimated strength, friendly and enemy casualties, and on and on. Many of the figures came from the latest HES Report.

Mr. Wilson had a reputation for being very difficult to brief and for threatening to have advisors relieved if they displeased him—and one sure way to displease him was if one did not know the material on those charts. There were legendary stories of what Wilbur Wilson said to, or did to, an advisor whose charts were out of date—or even worse, if the advisor tried to brief him with the charts and did not know what data was depicted on them.

As DDSA one of my jobs was to keep the charts up to date. Almost every day I got out the charts, updated the ones that needed to be updated, made sure the most recent HES Report security scores were recorded, kept plots of enemy unit locations, markings for mortar attacks, ground attacks, ambushes, and on and on. We never knew when Mr. Wilson might arrive, unannounced, at the district compound and want a briefing.

My trial by fire came one day in October or November 1971 when Major Kretschmar was on leave. At least I had a bit of warning—Mr. Kotzebue radioed to tell me that he was driving out to Hàm Long with Mr. Wilson and Colonel Kim, the province chief. I quickly set up the easel and slides, all in the correct order, gave myself a ten-minute self-brief about what was on them, and got ready.

Soon the small caravan pulled into the compound; LTC Sơn and I met the visitors and went into the Vietnamese TOC for LTC Sơn's briefing. Colonel Kim and LTC Sơn then retired to his private office, and I escorted Mr. Wilson and Mr. Kotzebue to the team house. Cô Bai had made coffee that she passed around as everyone got settled. Mr. Wilson began by asking me a lot of questions about myself—how long had I been in Hàm Long (three months), what my career background was, and so forth. "Okay," he said, "Let's have your briefing."

I flipped over the red cloth covering the charts and started my briefing. As I briefed each slide, I took it off the easel and laid it, in order, against the legs of the easel. I was not nervous because I knew those charts were up to date. Mr. Wilson never said a word as I went through the charts, and when I finished, I asked the usual, "Sir, what are your questions?"

Of course he had questions. "Let's see chart number three again," and tell me more about "this" or "that." The briefing lasted about 45 minutes. At the end, he stood up, came up to me and shook my hand. "Well done, Captain Haseman," he said. "You sure know your district." He was particularly interested in my combat experience as an MI officer in the tactical DDSA billet. Did I go on tactical operations (yes), how was my counterpart (excellent). He seemed to know more about me than he let on at first and let that knowledge out to me bit by bit. He had a ferocious reputation, but he certainly knew a lot about the people who worked for him. Like many senior officers, he turned out to be a very reasonable person to brief—as long as you knew your material.

Mr. Kotzebue was very pleased. It was the first time he had seen me do that briefing, and I think he might have been a tad worried since I was new in the province and he had not seen me brief before. I got a big pat on the back and some nice words of praise from him too.

… Happiness Is Translating the Monopoly Game into Vietnamese and Not Losing Your Shirt in Vietnamese Poker Games.

The team house had a batch of table games—a set of dominos and a Monopoly game, among others given to the team over the years. We did not have much time to play either game by ourselves, so we gave them to our interpreters. They particularly enjoyed playing dominos, an important game in Vietnam that was frequently played for not-insignificant sums of money. Neither Major Kretschmar nor I tried to compete.

Major Kretschmar and I had a bit of a leg up when it came to Monopoly. The three interpreters quickly understood the mechanics of Monopoly (dice, money, buying property, debts, get out of jail free), but names like

Marvin Gardens, State Street, and Mediterranean Avenue meant nothing to them, to say nothing of Boardwalk. So we decided to translate the street names and utilities into Vietnamese equivalents. I don't remember all of the new names, but I do remember that Boardwalk became Lê Lợi Boulevard—the wide main street in downtown Saigon. We did that for all the streets and taped the small strips of paper onto the appropriate streets. It took us several days of spare time, but we did it. Voilà! Vietnamese Monopoly.

The Vietnamese played many card games that were strange to Americans. LTC Sơn enjoyed playing cards with some of his staff and NCOs in the evening, and he frequently invited the advisors to join in. His favorite was a game of poker in which you were dealt 13 cards instead of five or seven, and there was no "draw"—you had to play each hand with the cards you were dealt. The requirement was to make three poker hands of five, five, and three cards, and your bet covered all three rows. It was very intricate because your strategy might be that your best hand was in the second row, not the first. So, you could win three times or lose three times or any combination between those extremes. And you could not drop out of a hand!

The Vietnamese were experts at this game, and rank had no privilege—the Vietnamese officers and even NCOs who were invited to play with the district chief were also allowed to beat their seniors—just like American soldiers. And, of course, they all loved taking money from the American advisors. My strategy was to take only a limited amount of piastres to the games, and when I lost it all (as I inevitably did), I was allowed to stop playing without losing face or causing offense. Then I watched the game and tried to figure out a winning strategy. Even our 12-year-old friend "Gangster," child of one of the RF soldiers, knew how to play the game. But I never did come up with any bright ideas, and I never won at that game.

… Happiness Is Payday on Pay Day.

Getting paid in Vietnam was complicated but is even more complicated when you are part of a small advisory team. In a perfect world, we could have been paid by having our entire pay automatically transferred to our Stateside bank checking account. A lot of people did that, particularly the married men, because that made it so much easier for their families. However, we all had a need for cash in Kiến Hòa. Remember, this was long before the arrival of ATM machines, and even credit cards were rare. So, in order to have cash, you had to be paid in cash.

It was even more complicated because Uncle Sam had given us a very valuable benefit—the right to establish a tax-free savings account into which we could put up to $10,000 and get 10 percent interest tax-free. (That was really huge in those days.) The catch was, you had to make payments into the account in cash. Therefore, many of us had arranged our pay so that most of it went by direct payment into our Stateside bank account, and we drew enough in cash to plus-up our special savings account and have a small balance of cash on hand each month for local purchases.

Every month someone had to be put on orders as paymaster, which took us away from our job for as long as four days. The pay officer had to drive to the MACV Headquarters Finance and Accounting Office the day before payday, pick up the payroll and return to Bến Tre and arrange everyone's pay. The easiest way was to wrap each person's pay in his pay voucher and file them in order by district. This detail fell to the captains in the province, and there must have been enough of us because I had to do this only a few times.

But, of course, "cash" was not U.S. dollar cash, it was Military Payment Certificates (MPC), a currency system that the U.S. government implemented to keep from overwhelming the Vietnamese economy with U.S. dollar cash, which could be used for all sorts of nefarious things. MPC came in denominations from, as I recall, five cents to $20. From time to time the series of MPC bills was changed on a no-notice basis to make worthless all of the unauthorized MPC held by Vietnamese. "Conversion Day" was a very deep secret and a very big deal. The large U.S. compounds got locked down tight to prevent unauthorized exchange of MPC from Vietnamese, who thronged base fence lines pleading to anybody to exchange their now-worthless MPC.

We needed Vietnamese piastres too. Merchants in our district towns wanted piastres. Our household staff expected to be paid on time in piastres. Most advisors needed to exchange some MPC for piastres—at the province team cashier's office in Bến Tre.

So Pay Day was a big deal. When I was on orders as pay officer, I went to Bến Tre two days before Pay Day, spent the night, drove to Saigon, always with two or three others who went to the PX, all of us armed with our M-16. I picked up the payroll, signed for the MPC cash, each person's pay voucher, and lots of deposit slips for the special savings account. After a visit to the PX, we drove back to Bến Tre—a full day's trip.

That night I prepared the payroll by counting out MPC for each person according to the amount specified on the payroll, wrapped their pay voucher around it, put everything in order district by district, and put everything very neatly into an attaché case. The next day, Pay Day, the swing ship flew me to each district and shut down. Somebody picked me up at their helipad and drove me to the team house, where I paid each person in private, gave them the form to fill out for their savings account, waited while they filled out the form and gave me back the right amount of MPC, wrapped the form around that money, and put it back in the attaché case. Quick trip back to the chopper and on to the next district. Then back in Bến Tre I held pay call for all the province-based Americans. If everything went right, everyone got the right amount of money, left over was the right amount of money for each person's savings account, and everyone was happy. The next day I repeated the drive to Saigon, turned everything back at Finance and Accounting, taking along two or three other men who wanted to visit the PX, another full-day trip.

Everything worked just fine IF we had payday on Pay Day. But several times during the year this did not happen, usually for either or both of two reasons: bad security prevented the trip to Saigon; or worse, there was no swing ship on payday. This caused problems. Our cook expected to be paid on Pay Day. Those Americans with, shall we say, "special friends," had to pay those sweet young things on Pay Day. If no pay call, no pay. And if you had not managed to save enough cash to cover a household staff person's salary, who knows what would come off the stove at mealtime!

... Happiness Is the Generator Starting on the First Crank.

Hàm Long's district power grid provided electricity to the local area, but it only operated from 0700 hours until about 1900 hours, when it was turned off to conserve fuel. Any light after that was by candle or lantern. To cover us during darkness, our team equipment included a small, gasoline-powered generator. We kept it in a CONEX container behind the district supply warehouse, the farthest it could be from the team house and the Vietnamese housing area in order to minimize the noise. The generator was connected to our team house, to the district chief's house, and to the TOC. As a favor to our counterparts and for goodwill, we also allowed our main counterparts to splice into the line.

The generator was hand-started the old-fashioned way—with a rope pull that one wound around the starter wheel, gave it a good yank, and hoped that the motor caught from the spark thus created. The yank required a good bit of strength. And most of the time it never started on the first yank. Sometimes it took many cranks to get it going. But it was usually worth the effort to have light in the team house, electricity for the fans and light in the sleeping bunker, and our Vietnamese friends had lights in their tiny quarters.

We could tell if there was too much of a load on the generator by a sudden "moan" instead of the usual low rumble, and all the lights dimmed and sometimes quit. We discovered that the S-2's wife was allowing other soldiers to splice into her line—for a price, of course—to spread electricity benefits to others in the soldiers' housing area. The problem was, the generator did not have enough capacity to run all of these extra lines. We kept telling Trung-úy Hương that the heavy load was going to ruin the generator and then nobody would have electricity, to no avail. Whenever the overload taxed the generator, one of us had to grab a flashlight, walk out to the generator hut, and disconnect Hương's electric line. The generator would immediately resume its normal "hum," and the illicit dim lights all through the Vietnamese housing area would go out.

Sure enough, after a short period of time, someone would go to the generator, reconnect Hương's line—and thus all the other illicit lines— and the same thing would happen again. Usually the second time one of us would go back to the generator and disconnect all of the lines except the TOC line, including LTC Sơn's line. In no time at all, one of his batmen would knock politely at our team house door and ask to reconnect the district chief's line. We always said yes; we always told him that we had to disconnect it to save the generator because so many "unapproved" lines had been hooked onto it, and we would appreciate it if something would be done to keep the heavy load off so the generator would not die. The word would go out to stop the illegal hookups, Hương's income would drop, and after a few days, it would all start again. Sigh! We started the generator up just after dark so we would have electricity and lights for dinner and early sleeping comfort. It had enough fuel to run all night, and then the first one up in the morning would go out and turn it off.

We really appreciated that generator and always hoped it would start on the first pull!

Our Pet Cats

Lots of American units—and advisory teams—had pets, usually a dog of indeterminate ancestry, even a huge python, sometimes unique animals like sun bears. Hàm Long had pet kitty cats. The Head Cat was always the oldest female cat, always named Cat. The several generations of Cat all produced many little cats that we had no trouble giving away to other advisors or soldiers on the compound. The PSA had one of Cat's offspring, as did the province PH coordinator. At some point we would lose Cat, but having kept at least one of the offspring, we just appointed a new Head Cat, which was very capable of finding a mate and eventually producing more little cats.

We hoped, overly optimistically, that Cat would keep mice and rats at bay. Not exactly. Many of the rats were considerably larger than Cat, and she was wise enough to leave well enough alone. She did account for a number of smaller mice and rats, so the system worked a little bit. Of necessity we also had a collection of large wire-cage rattraps. These locally made contraptions came with a heavy, spring-loaded trapdoor that also had a long, heavy wire handle. We placed bait well inside the trap and set them here and there in the team house and in our small community area. The loud "snap" let us know that the traps were working. One of us would look around for the trap with a rat and were often appalled at the size of the rat inside the trap. I wish I had a picture of Cat staring at one safely trapped and very large rat. One of Ông Hai's chores was to carry the loaded traps (by that strong wire handle) to a nearby canal or fish pond and drown the rats. We did not know, nor care, what he did with the remains.

A Quiet Day

There was so much operational activity that it was very nice to have a relaxing day with no operations, no emergencies, no medevacs. We still had plenty to do. There was always a daily operations and intelligence briefing in the TOC to attend, we always needed to clean our weapons and ammo, and there might be a local social activity that we had to attend with our counterparts. But there was still plenty of time to hang out in the team house, write letters, chat with each other. So here are some things we did when there was nothing more pressing to do.

We tried to stay abreast of the intelligence reports that the S-2 section sent us on a daily basis. They were always in Vietnamese. Some of them we could work out—enemy unit locations, for example. Most of them went to whichever interpreters were available. They hand-wrote a translation right on the original report. Most were historical in nature—something that had happened in the past, some VCI person had done something. Few were what we could term as "actionable," but they did provide a background tapestry of what was going on in the district.

If we had scrounged steaks or ribs, we had a cookout! SFC Logan definitely knew his way around a barbeque grill. Ours was a 55-gallon barrel cut in half and mounted on steel legs. We bought charcoal in the market, and SFC Logan made his own marinade from whatever he found in the kitchen. Barbequed water buffalo tasted just as good as American beef, and Vietnamese pork tasted MUCH better than the American version. He was also a terrific baker. He produced excellent cookies, cakes, and pies. This was a great way to spend Sunday, when Cô Bai had her day off.

I enjoyed strolling around the compound to chat with the soldiers and see what was going on. The soldiers were happy to attempt a conversation with me, and between my fledgling Vietnamese ability and their fledgling English, we communicated well enough to understand each other. It was a pleasant, short trip to the Tiên Thủy market for a bowl of *phở*, a chat with the people in the shops, and occasionally to do some shopping.

Fitting in at Social Events

An important factor in achieving a good counterpart relationship was the advisor's ability to adapt to Vietnamese culture. The advisors were observed and evaluated by representatives of many elements of Vietnamese society—the military and our operational counterparts, civilian officials, ordinary people of the district. We had ample opportunity to interact in a social environment. The Vietnamese enjoyed entertaining us, and we tried to reciprocate within the confines of our team house and our understanding of what our Vietnamese guests would like.

We hosted many informal get-togethers in the team house, usually on Sundays when it seemed that both the ARVN and the VC took a day off. We were able to provide beer, soft drinks, Vietnamese snack food cooked up by Cô Bai, and sometimes American snack food from our small store in Bến Tre. We also held parties when visitors—Americans and Vietnamese—came from province headquarters or from Saigon. Many of the district chief's programs were launched with some sort of social event—whether giving out Land to the Tiller ownership certificates or formally installing a newly elected village or hamlet chief.

Whenever we went to a village office, such as for interviews for the monthly HES Report, the village chief hosted us for lunch. These events almost always featured a wide variety of local food, ample supplies of beer, brandy, and potable water, and a lot of good fellowship.

Having Good Thoughts and, Sometimes, Deep Thoughts

There was always a lot of time set aside for personal thinking and sharing thoughts with others on the team. Sometimes serious, sometimes not, my own private thoughts covered the entire gamut of life as a district advisor. Some of them I wrote down. These short musings were all written while in Hàm Long or Mỏ Cày.

… The satisfying feeling I get when I realize I've adopted the Hàm Long RF/PF as my own soldiers. Seeing the steel and iron behind the continual grins and the grimness of honest patriotism and dedication beneath those

smiling faces. And realizing that not enough Americans had experienced this privilege.

… Climbing the watchtower at dusk for a few minutes of solitude, marveling at the deceptively peaceful sunset over the coconut trees.

… The great understanding of the soldiers, who realize after a particularly bad day that you want a few minutes alone, and who don't interrupt the lonely solitude of a concrete bunker roof. And then, at the right time, asking you down to the câu lạc bộ for a beer.

… Remembering the moment when, after two months in Hàm Long, I realized I had been accepted as a friend as well as an advisor.

… The privilege of observing the ordinary people's lives, the cycle of rice growing, the difficulties of life in a war zone, shopping in the market.

… Learning to like beer with ice, keeping up with the party, and not getting sick afterwards. Learning dozens of diplomatic excuses not to drink too much, and enough ways to pour out good beer or booze without being caught.

… Admiring the local village officials, many taking jobs that endangered themselves and their families, trying to serve a far-off government that often seemed not to care about them.

… Mischievously playing the role during trips to Saigon. Telling friends that it's time to leave because the road closes at 6 o'clock. Contempt for almost all MACV HQ people who simply do not understand what is going on in the field.

Officers, civilian officials, soldiers—all friends.

These next two were surely my most serious thoughts. I never spoke these aloud to anybody. This is the first time some of my friends and family will read, and know, these thoughts.

... the sudden peace that came in the one moment when I felt I would never leave Kiến Hòa Province alive, and not minding it.
... Discovering myself in the heat of battle, and the fear of myself for liking it.

... *Happiness Is Cô Bai's Chả Giò.*

Our cook, Cô Bai, fixed us excellent food every day. It was mostly western food because most Americans she had cooked for over the years wanted western food. She made terrific fried chicken, for example, and good fried and scrambled eggs. But her very best dish was her excellent *chả giò*.

Chả giò are deep-fried Vietnamese spring rolls, but the wrapper is especially made for *cha giò*. Some restaurants wrap *chả giò* in an egg roll wrapper (Chinese), which is really too thick for good results. Cô Bai used the thinner special-made *chả giò* wrappers and used our "fresh from the compound store" vegetable oil.

Chả giò ingredients include a variety of chopped meats and vegetables, depending on the cook and what the customers want. Usually the filling consists of fresh bean sprouts, finely cut carrots, some form of green fresh basil, and any combination of minced pork, chicken, shrimp, or beef. Cô Bai preferred minced pork and chopped shrimp.

The other crucial part of good *chả giò* is the dipping sauce. Plain *nước mắm* (fish sauce) is okay, but cooks can vary that with herbs and spices. It should never be too hot (spicy), but a little bit of piquancy is good, usually with finely ground red chili pepper. *Chả giò* should be served with a heaping plate of fresh greens (lettuce, basil leaves, other herb leaves) that the diner wraps around the roll before or after dipping in the sauce.

We never found out exactly what spices Cô Bai put into her mix of filling or exactly how she made her dipping sauce. We liked them so much she had to make a lot of them when she planned to serve them. Sometimes our dinner consisted only of *chả giò* and rice. But her *chả giò* were the best I've ever tasted, then or now.

... *Happiness Is Bò Lúc Lắc at the Hàm Long Câu Lạc Bộ.*

Câu lạc bộ is usually translated as "club," but that was a very grand description of my other favorite Hàm Long delicacy, the *bò lúc lắc* served at the soldiers' *câu lạc*, the Hàm Long *câu lạc bộ*. The compound "club"

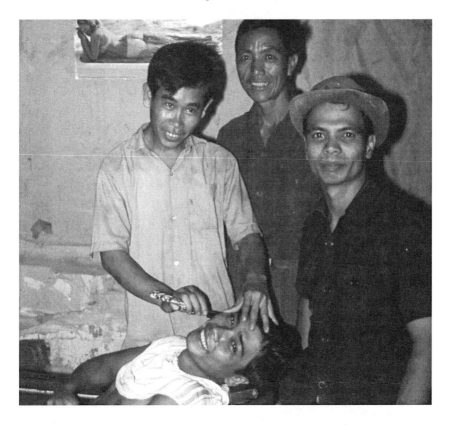

The district barber in his shop in the soldiers' housing area with three satisfied customers. I am in the "waiting, next" chair. Note the barber's good taste in the pinup.

was a rude hut in the soldiers' housing area. The "club" was very small and could hold perhaps eight or ten people max. There were a few very low, small tables and correspondingly small, low stools to sit on and a low food counter also with stools. Everything was rough, handmade, and the floor was packed dirt. The *câu lạc bộ* is where you went for a beer with friends or somebody else's cooking.

Bò lúc lắc has always been one of my favorite Vietnamese dishes. It is a mix of beef cubes (well, water buffalo cubes), tomato chunks, garlic, and onions all stir-fried together with oil and whatever other spices the cook likes. The cook at the *câu lạc bộ* made the BEST *bò lúc lắc*! Major Kretschmar and I often went there for dinner on Sunday, which was Cô Bai's day off. The place was always crowded with Vietnamese soldiers who always seemed very pleased that we came to share their food and drink with them (beer, more beer!).

... *Happiness is a haircut done with comb and scissors and straight razor. NOT with electric anything! Extra happiness because the Hàm Long barber was never found dead in the wire after a VC ground attack on a base camp or outpost, a tale that was told elsewhere by many U.S. soldiers.*

10

Beyond Hàm Long

Living with a small district advisory team required a close focus on the "here and now." There was enough going on to keep all three of us busy all of the time. That meant that we did not pay a lot of attention to what was happening in the other districts. We monitored the province radio net, so we had some idea of the routine goings-on as well as sudden emergencies, but there was little personal or professional contact between and among the other seven district advisory teams. We all got together in Bến Tre for monthly meetings of district chiefs and DSAs and for the monthly PH meetings. We might be in the province compound or TOC for business or for other chores like shopping in the small store for food and snack items, camera film, or liquid refreshments, so that usually gave us a chance to meet friends from other districts. But that was about all.

Two of my MASA classmates arrived in Kiến Hòa Province after me. One became the PH coordinator in Bình Đại District and the other in Đôn Nhơn District. But in all of my time I only saw them when I was pay officer or at the monthly meetings in Bến Tre. Occasionally we chatted on the radio. But from time to time something serious happened, or something interesting occurred, that would quickly be passed around the province radio net. Those serious or interesting things always involved courage or unusual events worthy of remembering.

Versatile and Effective Field Artilleryman

A province-level MAT Team, MAT-22 (officially called the Night Operations and Ambush Training Team), advised the Con Ho Training Center in Ba Tri District. Several of the Hàm Long District PF platoons underwent unit refresher training at Con Ho. A colleague and friend, Captain Mike Delaney commanded that MAT Team for several months. He told me that the training was good and the units there for refresher training benefited from their short visit. The main drawback was that the training center commander was very reluctant to actually conduct night-time training for fear of taking casualties from the VC.

When personnel strength reductions caused almost all of the MAT Teams in the province to be closed down, Captain Delaney was reassigned to the province team in Bến Tre. A Field Artillery branch officer, Mike became the province artillery advisor but spent most of his time as a shift duty officer in the province TOC. Because of his leadership, tactical skills,

Captain Mike Delaney at the end of an operation with RF soldiers. Ready for lunch, he "borrowed" a backpack with a live chicken for dinner (courtesy Michael Delaney).

and his ability to connect quickly with RF/PF soldiers in several different units, Captain Delaney was frequently assigned as a rotational advisor on *liên đội* operations in several different districts.

Having gone to Fort Sill for ROTC summer camp, I quickly identified with field artillerymen. The artillery section chief in Hàm Long was delighted to learn that I knew how to pull the lanyard on a 105 mm howitzer. Mike Delaney and I got together whenever we were both in Bến Tre at the same time. We have been good friends ever since.

An American Warrior Joins Advisory Team 88

Around Christmastime 1971 chatter and rumors began to spread through Advisory Team 88 that a true American warrior was going to join us. In January 1972 that rumor came true—Major Roger Donlon arrived at Advisory Team 88 and was assigned as DSA in Bình Đại District. In 1964 then-Captain Donlon was awarded the first Congressional Medal of Honor in Vietnam for his heroism in defending the Nam Dong Special Forces camp southwest of Huế in MR I. He was badly wounded in that battle and spent a lot of time in several hospitals for surgery and recovery.[1]

Medal of Honor recipients are routinely and carefully guarded by the Department of Defense in "safe" assignments, and Roger Donlon had several of those between attending both the Infantry Officer Advanced Course and the Army Command and General Staff College. However, Roger insisted that he was a soldier, and soldiers belonged fighting in Vietnam. He had enough horsepower to break through the protective barrier that senior army leadership had erected around him.

I met Major Donlon in January 1972 when he came to Hàm Long on his introductory orientation swing around the province (the orientation trip I never received). I felt honored to meet him and host him, but we spent exactly zero minutes discussing his past. Hàm Long was the first district he visited, and Major Donlon was interested in hearing about everything and what it was like to be a district advisor. Major Kretschmar was back home on leave over the holidays, so SFC Logan and I responded. I went through our standard briefing charts first and spent hours responding to his questions. I introduced him to Trung-tá Sơn and several of the officers during an informal party in the team house. I stressed to him how important the counterpart relationship was and the importance of trust in that relationship.

Many Advisory Team 88 personnel were excited at the chance to meet a person we had all heard or read about, and initially I was a bit awed at having him sitting in the team house and just talking. There were no heroic comments, no discussion of what I personally thought of a truly remarkable personal story. He was a relaxed, interesting, and thoughtful person who wanted to know what worked best for a district advisor. He shared dinner with us, we all shared a beer or three, and he spent the night with us in our sleeping bunker. After breakfast, the province swing ship arrived to take him to the next district on his itinerary.

Unfortunately, his time in Kiến Hòa was cut short due to injury. In August, during a mortar attack on the Bình Đại district compound, he hit his head diving into their bunker, and the next morning he discovered he'd lost vision in one eye. He was medevacked first to Saigon and then to Bangkok, where he was diagnosed with a detached retina in his left eye. His assignment in Vietnam was curtailed, and he was reassigned to the Joint U.S. Military Advisory Group–Thailand (JUSMAG-Thai) in Bangkok.

He and I had hit it off immediately. Happily we met again many years later and immediately renewed our friendship. He was my boss for several months during my assignment on the staff at the Army Command and General Staff College in 1981. He and his wife, Norma, and I have been dear friends ever since. They are two of the finest people I know.

Trúc Giang District Compound Almost Overrun

Trúc Giang was our next-door district. It was a strangely shaped political district that ranged from the Mỹ Tho River ferry landing at Tân Thạch, through the city of Bến Tre, down to a "tail" along the Hàm Luông River. The district compound straddled the main highway between Bến Tre and the ferry landing. The district's northern area and that southern "tail" were both areas of heavy enemy presence. Whenever we had to drive to Mỹ Tho or Saigon, we usually stopped off, coming and going, to visit with our friends on the Trúc Giang advisory team, so most advisors were familiar with the Trúc Giang compound. The DSA in Trúc Giang was a respected infantry officer; the PH coordinator was a fellow MI officer, Captain Bob Jones (not his real name).

On the night of 22–23 March 1972 we were awakened by the Hàm Long TOC duty officer banging on our team house door to relay instructions from the province TOC to go on alert and monitor the radio. The Trúc Giang compound was under heavy attack and in danger of being overrun by an estimated VC battalion. What we heard was startling. Captain Jones was on the radio calling for help from province assets and giving a minute-by-minute account of the battle and their situation. The DSA was on leave when this happened, so Bob was Acting DSA. The situation he described sounded very serious.

Province forces were hastily organized into a reaction force, with a province team captain as senior tactical advisor. The reaction force had stalled at the Ba Lai River bridge, just two kilometers south of the Trúc Giang compound. The RF force was hesitant to move across the bridge, fearing a VC ambush, but the American advisor did heroic work getting them across the bridge and on to Trúc Giang to engage the VC attackers. Meanwhile, Captain Jones had called in 7th ARVN artillery fire from Dong Tam directly onto the compound using airbursts that were highly effective because the friendly forces were in bunkers and the enemy was exposed in the open.

By the time the reaction force got there and succeeded in ejecting the VC force, there were heavy casualties among the Trúc Giang District soldiers. The combination of friendly artillery fire and the arrival of the reaction battalion saved the day. The advisory team operations NCO was wounded in the foot, the only advisory injury, but it was a very close thing. Both Americans received the Bronze Star for Valor for their courage and leadership of the beleaguered Trúc Giang soldiers. The advisory team house was completed destroyed by enemy sapper explosives and mortar fire, and it burned to the ground.

We didn't have all the details of the battle, but I made these notes soon after:

… Being awakened at 0300 on March 23, 1972, and told to monitor the net. Turning on the radio to hear Captain Jones' voice "There are sappers running all over the compound and most of the bunkers are gone, fires are everywhere. Get those reinforcements on the road, we need help." Trúc Giang District Headquarters, next door, overrun by a battalion of VC and for us an anxious time hanging on for the two Americans there. An American advisor leading the reaction force, pushing, arguing and cajoling fearful soldiers across the Ba Lai River bridge to the rescue. Seven medevac trips full of wounded and dead RF and PF taken to the Province hospital. 135 VC bodies found during the next two days.

Major Kretschmar and I drove over the next day, bringing as many spare personal items and civilian clothing as we had available, as did many of the province advisory team members. It could just as easily have been us.

The Kit Carson Scouts

By far the most mysterious unit working with Advisory Team 88 was the large Kit Carson Scout (KCS) company. Scouts were all former VC who had rallied to the GVN through the *Chiêu Hồi* program. A rallier was processed through intelligence and political channels, underwent extensive interrogation, and many of them accepted an offer to change sides by joining the ARVN or joining special operations teams sponsored by various other government agencies.

Scouts were particularly valuable working in the same region in which they had served in their VC units. They knew the VC areas of operation, base camp locations, supply and communications routes, and the identity of VCI cadre. Many U.S. tactical units had ARVN *hồi chanhs* assigned down to company and sometimes platoon level. Their knowledge of the territory in which they had served as VC was invaluable in spotting booby traps, providing intelligence, locating enemy weapons' caches and base areas, as well as training American soldiers in VC tactics.

Kiến Hòa's KCS company was large, with over 50 personnel, many of whom were very familiar with Kiến Hòa Province and both VC and GVN methods of operation and key personnel. The KCS company had their own very secure compound on the road from Hàm Long to Bến Tre, across from the Kiến Hòa airstrip.

The Kiến Hòa KCS company assigned a scout as chief scout. An American lieutenant commanded the KCS company, and several NCOs served as advisors and mission commanders. The KCS usually deployed in tactical teams; the size of a team depended on the anticipated enemy threat and the target of each operation. The scouts usually deployed in response to specific detailed intelligence. They were very good in operations against small VC units. They occasionally worked reconnaissance missions, but their primary mission was as a quick-reaction, hard-strike team.

The KCS despised the VC and were in turn despised by both the VC and by ARVN units, who never trusted them and viewed them as an enemy whose true loyalty was always in question. Their primary patrons were the U.S. "advisors" who selected and planned operations—and paid their salaries, which were considerably higher than the salaries paid to ARVN and RF/PF soldiers.

I met scouts on only a few occasions. The Chief Scout, Mr. Bom (not his real name), and a squad of the scouts came out to Hàm Long on one occasion to gather information and brief us on possible future operations. I was impressed by Mr. Bom—he was quiet but very clearly in charge of his subordinates. A very intelligent man who was college educated, his buzz haircut and slender stature gave him a mild appearance compared to the ragged haircuts and swagger of some of the other scouts. A former VC officer, he was tough, and I was very glad he and his team were on OUR side!

One of the advisors to the KCS was an outstanding young sergeant named Robert "Ike" Isenhour. We saw each other only sparingly, as he and the lieutenant spent a lot of their time at the KCS compound. On the occasions we met on the province team compound or at the TOC, I was impressed by his confidence, character, and his courage.

KCS operations were very close-hold, and the district advisory teams were rarely told if and when a team might be operating in their district. One giveaway were restrictions placed on the Hàm Long field artillery section, which received cryptic "do not fire" blocks around the area in which the KCS might be operating. The only operation I knew of in Mỏ Cày was one in which I escorted a wounded scout to the 3rd Surgical Hospital in Saigon (told later).

A few years ago I was able to reconnect with now-retired Ike Isenhour and ask what it had been like as an advisor with the KCS company. I was not surprised at his response, which was "busy and very active firefights almost every time." In a series of email exchanges, he told me more about his long-ago experiences. One of those operations is told here. It was a textbook raid to exploit very time-sensitive information.

One morning a young boy about 14 years old walked into the Bến Tre National Police office and said he wanted to *chiêu hồi*. He said he had been abducted from his family by the local VC and brutally put to work. The boy was homesick and did not want to fight for a cause he did not understand. Fortunately, only a few police and no ARVN military were aware of his arrival.

Advisory Team 88's operations/S-3 officer, Major Robert Stephens, happened to be on hand and recognized a good opportunity for actionable use of this young man and the intelligence that he could provide. At that time I had yet to meet Major Stephens, but Sergeant Isenhour and field officers described him as being highly professional, respected, and once I had the chance to meet him, I shared the others' respect for him.

The boy said his unit was located in an area called the Hữu Định, the name of a village in Trúc Giang District. However, this was also the name given to a much larger area that overlapped into parts of Giồng Trôm and Bình Đại districts; it was a VC-controlled area. Many scout operations had been run in the Hữu Định. The area was also very close to the Crossroads, where the Ba Lai River and the Giao Hòa Canal met in the shape of a cross. The Giao Hòa Canal was a key part of the maritime transport network that connected much of the Mekong Delta to Saigon and was a significant route for shipping rice from the Delta to Saigon and the rest of South Vietnam. During the time the U.S. 9th Infantry Division was based at Dong Tam and I was stationed in the 9th MI Detachment, the division conducted both ground and Mobile Riverine Force operations into the Hữu Định and along the Crossroads waterways. They made heavy contact with main force VC units every time.

Ike stressed that it was important to be careful when analyzing all intelligence reports because the VC were smart and could plant information in order to draw a unit into an ambush. He made a radio call to the KCS camp for the U.S. scout commander and two senior scouts to come as quickly as they could to the TOC. As soon as they arrived, they spoke very privately about using the boy and his information to run a raid on the camp location. Ike was chosen to lead the operation. His life and the lives of the scouts depended on being able to determine a true situation from a planted one. After questioning the boy for a while, Mr. Bom was satisfied that the boy's story was true and that the boy would be willing to guide a team to the location of the camp.

Before going further, Ike had to consider operational security. Many KCS operations were briefed to key ARVN officers in the TOC so that if artillery support was needed, it would be available, and no H & I artillery would be fired into their AO. ARVN support was also usually needed to arrange for insertion and extraction of the team. In this case the decision was made not to brief the ARVN side of the TOC to avoid leaks to the VC, since quick reaction was essential. Ike selected ten scouts, plus himself and the boy, and also decided to have the small team carry along a machine gun and an M-79 "just in case."

The team inserted by truck after several false stops to throw off any enemy observers. That meant a very long hike through heavy, jungle-like areas in the darkness to reach the target area. Despite the difficulty, the team reached the VC encampment just at dawn and quickly found that it was a much larger camp than they had expected. Ike could not praise the KCS enough for the skill they employed to reach the target area unnoticed by the VC. He wrote, "I might have been called an 'advisor' but in reality I was a student being taught by masters in combat operations."

The team was able to sneak silently to within 30 meters of the camp before opening fire on the enemy with all of their firepower. They achieved total surprise, quickly dispatched the closest enemy soldiers and raced through the camp searching the hooches. "We found a gold mine" in two ammo cans of documents, which later proved of tremendous value to intelligence. Ike was very glad he had thought to bring the machine gun and M-79 because that firepower proved to be an important reason the team was able to get in and out so quickly without any friendly casualties. "I believe our survival was mainly a product of the scouts' ability to break contact and retreat in a manner that was confusing to the enemy unit. I will never know how large the VC unit was but I do know that the VC commander should have been shot for being lazy with his security." Ike was modest in his own contributions to this picture-perfect raid and gave all the credit to the skill of the scouts.

The key factor I got from this story is the professional and personal relationship between the KCS scouts and their American "advisor." It was much like the feeling I had toward the RF and PF soldiers I "advised." It took a while for them to evaluate any new advisor and decide whether he was a worthwhile fellow warrior or a liability who did not know or understand them.

One difference between the KCS company and the RF/PF units was the command relationship. American district-level advisors did not command the RF/PF soldiers. However, the Americans working with the KCS company did command them and paid their salaries. Ike emphasized that the U.S.-VN relationship with the scouts was key. He had to temper "pure command" with a keen sense of personal dynamics. In this raid, like my own much-less-intense periods of combat, the unspoken trust between U.S. and VN soldiers had been earned through performance and leadership. Trust was not automatically given. Ike had earned the respect and the trust of his KCS comrades, and he, in turn, trusted them to protect him when the tactical situation turned very dangerous. Working directly with soldiers of another country is an art and a skill. Trust is not easily given; it must be earned.

11

Moving to Mỏ Cày District

In the spring of 1972 I requested a six-month extension of my assignment on Advisory Team 88. I emphasized that I wanted to remain assigned at the district level, not moved to a province-level position. However, Major Kretschmar's tour of duty would end in May 1972 when he finished his 18-month assignment as DSA. The decision was made to close the Hàm Long advisory team with his departure, so I would not be able to remain in Hàm Long. The reasons for closing the team included an improved security situation in Hàm Long and the continuing reduction in personnel strength in the overall advisory effort.

Farewell Lunch Hosted by the Tiên Thủy Village Council

Since the team was to be closed, Trung-tá Sơn arranged a farewell ceremony during which Major Kretschmar was awarded the Vietnam Cross of Gallantry for his service. The local Vietnamese leadership also wanted to honor the advisors for their service to the community, so they arranged an elaborate farewell luncheon held in the Tiên Thủy village covered market.

The lunch began with a speech from the Village Council Chairman thanking us for our work in the village, and small plates with snacks like peanuts and fried tidbits and several toasts celebrated with glasses of beer.

None of us was prepared when the main course was served. The chef and an assistant approached the large, round table carefully carrying a huge and obviously heavy, beautiful, huge ceramic bowl that must have been at least a meter in diameter. Inside was lunch—snake soup! It was a big snake. A REALLY big snake. It was beautifully arranged with the snake coiled neatly around the sides, with a variety of spices and fresh greens to flavor the broth and add color. I determined, when the village chairman began serving, that I did not have to eat the snake skin—he peeled it easily away, leaving white flesh that looked just like fish or chicken breast, except it was shaped like a snake. But when flaked off with a fork and placed in your bowl with broth, vegetables, greens, and rice, it looked like the flesh of a white fish and it tasted rather like a mild saltwater fish. If it had not been presented "in the skin," I probably would have not known exactly what it was. It was tasty and a very unusual farewell lunch.

I was sorry to see Major Kretschmar depart. He had been a marvelous boss, highly professional in his work, a steady mentor to me, personable with our counterparts and very effective in getting things done. His tenure included the construction of several small village health clinics, a two-story addition to the Tiên Thủy high school, and the start of plans for a village dispensary. He had also become a friend with whom the months had passed in companionship. He was a good man who served with distinction at the end of the American advisory effort. SFC Logan was within a couple weeks of his DEROS, so he was moved into the province team and processed for a slightly early departure. He had been a good companion, a great asset to our team, and he was ready to get home to his family.

New Assignment to Mỏ Cày District

Mr. Kotzebue approved my extension and reassigned me as DDSA in Mỏ Cày District. I was delighted because it meant I had earned my spurs in combat. Mr. Kotzebue showed his confidence in me by reassigning me to the toughest district in the province. I said goodbye to my many Vietnamese friends in Hàm Long and packed my bags. Mr. Kotzebue got approval from the province chief for Sergeant Bé to move with me, while Sergeant Tu was reassigned elsewhere in Kiến Hòa Province. Mr. Toi went back home to Saigon and continued with his mandatory national service elsewhere.

Getting to Mỏ Cày required driving through Bến Tre and then out along the Bến Tre River to the Mỏ Cày ferry landing, located where the Bến Tre River flowed into the Hàm Luông River. The riverside street was narrow, crowded with bicycles, pedestrians, animals, and sidewalk shops—there was no sidewalk; the shops were in the street. The ferry to Mỏ Cày was a "single-end" boat, which required drivers to drive out onto the ferry pier, reverse direction, and back onto the boat. It was easier getting off.

Once across the Hàm Luông River, the highway to Mỏ Cày crossed two long one-lane Bailey bridges over branches of the Hàm Luông River—the Mỏ Cày ferry landing was on a long, narrow island, the village of Thanh Tân. These two bridges were always a prime target for VC sappers—highly skilled saboteurs who specialized in silent, invisible attacks against bridges, base camps, barbed wire defenses, and isolated outposts. Mỏ Cày had outposts at both ends of the bridge and another one in the middle to watch the waterway for swimming saboteurs.

After crossing these two bridges, the highway was straight as an arrow to Mỏ Cày town. The main landmark was the Hòa Lộc Bridge about halfway to Mỏ Cày. This section of highway was dangerous. The heavily forested area between the road and the Hàm Luông River, most of it Định Thủy village, was full of enemy base camps into which RF and PF and even ARVN units rarely penetrated. The west side of the road was also heavily occupied by enemy forces. The highway had to be swept for mines and roadblocks every morning.

The most important bridge of all was the one-lane steel bridge that arched up high over the Mỏ Cày Grand Canal at the entrance to Mỏ Cày town. The bridge was the only land route into the town from the north and the only land connection onward to Hương Mỹ and Thạnh Phú districts. Needless to say, it was well guarded.

The move to Mỏ Cày in May 1972 could not have been more of a transition. I went from the relatively secure district of Hàm Long to the worst security situation in the province; from rural Hàm Long with no district town to Mỏ Cày, the second-largest town in the province after Bến Tre; from a district chief who enjoyed his relationship with his American counterparts to a district chief who prided himself on his testy relationships with colleagues, superiors, and counterparts; from a small team house to a large (but now almost empty) team house. I would need to meet many new Vietnamese counterparts and establish a good relationship with each of them. The easiest part was the physical move.

New District, New Boss, New Counterparts

Mỏ Cày District was larger in area than Hàm Long. It was further from the district town to the farthest reaches of the district. And those farthest reaches were, inevitably, full of enemy forces along the main rivers and the district boundaries with Đôn Nhơn on the north and Hương Mỹ on the south. It was ten kilometers from Mỏ Cày town to the Bến Tre ferry, almost 12 kilometers to the northwestern village of Tân Thanh Tây and onward to Đôn Nhơn District. The border with Hương Mỹ District was only six kilometers away, but those were difficult kilometers. I had to get used to new geography as well as new counterparts and a much stronger enemy force.

My new boss was the DSA, Major George B. "Byron" Reed. A native of South Carolina, he had just arrived in April. He was an Air Defense

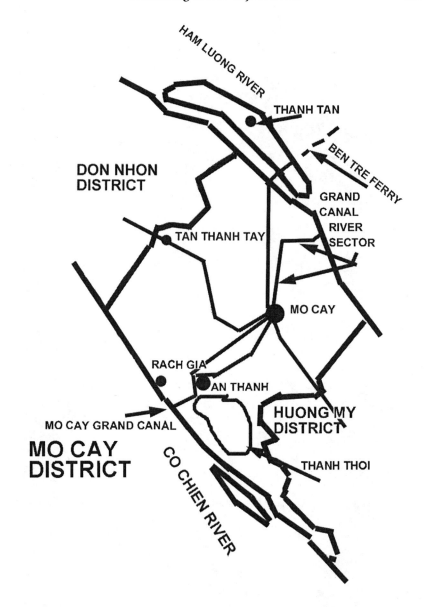

Map 4: Mỏ Cày District. Sketch by author from tracing, with towns, roads, and key water routes.

Artillery officer on his second tour as a district-level advisor. On his first Vietnam assignment he was the DDSA in Chợ Lách District of Vĩnh Long Province. Chợ Lách bordered Kiến Hòa's Đôn Nhơn District to the west. He had a wealth of advisory experience that was badly needed to restore

Major Byron Reed in the team's Boston Whaler en route to an HES Report interview session.

LTC Nguyễn Văn Cư and four of his ten children. The girl on the right is Yvonne, whom I was to meet again in Southern California in 2015.

a good counterpart relationship with the district chief. Taciturn but friendly, we enjoyed a good professional and personal relationship.

The Mỏ Cày District Chief was Lieutenant Colonel Nguyễn Văn Cư, a maverick of the highest order. He enjoyed thumbing his nose at his superiors and contemporaries alike, and he had a reputation of barely tolerating American advisors. He was badly out of sorts because his previous DSA counterpart was "only" a captain, despite that officer's high level of experience and maturity. Major Reed made it his mission to forge a good, mutually respectful relationship with LTC Cư. He did it through late-night discussions about Vietnamese history and culture but often branching out into other mutual interests. His superb sense of what was necessary turned the two men into friends as well as mutually respected counterparts.

The second member of the Mỏ Cày advisory team when I arrived was interpreter Sergeant Hùynh Đức Tuyến. He was a superb interpreter and a very courageous soldier. He had personal space and a bed in the team house, but he had his wife with him; they had a tiny home in town. He and Sergeant Bé knew each other, and they worked well together.

Mỏ Cày district headquarters compound was bigger than the Hàm Long compound. There was a large central area with a landscaped flagpole. The west side was crowded with the headquarters building and district chief's house, the TOC, and staff offices. The advisory team house was close against the offices and TOC with the back door leading directly onto the canal. A wire fence separated this part of the compound from the artillery compound at the tip of the peninsula. That area had howitzer gun pits and housing for the artillery and all others assigned at headquarters.

I immediately went to work getting to know the district chief and staff—and letting them get to know me.

Sergeant Hùynh Đức Tuyến and his wife outside their tiny home in Mỏ Cày. He was a superb interpreter and a very courageous soldier.

They knew of my Hàm Long experience and of my prior service in the U.S. 9th Infantry Division. I felt some trepidation meeting LTC Cư because I had heard from others how difficult it was to have a good working relationship with him. I need not have worried. He welcomed me to Mỏ Cày, and we got along well together. He understood from the start that I was the Deputy DSA and therefore more likely to be working with his staff than with him. That is how it worked out. He communicated only with Major Reed, whether planning tactical operations or development and pacification projects. In the few weeks before I left on my extension leave Major Reed and I went on several operations with him. I did not have enough time to establish a personal relationship with him as far as commander and counterpart were concerned. He was polite and professional with me in the few weeks that we lived and worked together.

My relationships with the Mỏ Cày staff officers were good but not as close as I had felt in Hàm Long. The S-2 was a young and inexperienced

This is a swing ship view of the western half of Mỏ Cày District compound. The large building in the center is the district headquarters and district chief's residence. The advisory team house is at left center with a dark-gray roof.

second lieutenant who had no authority to do much of anything. He was not nearly as professional and experienced as was Trung-úy Hương in Hàm Long. Trung-tá Cư was his own S-2. Thus, there was no opportunity to begin my assignment by accompanying the Mỏ Cày S-2 on field operations.

Sergeant Bé and I got unpacked and settled into the team house, which was much larger than the team house in Hàm Long. At one time Mỏ Cày had a large district advisory team with two or three officers and several NCOs. Now it was down to two Americans and two interpreters. Major Reed and I each had a separate room built in a small add-on building connected by a bunker to the main team house. I had much more personal space than in Hàm Long. The main disadvantage was that our two-room addition backed up to the fence separating us from the field artillery compound. The two 105 mm howitzers sounded like they were sharing our room when they fired, which was often!

Major Reed briefed me on the enemy situation, key personalities, and operational standards in Mỏ Cày. He told me there would be few opportunities to go on small unit operations because of the security situation. I do not recall a single operation to build new outposts or repair existing ones. Most tactical operations were large multicompany operations, mostly commanded by the district chief.

Although I was assigned to Mỏ Cày as the DDSA, I also had responsibilities to monitor the PH program. The Mỏ Cày DIOCC was located off the military compound in a small colonial-style National Police building in town. Although I initially put in some time at the DIOCC, it quickly became apparent that my DDSA duties had priority; I spent most of my time on regular military operations. The very active Mỏ Cày Police Special Branch chief was the DIOCC chief. Whenever I visited the DIOCC, he briefed me on new intelligence, any PH operations that had taken place, and sometimes on future planned operations. He frequently asked me to go with him on PH operations. As a result I went on more purely PH operations in Mỏ Cày than I had in Hàm Long.

Everything was different in Mỏ Cày from what I had become accustomed to in Hàm Long. Different Vietnamese counterpart personalities, different strength of personal relationships with them, different team house, different concept of operations. I was very busy getting used to my new situation and surroundings.

12

A New Environment
in Mỏ Cày

Mỏ Cày Town

Mỏ Cày was a real town rather than just a marketplace in the country-side—the second-largest town in the province. Rivers and the Mỏ Cày Grand Canal surrounded the town on three sides. It spread across a peninsula immediately adjacent to the district headquarters compound. The Mỏ Cày Grand Canal flowed straight from its junction with two rivers at the point of the compound. It was lined with schools, the town hospital, and warehouses for cargo boats traveling between Saigon and places in the lower Mekong Delta. The main market and shop areas were south and east of the district compound, separated from the compound by a low-lying area of ponds and vegetable gardens. A small grid of streets tied everything together.

Downtown Mỏ Cày and the market square were much larger than Tiên Thủy market in Hàm Long. Mỏ Cày had a huge open-air market building and parallel rows of two- and three-floor buildings on three sides. Vendors, buyers, sellers, baskets of vegetables, fruit, live and dead animals, fish, prawns, hunks of meat, casual shoppers, children, bicycles and occasional vehicles all competed for space. The town was badly damaged during the 1968 Tết Offensive, so much of the central town buildings had been rebuilt since then.

The main street connecting the district compound to the main high-way to Bến Tre was interesting as well. Sites along the canal side included a large school, the town hospital, and several warehouses. The province police station was on that street, as well as the small main office for the Police Special Branch and National Police Field Force (NPFF)—my main partners in the PH program in Mỏ Cày. I was living in a new place; there were lots of new things to see, learn about, and experience. I managed to see a lot in my spare time. Just living in a real town instead of in the coun-tryside was a big change.

Mỏ Cày town is situated on a peninsula surrounded on three sides by rivers and the Mỏ Cày Grand Canal. District headquarters is at the tip of that peninsula, accessed by a single street through the town. Most of the green countryside up to the Hàm Luông River was VC-controlled.

The All-Important Mỏ Cày High Bridge

The bridge across the Mỏ Cày Grand Canal was extremely important. Not only did it provide the only means to access Mỏ Cày by land, but it also connected Hương Mỹ and Thạnh Phú districts to the rest of the province. It was built high enough for large cargo boats to get safely under the bridge, although they had to carefully navigate the well-protected support pillars holding the bridge up and the security network of pillars and

An advisory team Boston Whaler view of the Mỏ Cày High Bridge with a large cargo boat just approaching.

barbed wire on both sides of the bridge. The bridge was good and sturdy, although only one lane wide. There was seldom a lot of traffic. In addition to military guards from one of the RF companies all around the land approaches, there was a military guard stationed in the center of the bridge. He kept a watchful eye on approaching boat traffic as well as for any would-be enemy sappers hoping to destroy one or both of the pillars. He also manned the traffic control sign—a large, round metal disk mounted on a swivel, painted red on one side and white on the other. White meant "GO" and red meant "WAIT."

Different Rural Environment

Unlike Hàm Long, which was primarily an area of rice paddies and coconut and other fruit orchards, Mỏ Cày had a much-more-varied agricultural environment. Although there were plenty of rice paddies, farmers emphasized other commercial cash crops such as tobacco, tapioca, market garden vegetables, and—yes—coconut groves. Besides being larger in area, Mỏ Cày District's population, almost 70,000, was twice as large as Hàm Long's. There were more roads, but many of them were unsafe to travel without a large security force. Some were in such poor condition as to be impassable to all but motorcycles and bicycles.

Flying over the district on a VR was a real education—most of the area was not safely accessible by either road or canal. Areas closest to Mỏ Cày town were heavily cultivated with tobacco, other market vegetables, tapioca, and coconut groves. Small hamlets were scattered with no discernable pattern. Further away the land was dedicated to rice paddies and smaller vegetable gardens and fruit orchards. There was no mistaking the dark and dangerous massive coconut grove areas along the major rivers. Both sides of the district were, simply put, VC-controlled.

... Happiness Is Curry Chicken for Breakfast with the Commo Section.

I cannot recall how I found the chicken curry restaurant in downtown Mỏ Cày. Perhaps I dropped in with Sergeant Bé or Sergeant Tuyển. One day I saw the NCOs from the TOC communications section enjoying their chicken curry breakfast there. They were surprised to see me having Vietnamese curry chicken at breakfast and quickly invited Sergeant Bé and me to join them at their table. After that, Sergeant Bé and I often went there for midmorning breakfast. The commo section guys would stick their head into the team house and announce, *"Cà ri gà, phải không?"* "Chicken curry, yes?" And almost always it was *"Ya Phải"*—"Yes, of course!"

This aerial view southwest of Mỏ Cày town shows the different variety of commercial crops in the district—tobacco, tapioca, garden vegetables.

The chicken curry was delicious. The curry was actually a thick soup, almost a stew, rather than the thin broth used in the national dish of *phở*—thicker with chunks of chicken meat and heavily seasoned with Vietnamese yellow curry spices. It was served with a plate of fresh greens, usually lettuce and basil leaves, and we always ordered a baguette of delicious Vietnamese *bánh mì*—which looked suspiciously like what Americans call French bread. *Bánh mì* was much tastier and always had that thick texture lacking in packaged American bread.

Along with the curry, I always had Vietnamese drip coffee, which I had learned to love when I was in Hàm Long. It is always served in a battered metal percolator set over a small glass—never a cup—with sweet condensed milk in the bottom. The wait staff brought this contraption already containing the correct amount of ground coffee and piping hot water. While we ate our chicken curry and bread, the coffee s-l-o-w-l-y percolated into the glass. When you thought it was ready, you took the percolator off the glass, took off the metal lid, turned it over and set the percolator on it to catch any latent coffee drippings. Stir the coffee and condensed milk, and drink. Very strong coffee! The glass was almost too hot to hold, but somehow we managed.

My regular trip to the curry chicken restaurant became common knowledge throughout the entire province advisory team. Some advisors thought I was wasting time and energy fraternizing with the commo section NCOs (or any other NCOs for that matter) and should be concentrating on the district staff officers instead. (I got in similar trouble with my commander in the 9th MI Detachment, but that's a different story.) I was delighted to cultivate the commo section NCOs because they kept us up to date on what was going on in the district that perhaps the district chief hadn't told us. I felt that any friend in Mỏ Cày was an asset. And chicken curry for breakfast was the perfect way to do that. Besides, the chicken curry was absolutely delicious.

... Happiness Is Being First in Line at the Ferry.

The only land route for Mỏ Cày and three other districts on the lower island of Kiến Hòa Province to reach Bến Tre was by ferry across the wide Hàm Luông River from Thanh Tân village to the outskirts of Bến Tre. The ferry boats were small, one-end boats, which required that all vehicles turn around on the ferry landing and back onto the boat. There were vehicles going to and from Bến Tre all the time, all of which required going back and forth on the small ferry boat.

There was always a line of trucks, cars, buses, motorcycles, bicycles, pedestrians, and animals that wanted to get on the boat. Military vehicles always had priority and could go to the front of the line. In principle, the

American advisors did not want to do that out of respect for everyone else who wanted to go on board (winning hearts and minds). We always waited in the line, sometimes for two or three boats if there was a big crowd. Waiting for the ferry was no big deal. We were seldom in a hurry; there were always at least two ferries going at the same time, in opposite directions. Plus, it gave us time to interact with the civilians, who were always curious about Americans. We also had to be very alert because undercover VC used the ferry too, and a grenade pitched into the jeep would ruin our day.

When it was our turn to board the ferry, we drove down the narrow, rickety access ramp to the steel floating dock, reversed around, and backed up the loading ramp, guided into place on the boat by one of the crew. Then we sat in the jeep (no benches on the ferry) for the crossing, which took about ten minutes.

But sometimes—not very often—we were first in line. That usually happened when we zoomed up just after a ferry had departed and had taken all the waiting vehicles. So we were first on the next boat. Being first in line was far more convenient. No jostling among the waiting pedestrians, vehicles, bicycles, motorbikes, and animals to drive out onto the pier. Of course, being first on the ferry also meant being last off, which *was* actually a good thing. The sight of all those pedestrians, vehicles, bicycles, motorbikes, and animals all trying to be first off the boat was quite amazing. We just sat and waited for things to calm down before driving off. Then the only trick was to hope that the policeman on the land end of the pier was able to hold back the waiting hordes of pedestrians, vehicles, bicycles, motorbikes, and animals all wanting to be first onto the boat at the same time we were trying to get off.

I never became as familiar with Mỏ Cày as I had with Hàm Long. My time in Mỏ Cày was shorter and fragmented by unforeseen events. The riskier security situation limited where we could go. The concentration of effort on larger tactical operations rather than on outpost-building and village office visits resulted in fewer occasions to survey the local situation. Still, I found much to keep me interested. The larger towns (Mỏ Cày, An Thạnh, Rạch Dầu) had historic examples of VC/NLF presence, and the varied geographies were all new to me. Although I wanted to get out and about more than I could safely do, I still experienced a lot of new and interesting sights and sounds. Mostly friendly.

13

Mỏ Cày's
Higher Operations Tempo

The biggest operational difference between Hàm Long and Mỏ Cày was the scope of operational tempo. Hàm Long operations were small, usually by several platoons of PF forces or company-size operations by the two RF companies. Mỏ Cày had a far-more-dangerous security situation, with enemy forces in battalion strength in several parts of the district. Most operations were at least company size and usually involved two or three companies. Mỏ Cày joined some other districts in forming two or more RF companies into battalion-size formations called *liên đội,* which made the district chief's command span of control smaller and easier to handle.

Thus, there were fewer operations but much larger ones. Because of the size of operations, the district chief did not go out to the field as often as in Hàm Long.

... Happiness Is Going on an Operation in Thành Thới and Not Getting Shot.

I arrived in Mỏ Cày in May 1972, the start of the rainy season, so the rice paddies were flooded. In many places the paddies were deserted and unkempt because of poor security. In those areas the "rice paddies" were often fields of tall grass and weeds, with a few earthen dikes here and there. Those fields filled up with waist-deep water because nobody maintained the complex irrigation system. So we got very wet.

Thành Thới was a large village in area size but with a small population. Much of it provided the enemy with almost full-time mini-base areas. District forces operated in force on the fringes of this unfriendly and dangerous village, primarily to prevent easy enemy access to the more secure areas of adjacent An Thạnh and Đa Phước Hội (including Mỏ Cày town) villages. Major Reed was pleased to have a second advisor to go with him on such operations. I recall going on two similar operations in early

Major Reed and I waded a long way in this abandoned and flooded rice paddy. LTC Cư is in the group in front of us.

June 1972 in Thành Thới with Trung-tá Cư and Major Reed, both of which passed through extensive fields of neglected rice paddies that were overgrown with wild grass and scrub brush that easily concealed booby traps and potential ambush sites.

Progress was necessarily slow, slogging through often waist-deep water, deep, soft mud, and narrow, muddy pathways. None of those operations resulted in enemy contact, which was a relief. Circumstances led me to believe that those operations were planned that way, with tacit agreement from the enemy, which saw no gain in attacking a patrol that did not threaten their established safe zones.

… Happiness Is All of the Incoming Landing in the Canal.

During the time I was in Hàm Long, the district compound was mortared infrequently. It was a different story in Mỏ Cày. Because of poor security in most of the district, the enemy was able to get close enough to mortar the district compound from any number of places, and we experienced many mortar attacks, usually at night. Fortunately, there was little damage and few casualties.

The large advisory team house in Mỏ Cày had two bunkers, one built inside the main team house in a room that had once been sleeping quarters when the team was much larger. The other bunker was also inside the team house, between the original building and a new, small add-on that held two sleeping rooms for the DSA and DDSA. When a mortar attack began, we all sprinted to a bunker. Sergeant Bé and Sergeant Tuyến slept in the main part of the team house, so they used the bunker in that adjacent former sleeping area. Every night we moved our PRC-10 radio into the bunker so we could get quick communications with the province TOC. One of us would go to the TOC to find out what we could about casualties, damage, and return fire.

The Mỏ Cày district compound was on a point of land surrounded by a canal and rivers on three sides. Two of those three sides were definitely bad country; the third was along the highway to the Bến Tre ferry and had somewhat better security. If the VC wanted to mortar the compound, they had to be skillful enough that their mortar rounds sailed over the rivers or canal and into the compound. They did not particularly want to mortar the district town because so many residents were VC sympathizers, openly or secretly. The best possible result for us, therefore, was for the mortar rounds to be "short" and fall into the rivers and canal on the three water sides and thus causing neither casualties nor damage. Sometimes the rounds exploded on impact with the water, causing a spectacular water display; sometimes they sank without exploding.

Knowing Which Canals Are Safe and Which Are Not

Because of the geographic shape of Mỏ Cày District and the poor security situation, the major rivers were not secure for operational transport. Almost all of the territory along the Hàm Luông River on the northeast side of the district was enemy territory; similarly, the Cổ Chiên River on the southwest side was also very dangerous for friendly forces. Still, those rivers were important national lines of communication, especially for moving rice from the Mekong Delta to Saigon and to the rest of South Vietnam. The VC stopped and taxed those rice boats and water taxis and then sent them on their way.

The most important water route in the district was the Mỏ Cày Grand Canal, which ran from the river junction at the district headquarters compound, straight across the district to An Thạnh village and then jogged a bit to the Cổ Chiên River. The French had used corvée labor to build the large canal during the colonial era. The canal is part of a system of connected river and canal routes designed to move rice from the lower Delta to Saigon without boats and barges having to enter the South China Sea. The route ran right past Mỏ Cày and Bến Tre, through rivers and canals to the Mỹ Tho River, the Cho Gao Canal and on to Saigon. The Mỏ Cày Grand Canal was wide and deep and had been designed to allow inland boats to pass unobstructed by depth, width, or bridges—that's why the bridge entering Mỏ Cày was so high. The spoil from construction was so much that both banks were a meter or so higher than land further away from the canal.

The canals and the rivers went through enemy-controlled territory that advisors seldom saw because Mỏ Cày's forces were too small and ill-equipped to conduct major clearing operations in tough country long controlled by the VC. Merchants shipping rice, boat captains who carried cargo, and water taxis with passengers all had to pass through enemy-controlled areas and pay a toll each time. The VC seldom attacked those private commercial boats because they were a source of income for the VC, and many times the boats were also carrying VC or VC sympathizers from point to point. All kinds of boats sailed up and down the Grand Canal. On the occasion where a passing boat was attacked, it usually meant that the crew had earlier failed to pay a sufficiently large "toll" to the VC.

Whenever a major operation was planned along the Grand Canal or adjacent to the Cổ Chiên River, or if we had to cross the canal, the district "chartered" enough water taxis to carry the entire force. The soldiers loaded into the boats and onto the roof, and away we chugged.

Troops in a string of outposts along the canal were supposed to provide security and control and inspect traffic along the canal. Well, sometimes they did, and sometimes they didn't. Ubiquitous solid wood water taxis carried cargo and passengers and stopped wherever passengers or cargo wanted. People along the bank had flags on long bamboo poles to signal the boat to stop.

Nice Try, But No Village Upgrade

Thanh Tân village was a long, narrow island in the Hàm Luông River, separated from mainland Mỏ Cày by a narrow channel that was considered too dangerous to travel in by boat or sampan. Thanh Tân was an important village because the ferry across the Hàm Luông River to Bến Tre landed at Thanh Tân, and it was connected to the rest of Mỏ Cày by well-built iron bridges.

Trung-tá Cư and Mr. Thoi (not his real name), the Deputy District Chief for Development, told us that the "D" HES rating of the village was much too low. They both insisted there was no VC presence there and it should be upgraded to "C" or even "B" level. They claimed it was so secure that we could walk along the main road to the village office without a security force. To prove their point, they scheduled an operation to do exactly that—we would walk from the highway near the ferry landing to the

Thanh Tân village office to do HES Report interviews. Mr. Thoi would go with us, and we would go without a security force. We had no choice but to agree to go with them.

A small convoy of jeeps drove us to the drop-off point and waited for us at the ferry landing. Major Reed carried a submachine gun, and I carried my M-16, and we both had .45 pistols with lots of extra ammunition for them and pockets full of hand grenades. We set out on the designated path. Although described to us as "the main road to the village," this main path was suspiciously small—wide enough to walk in single file or ride a bicycle or even a motorcycle, but it definitely did not look like the "main road" to a supposedly secure village.

It was a relatively short four or five kilometers to the village office, a pleasant walk through coconut groves and along small irrigation canals. After about 30 minutes into the walk, Major Reed and I spotted a column of soldiers about 100 meters through the trees to our left. We immediately pointed them out to Mr. Thoi and asked if they were VC or friendly forces. Caught, he admitted they were part of a platoon of PF soldiers providing flank security for us. Thanh Tân was not nearly as secure as promised! We continued to the village office, met with the village chief and a large contingent of PF soldiers, and conducted HES Report interviews. We did not upgrade the village and received no argument from Mr. Thoi.

Here's how I remembered it:

... Being invited by the Deputy District Chief to visit northern Thanh Tân island, a "D" village. Being escorted by only village and hamlet chiefs up the trail for five klicks. Mr. Thoi asking if we saw any signs of VC activity and showing how we could walk around without any security troops. And asking why the village couldn't be upgraded to C. But then, the platoon leader of our out-of-sight security platoon moved too slowly and got spotted as his ring of troops got too close to us. Tactfully saying nothing, not raising the village rating, and not getting any argument.

HES Report Interviews, Mỏ Cày Style

Mỏ Cày's geographic expanse, number of villages, and major security concerns quickly educated me on the difference between Hàm Long HES Report interview operations and Mỏ Cày HES Report interview operations. In Hàm Long we had visited every village office over time to conduct those interviews, except for Phú Túc, which did not have a village office.

In Mỏ Cày only a few of the village offices were easily reachable by road or canal boat. Two of the worst, security-wise, were Định Thủy and

Phước Hiệp villages, adjacent to each other between the Hàm Luông River and the rivers at Mỏ Cày town. The district chief had no wish to establish a huge security force to protect us in order to visit the official village offices of those two places. When it was time to meet the village officials of Định Thủy village, they were summoned to the Hòa Lộc village office on the highway to the Bến Tre ferry, or all the way to district headquarters. Phước Hiệp's "temporary" village office was in a tiny hamlet directly across the river from Mỏ Cày main market square. It had once been connected to the Mỏ Cày market by a large steel bridge, long ago destroyed by the VC. I went on only one visit to Phước Hiệp the entire time I was in Mỏ Cày. Major Reed, Sergeant Tuyến, and I took our Boston Whaler across the river and met the deputy district chief at the village office, did the interviews, and returned to the team house. Phước Hiệp's village chief lived in Mỏ Cày town and was seen in the official village office only for those HES Report visits.

Unlike in Hàm Long, where I had visited all of the village offices, in Mỏ Cày I visited only a few village offices. Our counterparts did not arrange the necessary large security operations in order to visit the most dangerous villages. Instead, the village chief was summoned to the district compound, and HES Report interviews were done in the district headquarters' offices. In all of these cases, the most embarrassing question was, "Does the village chief stay overnight in the village?"

… Happiness Is a Glass of the Rạch Dầu Priest's "Wine."

Rạch Dầu village is a settlement of Catholic refugees, most of whom were families that came south in the 1954 partition of Vietnam. It was one of the few village offices I was able to visit in Mỏ Cày. The village lay along the north bank of the Cổ Chiên River and was a prosperous small town with excellent security—adjacent to some of the worst areas of Mỏ Cày. The VC left Rạch Dầu alone for several reasons. One was the frequency of district operations in and around Rạch Dầu. Another was the good local security backed by staunch support from residents of the village. And perhaps the third was the personality of the preeminent leader in the village— the priest in the large Catholic church in Rạch Dầu. He was one of the most interesting people I met during my stay in Mỏ Cày. He was physically fit and spoke English and French excellently. His leadership went far beyond his priestly duties. His impressive church with a tall steeple was a landmark in that part of the district, and the youngish priest—I'd guess he was in his 40s when I knew him—was firmly in control of the village population.

As staunch Catholics, the populace was strongly anti–VC, and they maintained their own security with a combination of district PF outposts and the village PSDF unit. In most places the PSDF were a rag-tag, poorly armed and poorly trained militia force, usually consisting of men too young or too old for regular military service. However, in some locations, most notably in Tân Lợi village, Hàm Long and in Rạch Dầu, the PSDF were disciplined, well-armed, and acquitted themselves with courage and skill against VC/NVA forces. Rạch Dầu's PSDF patrolled only within their village area and did not conduct offensive operations outside their area. They were good enough that the VC/NVA did not bother them.

Mỏ Cày's district chiefs frequently visited Rạch Dầu, together with a rather formidable security force. On this operation in June 1972 both Major Reed and I went along. We drove to An Thạnh village and boarded a flotilla of three water taxis, then sailed down the canal to the Cổ Chiên River and then upriver to Rạch Dầu. Meanwhile, a large force of RF/PF soldiers conducted an overland security operation on the north side of the Mỏ Cày Grand Canal and provided a security screen on the landward side of Rạch Dầu. The visit to Rạch Dầu gave us the opportunity to ask the HES Report questions and included a long meeting with the priest. In addition to his religious role and as community leader, he also had a good personal intelligence network that he shared with district authorities. He greeted us wearing his priestly garments, a long black cassock that reached to the ground. That belied his other persona, which was that of a skilled anti–VC fighter who often led the security patrols through his village—always dressed as a priest, not as a soldier.

The Rạch Dầu priest was not shy about his love of good brandy. We were served a midday meal prepared by the women of the church, accompanied by "pale wine," which was, of course, good brandy. Most Vietnamese food shops stocked brandy, the true origin of which was sometimes in doubt. I never knew where the priest obtained his full stock, but whenever advisors went to Rạch Dầu, it was tradition to carry a couple bottles of good brandy purchased in the province compound store to help the priest maintain his supply. The brandy we were served was always declared to be "pale wine." Very enjoyable at lunch, and we did not have to drive home.

Northwestern Mỏ Cày

The northwestern part of Mỏ Cày was a difficult region. Mỏ Cày town was connected to Đôn Nhơn District by a "road" from Mỏ Cày town west across the district and then north toward Đôn Nhơn and further to the Chợ Lách District of Vĩnh Long Province. It was a very rough rock road (as opposed to dirt or gravel) on which we had to balance speed and safety when we drove—fast enough to avoid an ambush or sniper fire but not so fast that we blew out the tires or otherwise damaged the jeep. The several-kilometer-wide area between this road and the parallel main highway from Mỏ Cày to the Bến Tre ferry landing was extremely difficult, frequently used by the enemy for small base camps. There was no "cross road" through that dangerous area; land movement was only on a network of pathways. The entire area was heavily booby-trapped. Major Reed told me a couple tales of operations in that roadless part of the district. I never had a chance to see the area for myself.

Tactical operations along the "road" to Đôn Nhơn required at least a company-size security unit and often a company on both sides of the road. One operation took place in late May or early June 1972, just shortly after I had transferred from Hàm Long to Mỏ Cày. Trung-tá Cư commanded the operation, and both Major Reed and I made the long walk with him. We drove to Kinh Ngang outpost and then walked up this road. The mission was to finish up repairs to the new market building in Tân Thanh Tây village, just before the border with Đôn Nhơn District, and then officially open the new facility with an appropriate ceremony. The original market building had been badly damaged by the VC. Fortunately, the operation was uneventful. Except for that long walk.

Preparations for Extension Leave

Once settled into my new team house, becoming comfortable with my new boss, starting to work on counterpart relationships, and getting my feet wet (literally) in the field, I had to address the seemingly simple issue of getting orders approving the extension of my tour of duty, assignment of a new DEROS, and orders for the 30-day free leave awarded for making the six-month extension. This turned into a major problem. With constant personnel turmoil at MACV Headquarters because of the ongoing personnel drawdown, those orders got lost somewhere in the proverbial crack. Finally, in late June the province team chief of staff took me and my baggage to MACV Headquarters and told the personnel people that we were not leaving their office until my orders were published. His extra horsepower as a lieutenant colonel was worth much more than my mere captain's bars.

It was an important issue because the free 30-day leave program and accompanying free transportation to and from the leave location was going to expire at the end of June 1972, only days away. I had already told Mr. Kotzebue that I would honor my extension even if the leave fell through, but he was determined to make this all work. It took three days in Saigon, but finally I had my extension orders, a new DEROS for my assignment—7 February 1973—and my leave orders. After a short stay at Camp Alpha, I was on my way.

I left for Australia and New Zealand on 27 June 1972, with no premonition of the difficulties that would strike in Mỏ Cày, Hàm Long, and Kiến Hòa Province as a whole while I was away.

14

Tragedy and Courage
in Thành Thới

While I was enjoying my 30-day extension leave in Australia and New Zealand, bad things happened back in Hàm Long and Mỏ Cày. In July 1972 the VC/NVA forces began a summer offensive in Kiến Hòa Province. Hàm Long and Mỏ Cày Districts were hard hit by main force NVA battalions that infiltrated across the rivers from Định Tường and Vĩnh Bình provinces, respectively. In Mỏ Cày at least seven separate VC/NVA battalions deployed against Mỏ Cày's RF\PF forces. On 1 July the 996 RF Company was ambushed in Thành Thới village and suffered major casualties. On 10 July sappers attempted to infiltrate the district compound but were repulsed with heavy casualties.

Insulted Pride and a Doomed Operation

In an attempt to respond to the NVA invasion, on 7 July a province-level *liên đội,* consisting of several RF companies, began operating in the Định Thủy and Phước Hiệp villages of eastern Mỏ Cày. Both the VC/NVA and friendly forces suffered heavy casualties. Very annoyed at a battalion-size unit operating in "his" district without having any command responsibility for it, on 17 July Trung-tá Cư launched his own operation into Thành Thới village. LTC Cư told the province chief that it was only a small operation to recover an outpost that had been overrun. In fact, he assembled a substantial force of RF *Liên Đội* 14—the 468 RF Company and the 756 RF Company, plus two PF platoons, with a total of about 100 soldiers. The operation was targeted at the VC/NVA's D-263 Battalion. The operation was a mistake, an action that Major Reed urged him not to take. But the operation went on, and Major Reed and Sergeant Tuyển went with the district chief and his command group into a very dangerous part of Thành Thới village.

161

The operational forces boarded three VN Navy assault boats and traveled west on the Mỏ Cày Grand Canal past An Thạnh village and out into the Cổ Chiên River, then turned south for several kilometers. At the designated spot the force landed, cut its way through very heavy jungle growth, and waded through chest-deep streams to approach the target area where the enemy force was believed to be located. The Mỏ Cày units arrived at Thới Khương outpost, the outpost that LTC Cư had told the province chief he was going to recover and re-man around noon. The outpost had been burned by the NVA, and there were no bodies, a sure sign that the soldiers in that outpost were traitors and had abandoned the outpost to the NVA.

As the force continued forward, it soon neared a raised dirt road with a very large open area on the other side of the road. The force began taking sporadic fire and then increasingly heavy fire from enemy forces of unknown strength. A combination of light jungle, rice paddies, and a series of small villagers' straw-built field hooches all provided cover for what turned out to be a very large enemy force.

The Mỏ Cày forces took cover in a deep ditch along the road and began firing across the road. Province had arranged a FAC to cover the operation, which was of major importance. Major Reed directed seven air strikes against the enemy positions, bringing the bombs "danger close" to the friendly forces in the ditch. Sergeant Tuyến reported that he saw "too many" enemy moving through the jungle, in and out of hooches, all across the large open area across the dirt road directly in front of the friendly forces. They even spotted a bugler on one enemy flank and a female carrying a large NVA flag on the other flank. Despite those air strikes, the enemy was still waiting.

In Major Reed's words,

> Out of the jungle marched the North Vietnamese regiment that everyone had been hunting. Almost a thousand soldiers, in uniform, with battle-flags flying. They were formed in three battalion-size columns of about 300 men each. It looked like an ROTC drill formation. On the right was a big red battle flag and on the left was a bugler. We opened fire on the huge formation of the NVA main force regiment. They answered with bugle calls and a beehive of shots that sang into the bamboo around us, and then they broke ranks into a battle line that swept toward us.

The Mỏ Cày forces, outnumbered probably ten to one, fought well and inflicted heavy casualties on the advancing enemy regiment. Unfortunately, there were no more aircraft to continue air strikes against the enemy. Instead of one enemy battalion that LTC Cư expected to find, a much larger force—a full NVA regiment—had successfully gathered, unknown to friendly intelligence, in Thành Thới village. When the NVA battalions opened fire, Trung-tá Cư's courageous actions on the battlefield began to rally the beleaguered district forces. Major Reed personally used his M-16 to silence enemy machine-gun fire that had prevented Mỏ Cày forces from withdrawing on the road. The 468 RF Company fought well, but Mỏ Cày's forces were badly outnumbered.

Then an enemy B-40 rocket grenade struck LTC Cử, and he was killed instantly, as were his four-man personal security force. The blast blew Major Reed up onto the road, unconscious and wounded by shrapnel in both legs. The soldiers thought he too had been killed. The brave 468 RF Company commander rallied the remaining troops together and began to withdraw on the road, away from the ambush and toward a distant outpost where they could find cover. Looking back, as he retreated with the RF forces, Sergeant Tuyến saw Major Reed begin moving on the road as he regained consciousness. He raced back to help him up and walk him out of the ambush site before the advancing VC could capture him.

Major Reed and Sergeant Tuyến urged the friendly element to move out of the ambush, carrying as many wounded as they could. All of Mỏ Cày's officers were either dead or wounded. Major Reed took the lead, getting all of the soldiers into a tight formation as they kept up their slow withdrawal while also fighting off the advancing enemy. SFC Tuyến said he could see strong NVA forces on three sides of the friendly units, some as close as 50 meters. Eventually, the small force reached a mud PF outpost where they could take cover. By then Vietnamese attack helicopters arrived to assault the NVA force, and medevac helicopters arrived and began to take out the wounded soldiers.

Mr. Kotzebue, the Kiến Hòa PSA , flew in on one of the medevac helicopters and joined the defenders in the outpost. Major Reed remembered handing him his rifle and pistol, both empty—he was completely out of ammunition—before he collapsed and was carried onto the last departing medevac helicopter.

Of the 100-man friendly force, Vietnamese press reported seven were killed and 53 wounded. Major Reed thought there might have been as many as 90 RF wounded. Enemy casualties were estimated at 40 or more killed by air strikes and close combat. One day later a B-52 raid struck the area of contact and virtually annihilated the enemy regiment; it was not heard from again. But the damage was great—the KIA included the district chief and the intelligence section leader; the wounded included the DSA and the district S-3.[1]

Major Reed was evacuated to the 3rd Surgical Hospital in Saigon, where he remained for almost two weeks. Surgeons removed 22 large pieces of shrapnel from his legs and stitched up the wounds but left dozens of tiny pieces in his legs. Major Reed credited Sergeant Tuyến with saving his life: "If he had not run back and helped me out, the NVA would surely have captured or killed me on the side of that road," he said. Sergeant Tuyến was awarded the U.S. Army Commendation Medal with "V" device for valor. Major Reed was awarded the Silver Star, one of the last awards for valor awarded to American soldiers in Vietnam.[2]

I Return to a Vastly Different Mỏ Cày

I returned from my extension leave on 25 July 1972, just a week after the battle in Thành Thới village, to be met by the shock of LTC Cư's death and Major Reed's injuries. News of the battle had obviously spread widely. I learned of the fight even before I got back to Kiến Hòa. Talkative passengers on the Vietnamese civilian bus I took from Saigon to Bến Tre told me several versions of what had happened. I got an official update when I checked in at the advisory team compound in Bến Tre.

When I returned to Mỏ Cày, Major Reed was back from the hospital, but he was almost immobile and unable to go to the field until his legs healed. I remember seeing him painfully extracting bits of shrapnel from his legs in the evenings as the tiny bits moved near the skin and he used tweezers to pull them out.

I felt terrible about not being there when all of this happened. He went out of his way to alleviate my feelings of guilt. He told me that had I been there he would have assigned me to remain at the TOC as a radio relay, standing by immediately to call for the medevac helicopters he was certain would be needed. Thus, I would not have been in the field with him and the district chief. His words were kind and heartfelt and made me feel better.

… Major Byron Reed, wounded in a bad action in which his district chief was killed, unwrapping his leg bandages every night to painfully clean the tiny pieces of emerging shrapnel, never complaining, never shirking. An inspiring boss.

Now a dangerous and strong enemy force was striking almost at will throughout the district. The demoralized district staff was now working for a temporary district chief who normally worked as an operations officer in the province TOC. He was the "circuit rider" who customarily filled in when district chiefs went on leave, or in our case, where there was an unexpected vacancy.

The Mỏ Cày RF/PF forces and interim district chief had little respite from the NVA offensive. The large number of invading enemy battalions showed in the heavy contact experienced by the province-level *liên đội* in eastern Mỏ Cày's Phước Hiệp and Định Thủy villages. The soldiers and officers on the compound were still in shock from the ambush in southwestern Thành Thới village that killed LTC Cư. On 9 August the newly arrived NVA three-battalion E-2 Regiment launched a major attack against Tân Thanh Tây, Tan Binh, and Thành An villages in far northwestern Mỏ Cày. The enemy cut the only road between Mỏ Cày and Đôn Nhơn Districts for about a week and overran the Tân Thanh Tây village office and held it for two days. Province-level forces deployed into the region and had heavy enemy contact for much of August, until the enemy regiment broke contact and split into separate company-size units for rest and resupply. Major Reed and I split our time between the team house and the TOC, working with the district staff to request and deploy tac air strikes and try to keep up with the rapid pace of events.

A Medevac Portends Another Big Change

I took part in one of the most significant of my many medevac operations a week or so later. The Province Kit Carson Scout platoon conducting an operation in eastern Mỏ Cày made contact with the VC and took one serious casualty. The Americans promised that any KCS wounded in action would be treated at an American military hospital, not a Vietnamese one, since conditions were better in the American medical facilities. But the only way to insure the Vietnamese KCS would be admitted to a U.S. hospital was for an American advisor to accompany the casualty to the hospital.

The two Americans with the Scouts could not leave the operation to escort their wounded man to a hospital. We were monitoring the radio during this operation, so we heard their call around the radio net for a volunteer to pick up the wounded man and escort him to Saigon. It was our district, so I volunteered to go. The swing ship picked me up at our district helipad on the edge of town and took me to the scene of the contact, where the KCS had designated a landing zone adjacent to some damaged and abandoned buildings but warned the pilots that it could be hot. The pilot flew as if it was a hot LZ, and the door gunners were firing like mad, but there was no return enemy fire.

I hopped out and immediately fell into a water-filled, waist-deep defensive trench, then climbed out to get the information I needed from the advisors while KCS men carried the casualty to the helicopter. Then we lifted off and flew to 3rd Surgical Hospital in Saigon. When the pilots landed across the street from the hospital, I explained to the orderlies meeting the helicopter that our KCS was authorized to receive U.S. medical care.

On the return flight from Saigon to Mỏ Cày I noticed a large cloud of smoke rising from the area in Hàm Long that I knew was the location of Tân Lợi village. When I got back, I mentioned it to Major Reed. He told me that there was a major enemy offensive underway in Hàm Long, and the PSA was planning to send the Province S-2 advisor, Captain Bill Chandler, out to Hàm Long as a temporary advisor. I filed that away.

In Mỏ Cày the increased pace of widespread enemy activity meant very few field operations for the acting district chief and his staff, which was a welcome respite for Major Reed and me. Still, there was much to do—coordinating air strikes, reviewing the security situation and updating the threat posture to the many friendly units and outposts. The district compound felt the increased enemy threat by several mortar attacks and at least two foiled sapper attacks.

On 13 August 1972 the compound came under a combined small arms and mortar attack. A sapper unit swam most of the way across the river on the southeast corner of the compound but was spotted by an alert sentry who opened fire and either killed or wounded whoever was in the water; no sappers made it to the riverside perimeter. One RF was wounded by mortar fragments. This attack appeared to be part of a strong attempt to overrun Mỏ Cày town as well as the district compound as part of the summer NVA offensive in Mỏ Cày; intelligence believed that the enemy forces included the C-1 Sapper Company and the D-263 LF Battalion (NVA)—the original, incorrectly identified objective of LTC Cư's ill-fated operation in Thành Thới village.

… Gratitude to the alert artillery sentry who spotted a straight line of vegetation in the river, then spraying the area with his machine gun and literally turning the canal water red, thus destroying an attempted sapper attack.

Enemy attacks against Mỏ Cày town continued unabated. On 14 August, just before midnight, the TOC watch officer told us that the enemy had launched a ground attack against the town and the district compound had come under a sustained mortar and—for the first time—rocket attack. That confirmed that NVA artillery units had joined the offensive against Kiến Hòa Province. The ground attack again launched from southwest of the town and got within 200 meters of crossing the main highway and entering the built-up area of town. Mortar and rocket fire came from the northeast, east, and southeast directions from locations across the river in Phước Hiệp village. TOC estimated that two enemy battalions were involved in the attempt to enter the town. Fortunately, concentrated friendly artillery fire stopped the attacking ground force before it could enter Mỏ Cày. The battle lasted well over an hour before the attacking ground force retreated. It had been an anxious time.

…Running to the bunker at 0100 in the morning…. The grim discovery that there is an NVA battalion attacking from 200 meters south of town; satisfaction when our artillery surprises THEM trying to surprise us.

In Retrospect: The Maverick of Mỏ Cày[3]

Years after I returned from Vietnam I wrote several articles for publication about some of my remarkable, able, and courageous counterparts, men whose leadership and character left a lasting impression on me. I have had a 50-year-long eagerness to tell these men's stories to illustrate the courage and tenacity of the ARVN soldier. This is Nguyễn Văn Cư's story.

Nguyễn Văn Cư was a man who called forth strong emotions from all who knew him. Vietnamese found him to be a good friend and a ruthless opponent. American advisors found him unpredictable, effective most of the time but seemingly immoveable at others. Outspoken in a society that valued discretion, argumentative with superiors in a culture that valued hierarchy and status, breathtakingly courageous on the battlefield, Nguyễn Văn Cư was an enigma to all who knew him. Above all else he was a patriot who deeply loved his country and who believed in his people's strength and dignity. He was a man of unpredictable moods who kept his own counsel, approachable at some times but inscrutable and unreachable at others.

Cư was an engineer by education and an army officer by choice. He thought with the ordered mind of the technician when it suited his purposes. But he also thought with the processes of the local fortune tellers, who are a foundation of Vietnamese village society. He had a volatile temper but was capable of quiet introspection, a black belt karate expert who worked off his frustrations on a canvas-covered, padded telephone pole behind the district headquarters. Above all else Nguyễn Văn Cư loved his country. He was a genuine Vietnamese patriot.

LTC Cư presented a real challenge to his American advisors. He was a man of great ability, vision, and depth. He was also ethnocentric to a high degree, a tremendous egotist, and made his own order of priorities. As a result, the counterpart relationship between him and his advisors had been a stormy one that ranged from close cooperation to open conflict. Earlier in his career LTC Cư had attended military courses in the U.S., and he spoke English excellently—when he wanted to. He was knowledgeable about American military strength and technology, and he was frustrated that his own country could not achieve similar levels.

He never hesitated to disagree with his advisors, his fellow district chiefs, or his superiors. His ability to get things done despite this constant series of confrontations won him the secret admiration of his peers even when he was using assets originally scheduled to be used elsewhere in the province. He held firm views on the relative roles of district chief and the American advisory team assigned to assist him, and often his views conflicted with the official line laid down by his superiors. He was astonishingly corrupt, but at least for advisors there was nothing that could be proven. Despite all the controversy about his methods, there was little question about his ability. LTC Cư's leadership was often spectacular, and he controlled his military forces with an iron hand. Other advisors told me that he was the equal of any American commander, but he lacked the extensive modern training and equipment available to American forces. He became angry when he could not accomplish a task because of a lack of tactical assets and reflected his frustrations by deliberately ignoring his advisors or defying his superiors.

Into this unusual situation came a remarkable American officer in April 1972 as the new DSA in Mỏ Cày. Major George B. "Byron" Reed was a prematurely gray Carolinian with a wealth of prior advisory experience. On his first Vietnam assignment he was DDSA in nearby Chợ Lách District, Vinh Long Province. He rapidly developed an effective counterpart relationship with LTC Cư. A student of Vietnamese history and culture, Major Reed was able to discuss these subjects intelligently, and the two men often talked together late into the night. Their mutual love of history and philosophy cemented their association into firm respect and friendship. While history and philosophy are strange subjects on the battlefield, they rescued the advisor-commander relationship in Mỏ Cày that was in danger of complete collapse.

An animist as well as a Buddhist (as are many Vietnamese) Cư believed that he would return to fight his enemies in another life. He often referred to events far in the future with the phrase "when I return," invoking the Vietnamese belief in reincarnation. Such animistic reasoning by a modern, well-educated engineer officer was difficult for some Americans to understand. Because of his belief that he would return to fight again after death, LTC Cư was absolutely fearless on the battlefield. He strolled along almost casually on tactical operations as if daring the enemy to shoot him. Major Reed vividly described one operation through a heavily booby-trapped enemy base area without casualties; on another operation he took the point on a night march, disregarding the danger of mines, booby traps, and enemy snipers. Of such performances are legends made.

It is fitting that Lieutenant Colonel Nguyễn Văn Cư died as he had lived: with pride, leadership, and love of his country foremost in his mind, directing his men to victory over an enemy he had fought with all his heart and soul for a lifetime.

Nguyễn Văn Cư was indeed a maverick. His views often conflicted with those of his superiors, his peers, and his advisors. He spoke his mind as he saw fit and expressed himself forcefully in a quiet-voiced society. Cư was proud of his country and its heritage and was determined to defend them. He was proud of his patriotism, his people, and his culture. He was determined that no enemy would subvert them. He was a man of great contradictions who stood up for his beliefs. When the moment of reckoning arrived, he died fighting to preserve those things in which he believed most. No man can do more.

I am sure that many people who knew him are waiting for him to return again.

North Vietnamese Army Invades Hàm Long District

The Town of Tân Lợi

Tân Lợi was the largest town and marketplace in Hàm Long District. The road to Tân Lợi branched off from the main road from Bến Tre just before the district headquarters compound and led six kilometers west to Tân Lợi. During my ten months as DDSA in Hàm Long, the road to Tân Lợi was secure; it had not been interdicted by enemy forces nor damaged by roadblocks or mines. RF/PF forces regularly patrolled the area between the district compound, past the iffy village of Quới Thành, and on to Tân Lợi. On the other hand, north of the road it quickly got tricky. Quới Thành was an edgy "C" or "D" village, and Phú Đức was a "D" rated village, and most of our trouble came from these two areas. Further to the northeast, Phú Túc was a solid "D" village. Enemy units had base areas, supply and communications trails, and hidden bunker complexes throughout those villages.

Tân Lợi was a pleasant small town with a clean market area and all of the expected infrastructure—school, medical clinic, and other public buildings. The main temple was across the narrow Tân Lợi River, which was an important connector to the Mekong River branches on both the north and south sides of the district. A very large dome-shaped PF command bunker dominated the eastern end of the market square, which was to play a major role in the successful defense of the town during the July 1972 NVA invasion.

The Battle for Tân Lợi

The 1972 NVA Easter Offensive hit hard in Quảng Trị, Kontum, and Bình Long provinces further north but was late coming to the Mekong

Commerce and families sail along the Tân Lợi River at the edge of the town; the stately Buddhist temple stands across the river.

Delta. While major battles were taking place in those areas, the Delta was actually quiet. That ended in July 1972, when NVA regiments crossed from Vĩnh Bình Province into the Mỏ Cày and Đôn Nhơn districts in July and from Định Tường Province into northwestern Hàm Long in early August. In Hàm Long the NVA moved southeast toward their first major objective, the small town of Tân Lợi. When I flew that medevac flight for the wounded KCS from Mỏ Cày to Saigon, I saw plumes of smoke coming from where I thought Tân Lợi was located. I was correct. NVA forces had surrounded Tân Lợi and had commenced several days of attacks against the village. Artillery, close-quarter fighting, and later tactical air strikes caused widespread destruction. Meanwhile, other elements of the invading Đồng Tháp I Regiment spread out through Quới Thành and Phú Đức and closed the road to the district headquarters, making it impossible to reinforce Tân Lợi's defenders by road.

The courageous defense put up by local soldiers and civilians in defense of Tân Lợi is another story about the courageous and oft-maligned Vietnamese local forces.[1] The battle pitted a small force of RF/PF soldiers, PSDF, RD Cadre, police, and other volunteers against a battalion of the invading Đồng Tháp I Regiment, which was fully manned by NVA soldiers infiltrated down the Hồ Chí Minh Trail. The town's defenders received valuable support from Hàm Long's artillery and from occasional tactical air strikes, and the NVA used mortars and rockets throughout the battle.

The fight at Tân Lợi was not typical of the actions that were heretofore fought by the Hàm Long RF/PF. They were experienced fighters in short violent clashes, generally in isolated rural locations. On the contrary, most of the Tân Lợi battle was fought in, and adjacent to, a built-up small town composed of well-built cement two-story buildings and single-story infrastructure buildings (school, clinic, etc.). The struggle was fought in international anonymity. There were few reporters who bothered to cover or record such small and remote battles. One Vietnamese-language newspaper devoted a page to the Tân Lợi action after the fact, but no foreign language papers took note of the battle.

The Battle of Tân Lợi, Phase I

The Battle of Tân Lợi began on 6 August 1972 when the NVA Đồng Tháp I Regiment (DT-1) infiltrated south across the Mỹ Tho River into Hàm Long District. Two battalions of the DT-1 were assigned to attack the Hàm Long District headquarters, while the D-261B battalion was assigned to attack and occupy Tân Lợi. The regiment would then move further east to seize Bến Tre, the primary objective of the attacking NVA forces. Two days of increasing enemy pressure in outlying areas of the village gave most of the population time to flee rather than support the enemy. It also gave local security forces time to prepare their defense.

The Tân Lợi village chief was a quiet and able man, considered the best of Hàm Long's village chiefs. I knew him well, having made many visits to Tân Lợi during my ten months as Hàm Long DDSA. Discussions with him were always informative; he knew just about every person and every thing in Tân Lợi. He commanded all local security forces in the village—a total of 22 PF soldiers, six National Policemen, three Rural Development Cadre (RDC), and 18 People's Self-Defense Force (PSDF) militiamen armed with old M-1 and M-14 rifles. The village chief had the good fortune to have an able and courageous PF soldier as the village military chief. I had accompanied him on visits to several of Tân Lợi village outposts, where his strong leadership and no-nonsense attitude reminded me a lot of U.S. Army First Sergeants.

With several days of advance warning, the small force of defenders reinforced the village defenses. Platoons in several PF outposts around Tân Lợi (including Tan Bắc, mentioned earlier) were either withdrawn to Tân Lợi or sent to reinforce other outposts. Soldiers upgraded and built new bunkers, quickly prepared covered fighting trenches and smaller bunkers, double-checked defensive wires, and completed preparations. The early evening of 10 August was quiet but tense. Everyone knew that the D-261B battalion was tightening the noose. Enemy forces interdicted the road to Hàm Long and the Tân Lợi River north to the Mỹ Tho River. Nevertheless, the village chief continued to send out regular small reconnaissance and ambush patrols from the large PF outpost at the eastern end of the Tân Lợi market square.

At 0200 hours on 11 August one of those ambush patrols made contact with an NVA sapper unit trying to cut the village's perimeter wire only 30 meters south of the outpost. At the same time the enemy began to fire 82 mm mortar rounds into the town. Two PF were killed in the firefight with the sappers, but the rest of the patrol got safely back to the outpost. The village chief deployed ten PF and PSDF into the second-floor windows of houses on the north side of the market square. At the same time the PF platoon leader sent a few PF and PSDF into newly built bunkers north of the market. An RD Cadre leader took a small group of PSDF and RD Cadre to the bunkers south of the market. At first light this small force took the brunt of the first enemy ground attack. One NVA platoon, supported with B-40 rocket fire, got within 20 feet of friendly positions before being driven back by accurate small arms fire. For most of the PSDF it was the first time they had fired their weapons in anger.

By then it was near dawn, 0530 hours on 11 August. While the NVA platoon continued to probe the south side of the PF defenses, an enemy company attacked the market from the north. This much larger force broke against a single newly built mud and coconut log bunker manned by three PF soldiers and a squad of PSDF about 100 meters north of the outpost. Using only rifle fire, the small band of defenders, supported by PF soldiers in the upstairs windows of houses behind them, held off the attacking enemy company for almost an hour. Sporadic supporting field artillery from the 105 mm howitzers at the district compound helped the defenders, but the artillery soldiers also had their hands full with fire missions against the two NVA battalions attacking closer to the district headquarters. The small party of PF defenders finally had to withdraw after suffering eight wounded, but all of them made it back to the main PF outpost.

By daylight on 11 August, the NVA had surrounded Tân Lợi. They began a steady barrage of rifle and mortar fire. Except for the small group south of the market, all of the defenders regrouped in the PF outpost, where they had good overhead cover and better protection from the steady pounding of indirect fire. Stymied by the unexpected level of opposition, the NVA stopped the ground attacks, and the tactical situation settled into a siege that lasted almost 36 hours.

Death of a Dedicated American Advisor

Meanwhile, the province leadership was very concerned about the deteriorating situation in Hàm Long while also dealing with a major invasion of Mỏ Cày. On 9 or 10 August 1972, the PSA called Captain Bill Chandler, the province S-2 advisor, to his office. Since the advisory team in Hàm Long had been closed down the previous May, the PSA needed an American in Hàm Long to help the district chief coordinate air strikes against this major new enemy threat. Mr. Kotzebue ordered Captain Chandler to deploy to Hàm Long District headquarters to assist LTC Sơn. Bill was a Military Intelligence branch officer, but earlier in his career he had been in the infantry branch, including combat duty in the U.S. 9th Infantry Division. Bill had transferred to the MI branch after his 9th Infantry Division assignment. The PSA selected him to go to Hàm Long because of his infantry background and combat experience.

Mr. Kotzebue personally drove Captain Chandler to Hàm Long and introduced him to LTC Sơn. The PSA stressed the seriousness of the security threat, as did LTC Sơn. Captain Chandler took the right equipment and knew of the danger. Mr. Kotzebue took a picture of Captain Chandler sitting on his steel helmet just before he drove back to Bến Tre. I have a copy of that picture; it haunts me to this day.

LTC Sơn had his hands full. On 11 August he led an operation of two platoons of RF soldiers, accompanied by Captain Chandler, in an effort to reinforce Tân Lợi. Unfortunately, neither he—nor province headquarters—had sufficient intelligence about the strength and disposition of the invading regiment. The full nature of the enemy threat had not been developed. Unknown to Hàm Long's forces, two enemy battalions spread out north and west of district headquarters. An unknown-size NVA force was hidden in a grove of coconut trees south of the road and west of the Tre Bông River, only one kilometer from the district compound. Just after crossing the Tre Bông River bridge and passing through several coconut groves on both sides of the road, the Hàm Long command group emerged into an open area with broad rice paddies on both sides of the road. Unbeknownst to the Hàm Long forces, the enemy had established an ambush zone and was waiting to spring their ambush.

LTC Sơn later told me that they had been moving toward Tân Lợi along the road, which at that point ran on a diagonal from southeast to northwest. However, his security element on the south side of the road was aligned due north-south (on line with the grid lines on the maps) rather than perpendicular to the road. That misalignment of flank security forces gave the enemy a clear shot at the command group, and the NVA opened fire with AK-47 rifles and B-40 rocket launchers. Many of the district soldiers were able to take cover in the rice paddies on the north side of the road, protected by the height of the road above the paddies, but many were killed and wounded before they could get to cover. Sadly, Captain Chandler was killed instantly by the blast of a B-40 rocket-propelled grenade while still on the road. The outnumbered district force quickly retreated back to the compound in disarray.[2]

During the same time, the 18th Regiment, 9th ARVN Division, had just deployed to Kiến Hòa Province to assist province forces in repelling the NVA invasion. The division's units had been steadily and heavily engaged elsewhere around the northern part of the Mekong Delta, so it had taken almost three days before a force could be freed from other conflicts and deployed to Kiến Hòa Province. Two of the 18th Regiment's battalions were operating to the north and east of Hàm Long's district compound, in the dangerous areas of Tương Dạ village of Hàm Long and in adjacent Trúc Giang District. A reaction force from the 18th Regiment responded to the attack against LTC Sơn's outnumbered forces and forced the enemy to retreat into the heavily wooded areas of Quới Thành and Phú Túc villages.

Regiment soldiers recovered Captain Chandler's body, and with great respect, the regimental senior advisor arranged for movement of Captain

This photograph shows the location where Captain Chandler was KIA in the area marked "Troops here." The district forces were only one kilometer west of the district headquarters compound (northwestern corner shown at lower left corner). Captain Chandler was the last American soldier killed during the long U.S. presence in Kiến Hòa Province.

Chandler's remains to the U.S. mortuary at Tân Sơn Nhứt Air Base, Saigon. Two of Bill's close friends on the province advisory team had the sad duty of gathering and packing up Captain Chandler's personal property for shipment to his family. One of them, my friend Captain Mike Delaney, the field artillery advisor, told me that it was the toughest thing he had ever done.[3]

The Battle of Tân Lợi, Phase II

After more than a day of quiet, at about 0300 hours on 13 August the NVA began a coordinated ground attack against Tân Lợi's defenders. A squad of PF soldiers climbed back into the second-floor windows along the market square; the platoon leader himself directed fire from the roof. They surprised another enemy sapper squad trying to breach the perimeter wire and drove them off. At first light the NVA launched a two-pronged attack. One element moved down a narrow side street along the Tân Lợi River on the west side of the village and emerged directly into the western end of the market square at the opposite end from the PF outpost. Another NVA element attacked from the northeast, crossed the road leading back to Hàm Long, and attacked against the large fortified PF outpost.

At this point the village chief made a crucial and courageous decision—he requested variable time fuse (VT) artillery concentrations directly over the beleaguered village. Hàm Long's two-tube artillery responded with accuracy. Its fire halted the enemy attack less than 50 meters from the outpost. The few PF still in second-floor windows rolled grenades onto the enemy flank in the cramped alley on the west side of the market. Although it forced the enemy to retreat, the artillery did massive damage to Tân Lợi homes, shops, and infrastructure.

At around 1100 hours elements of the ARVN 18th Regiment conducted a helicopter-borne air assault and landed west of Tân Lợi. Faced with this new and much-more-serious opposition, the NVA withdrew from the immediate area of the Tân Lợi market and moved to more secure areas in northern Phú Đức and Phú Túc villages, about six kilometers northeast of Tân Lợi. That retreat lifted the siege of Tân Lợi for the moment. They left behind 41 bodies in and around the market square.

Tân Lợi's defenders suffered two killed—in the very first contact with sappers south of the outpost—and 12 wounded. Elements of the 18th ARVN Regiment swept east, crossed the Tân Lợi River, and assaulted the rear of the two battalions poised to attack the Hàm Long District headquarters. The combat was fierce but short, and the enemy forces fled north to avoid being overrun and defeated by the ARVN force.

While the D-261B battalion had been hurt, it had not been killed. Several days later, after most of the ARVN 9th Division units had redeployed further east in Kiến Hòa Province, the D-261B battalion again began moving toward Tân Lợi. LTC Sơn had used the short breathing space provided by the arrival of the 9th ARVN Division units as best he could. He sent the 890th RF Company from district headquarters to Tân Lợi, accompanied by a number of volunteers from headquarters' soldiers. The 890th RF Company set up in positions around the ruins of the Tân Lợi school northeast of the PF outpost and built a large new bunker 200 meters west, across the Tân Lợi River. The Tân Lợi PF constructed a small squad bunker in the side street at the west end of the square (the area of advance previously used by one of the NVA elements) and a larger bunker in the main road just north of the outpost.

On 22 August—after a week of quiet—that new side-street bunker was manned by seven Tân Lợi PF and district staff soldiers under the command of an NCO from Hàm Long District headquarters. At first light enemy mortar fire began falling, and NVA forces began firing B-40 rockets straight down the narrow street. The NCO watched 15 NVA run across the footbridge over the Tân Lợi River and take up positions in the houses across from the bunker. The PF could not direct effective fire against the well-covered enemy until a platoon of NVA started walking straight down the narrow street toward the bunker position. One of the Claymore mines set out by the defenders was disabled by shrapnel, but they were able to detonate the other Claymores with devastating results—the lethal hail of pellets halted the enemy advance down the narrow street.

However, soon the small force of PF defenders in that bunker was drawing heavy B-40 fire. Fortunately, the village chief had directed everyone to erect webs of barbed wire mesh supported by steel stakes outside all of the bunkers, so many of the enemy rockets detonated prematurely, but the intense fire wounded all seven of the men manning the bunker. This small firefight raged for more than two hours and in the process started a fire in the houses along the street. The flames forced the NVA to retreat. The PF soldiers were finally rescued when the village chief and another PF squad, responding to check out the fire damage, found them still alive in the bunker. The rest of the defenders thought they had all been killed.

In another part of Tân Lợi soldiers from district headquarters were assigned to man a defensive position on the roof of the row of houses along the north side of the market square. They quickly became the target of B-40 fire from enemy shooting from a grove of coconut trees north of the village. In dire straits, the men in the row of houses called for help. By now having good radio communication with district headquarters, the village chief was told that tactical air support might now be available. Tac air could not be used for several days because of clouds and low ceilings. Fortunately for the tiny force in Tân Lợi, improved weather brought several sorties of VNAF fighter-bombers for use against the attacking NVA. Three of the soldiers were lightly wounded, and after the battle, one of them was proud as a peacock to show off the scars on his buttocks. Many of the soldiers credited the PF platoon for bringing desperately needed ammunition, helping to direct fires, and moving wounded men to safety.

The NVA attempted one more assault against Tân Lợi, this time against the new bunker in the road north of the market square. More than 20 B-40 rounds fired at the bunker finally collapsed the roof. One witness recalled the scene when a tearful policeman told the village chief that his son must have been killed in the fierce pounding. A small reaction force later found that, miraculously, none of the five men in the bunker had been killed, although all were badly wounded.

NVA Regiment Withdraws from Kiến Hòa Province

The attempt to overrun that bunker was the NVA's last gasp in the battle for Tân Lợi. For two more days the enemy continued to pour mortar and rocket fire into the village before what was left of the DT-1 Regiment withdrew back across the Mỹ Tho River, badly mauled by air strikes, artillery, and heavy pressure from the 18th ARVN Regiment. The NVA left behind over 30 bodies from the second phase of fighting plus an unknown number of casualties dragged from the battlefield. In addition to its personnel casualties, Tân Lợi village lost 14 homes, the medical dispensary, most of the elementary school, the roof off the market, a large rice mill along the river, and several smaller buildings.

When asked how his small force of men had been able to hold at bay a full NVA battalion, the courageous village chief had a simple answer: "This is our home."

To a man, the defenders of Tân Lợi credited their success to the leadership provided by the village chief and the village military chief. When tasked to single out individuals for heroism medals, the chief refused to select anybody. "All, or none," was his reply. LTC Sơn and the province chief agreed. Every man who fought at Tân Lợi was decorated for valor. Tân Lợi's village chief was called to Saigon and personally commended by President Nguyễn Văn Thiệu.

The NVA battalion command structure was its own worst enemy in this battle. The chain of command violated several important principles of war that led directly to defeat. One of the most significant of these was moving to the attack with insufficient intelligence. While most post-battle analyses concluded that the NVA probably had detailed information about the disposition of the RF/PF forces in Tân Lợi, they did not understand the factors of morale and determination that helped the outmanned defense force to remain in place and fight. Most importantly, the NVA commander committed his forces piecemeal into the fighting. This was probably done to avoid concentrating forces that might attract air strikes or artillery fire. A determined multipronged attack by the battalion's three companies probably would have overwhelmed Tân Lợi's defenders. By committing forces piecemeal in time and space, the NVA battalion commander squandered his advantages of size and superior fire power.

The battle for Tân Lợi was the biggest fight in Hàm Long District during the Summer 1972 NVA invasion. Security forces conducted a magnificent defense and prevented the enemy from gaining control of the town. The arrival and deployment of the 18th Regiment, 9th ARVN Division forced most of the attacking NVA forces out of Hàm Long and back across the Mỹ Tho River to habitual base areas in Định Tường Province and the Plain of Reeds. But the task of reasserting security in Hàm Long was going to be a struggle. The combination of artillery fire and close combat wreaked severe damage on Tân Lợi. Many buildings were destroyed in order to overcome enemy forces that had taken cover inside them. The school, the dispensary, and many homes were destroyed, but the market center suffered only minor damage.

... But the hardest loss of all—a friend sent to help out in Hàm Long, and killed shortly after he got there, in an ambush and firefight so heavy it took a day to recover his body. My gut knots when LTC Sơn told me what happened.

16

District Senior Advisor, Hàm Long District

New Orders: Return to Hàm Long

In mid–August Mỏ Cày received a radio message for me to come to Bến Tre and report to the PSA right away; the swing ship was already on the way to pick me up. When I reported to Mr. Kotzebue, wondering what was up, he somberly told me that Captain Chandler had been killed in an ambush and firefight just outside the Hàm Long District compound, and he wanted me to return to Hàm Long as DSA.

I was stunned, first at the death of a fine officer and friend, and second because I did not want to leave Major Reed by himself as he continued to recover from his wounds. Mr. Kotzebue told me that he had discussed it on the radio with Major Reed while I had been flying up to Bến Tre and had gotten his okay for me and Sergeant Bé to go to Hàm Long "for as long as necessary."

He briefed me on the circumstances of the tragic death of Captain Bill Chandler and on the dangerous tactical situation in Hàm Long. He stressed to me that he knew he was sending me into harm's way and that he was confident that I could handle the mission. He told me my main mission was to "buck up" the distraught district chief, who had lost confidence in his soldiers and his own leadership; aggressively to direct tactical air and attack helicopter strikes; and "go everywhere" with the district chief. He also told me to coordinate with the 18th ARVN Regiment elements and their advisor still in Hàm Long but that I was "in charge" of American support to the Hàm Long District.

I was shocked and saddened by the news of Bill Chandler's death but also was prepared to go back to Hàm Long. It was an honor to follow in Bill's footsteps. At the same time I felt extreme regret that Bill Chandler had been sent to Hàm Long first, instead of me. As near as I can determine, the reason was because I was needed as DDSA in Mỏ Cày. The district was in a worse tactical situation than Hàm Long, had only an interim district chief, and Major Reed was immobile because of the injuries he had suffered in July. Although he had changed to the MI branch, Captain Chandler had prior experience as an infantry platoon leader and company commander in combat. He was nearby, available, qualified, and was the logical choice given the chaotic situation in Kiến Hòa Province. Mr. Kotzebue told me in confidence many weeks later that he was personally devastated at Bill's death and had second-guessed his decision many times. Each time he concluded he had made the correct decision to send Captain Chandler to Hàm Long. I agree.

I arrived back in Hàm Long on 24 August 1972 with myself as DSA and SFC Hồ Văn Bé as interpreter. A few days later Mr. Kotzebue sent SFC Harvey Jones (not his real name), one of the TOC operations NCOs, to join us. He was a valuable addition to our team. I used him primarily as a radio relay monitor since much of western Hàm Long was out of reliable PRC-25 range to the TOC in Bến Tre. To his credit SFC Jones also concentrated on forming a solid relationship with the district chief and staff so he could work with them when I was away.

The 18th Regiment mobile command post (an awesome large box truck full of communications gear and work spaces) was still on the Hàm Long compound when I arrived. I had time to meet and coordinate with the regimental senior advisor and regiment commander before they deployed their mobile CP to a more central position further east at the Bến Tre airfield in Trúc Giang District. Just days later we would work together again.

My friends at Hàm Long were very relieved when we arrived. As promised, LTC Sơn was ready to receive us. He was very distraught and near tears when I reported to him in his office. Leaving the account of the combat action that had caused my friend's death until later, he got our team settled into what had been the administrative TOC and briefing room. Our former team house had been transformed into a new and much-more-spacious *câu lạc bộ* for the compound soldiers. The room he gave us was across a walkway from the main military office section and LTC Sơn's office and private quarters, just steps from the district staff offices, and adjoined a large, covered gathering spot used for briefings as well as relaxed conversation. Sturdily built from concrete cinder blocks, our new quarters had a reinforced roof for protection against incoming mortar rounds as well as a strong blast wall protecting the entrance doors.

We had enough space for our cots and mosquito nets, a PRC-10 radio from the Hàm Long District commo section, our own PRC-25 radio I brought from Bến Tre, footlockers made of wooden artillery shell boxes for our personal gear. We bought a tiny kerosene stove in the market to

LTC Sơn stands in front of the administrative TOC. This room became the
advisors' home August-November 1972.

warm C-ration cans and heat water for shaving. It was quite secure—concrete block walls rose almost head high, with heavy, screened, open windows above and a sandbagged roof. It was all we required. We used the
former advisory team latrine and shower room, now a bit further to walk
to, but still serviceable.

The 18th Regiment, 9th ARVN Division, was the strong force instrumental in driving most of the invading NVA regiment back across the Mỹ
Tho River. Now the Hàm Long District RF/PF forces were left to deal with
the strengthened, emboldened, and better-armed enemy local forces that
had been reinforced by NVA replacements.

Being a Strong Right Arm

The months of July and August 1972 were a real scramble for me. First,
returning to Mỏ Cày from extension leave to discover my DSA wounded
and district chief killed in action; then dealing with the NVA invasion of
Mỏ Cày District; then learning of Captain Chandler's death in Hàm Long;
and then called by the PSA to return to Hàm Long as DSA. To say the
least I had many things on my mind. What about Mỏ Cày and Major Reed,
still in pain from the wounds he received in July, and with a temporary

district chief to replace LTC Cừ, killed in action? Most importantly to me on a deeply personal level was the death of my friend Bill Chandler, KIA in Hàm Long only a day or two after he was sent there to assist the district chief. Like many who lost a friend in combat, the "why him and not me?" issue whirled around in my brain and reappeared with discomfiting frequency. I was able, over time, to reconcile that issue, but 50 years later it still reoccurs.

Was I good enough, experienced enough, and—perhaps—lucky enough to be successful as DSA in a district I knew well and at the same time not so well? Regardless, I had a job, I had my orders, I had a loyal interpreter to help me, and I knew most of the men I would be working with. I went as ordered, full of anticipation. It was a very different Hàm Long that I was now charged with helping. When I arrived back in Hàm Long, I found that most of the northern part of the district had earlier been occupied by the NVA's Đồng Tháp I Regiment. While that main force NVA regiment was now gone, having withdrawn to Định Tường Province after suffering heavy casualties from the 18th ARVN Regiment forces and several B-52 strikes, they had left reinforcements for the local VC units, which were already manned largely by NVA soldiers in any case.

The NVA invasion had quickly overrun many of the outposts in western and northern Hàm Long—some lost in battle and some from which the friendly forces had been evacuated ahead of NVA advances. Despite strength in numbers and weaponry, the enemy regiment had failed to overrun or capture any of Hàm Long's village offices or the district headquarters, which had been its primary mission. The security challenges we now faced were to retake the lost ground, rebuild the outposts, re-establish forces in all of them, and by these tactics regain the security lost during the previous month of combat. The enemy forces were more aggressive than in the past, encouraged by the gains of July and August. We had our work cut out for us.

And there was the issue of Trung-tá Sơn's emotional state. Mr. Kotzebue had told me he was distraught, having lost confidence in himself and his soldiers, and almost in shock from the losses inflicted on the district and its people. He was nearly in tears when I arrived and met him in the privacy of his office. He was older than me, more senior than me, more experienced than me. Yet my instructions were clear: I was to buck him up, restore his confidence in himself and his soldiers—and confidence in him by his superiors and his soldiers.

I did not come prepared with a rousing speech. I was not about to shame him with critical commentary, least of all about the death of Captain Chandler and the fact that it had taken a day for the 18th Regiment's men to find and recover his body. I told him I was glad to be back in Hàm

Long, that I looked forward to working with him and his soldiers, and asked that he tell me whenever he needed anything from me—equipment, air strikes, whatever. His response encouraged me: "I am very glad they sent you back here to help us; we trust you, and we will work very well together." That short sentence settled me down with relief and reinforced my confidence—the Vietnamese lieutenant colonel was going to treat the American captain as an equal. Even so, I knew that it was critical to success that I defer to him as district chief and accord him every respect as the senior officer.

Trung-tá Sơn's priorities were to rebuild and re-man the many outposts lost to the enemy offensive. He also had to retake the area between Hàm Long and Tân Lợi still partially controlled by enemy forces. With an RF company now in Tân Lợi and much of that village badly damaged by combat action, I felt that restoring the secure ground transportation link between the district headquarters and Tân Lợi was important, but he wanted to delay that task for some reason never made clear to me. In any event, he was the commander, I was the advisor, and his priorities became my priorities. Little did I know that I would be involved in more combat with the enemy during my three months as DSA in Hàm Long than I had (and would) experience during the other 15 months of my duty in Kiến Hòa Province.

Bodyguards to Watch My Back—Then and Later

When Sergeant Bé and I arrived back at Hàm Long District and had barely enough time to unpack our trailer and jeep, right away LTC Sơn sent for two soldiers. "They will be your bodyguards," LTC Sơn explained. I recognized both of them from my earlier time in Hàm Long. The details were, they would be part of a guard force for our quarters at night, and they would be my bodyguards wherever I went. They would carry my radio when we went to the field. I could not refuse the bodyguards, but I did keep the radio for myself, as had been my preference all along. I did not want to wonder where it was should shit hit the fan and I needed quick commo.

Sure enough, every night one or both of those soldiers was on armed guard outside our quarters. I could see or hear them before I slept or if I woke up in the night. It was a comfort having the protection even though I was sure there was no threat to us other than that posed by a mortar attack or ground assault on the compound. But clearly LTC Sơn thought there might be an enemy agent among his soldiers who might be ordered to attack the advisors. I was more unsettled by his obvious assumption that the VC already had people under cover among the RF and PF soldiers on the headquarters compound than I was about needing a bodyguard.

During our tactical field operations, one or the other of those two soldiers was always with me. He walked directly behind me in file and took up a position close to me during rest stops or administrative meetings, mealtimes in the field, during outpost construction, or when we had firefights with the VC. One or the other was very close to being my shadow for the entire three months I was deployed to Hàm Long. Whether on "walk in the sun" visits to village offices and outposts, or in the many firefights with the enemy, I was relieved to know that someone's mission was to attempt to keep me safe, alive, and unwounded.

Decades later, during one of my frequent visits to Saigon, a former Province interpreter told me of his postwar life. We also reminisced about "the good old days." On an earlier visit I had asked him how long he had spent in a "re-education camp" because he had been an ARVN NCO. He was silent for a moment. Then he told me that he had been incarcerated for only two months, and then a sister, who had been a VC cadre throughout the war, got him released. He swore he had been a loyal ARVN soldier and loyal to the Americans he worked with. If he had told anybody about his sister's position in the VC, he would not have been allowed to enter ARVN or to work with Americans as an interpreter.

Life after the war had not been kind to him, even with the family connection to a VC cadre. As a former ARVN NCO, he was barred from working in any government position—he had wanted to be a school teacher. He made his living as a private English language tutor, which provided enough income to keep his small family in relatively comfortable surroundings and to own a motor scooter to get to and from his tutorial clients.

On this visit I was finally bold enough to ask him who I knew personally who had turned out to be a VC. Most of the advisors assumed that about one-third of the officers and soldiers in the province were either VC or VC supporters. We weren't wrong as it turned out. I was surprised at some of the names he gave me.[1] But the real surprise was when he told me that the two soldiers assigned as my bodyguards were secretly VC all along. That meant that the two men to whom I had literally trusted my life had been enemy agents.

"Why am I still alive?" I asked my Vietnamese friend. "Those two guys could easily have killed me either while I slept or during enemy contacts on our tactical operations."

"Well, Đại-úy," he said, "there are several reasons." He went on to explain them.

First of all, the VC did not want to assassinate American advisors because a major, intense investigation would take place. The VC believed that undetected agents were more valuable than assassinating advisors. Even if the assassin escaped detection, a detailed investigation might turn up *other* VC assets.

Secondly, VC spies gained valuable bits of information about advisors' strategic and tactical plans, daily routine, relationships with counterparts, operational techniques, codes, and equipment.

And finally, "Đại-úy, you are a nice man. Everyone liked you, even the VC. A lot of people would have been very upset if you had been killed."

I never had the slightest inkling that my two bodyguards were anything other than loyal soldiers. I had known them well during my earlier ten months in Hàm Long. I was very surprised to learn that they had been VC all along. I am also very glad I was considered a nice man. It may very well have been a major reason why I was able to leave the war zone alive.

This account made sense. Many advisors in Kiến Hòa believed that the enemy was deliberately not targeting advisors for assassination. With their access to us, they could have taken us any time they wanted. I found it interesting that the VC did not assassinate advisors, but it was okay to kill them during tactical firefights.

It is just as well I had waited more than 30 years to learn that information. Had I known at the time who the clandestine VC were it would certainly have made a difference in my attitude!

Norris Nordvold and Ahn Hung

Norris told me another similar story that illustrates how open advisors were to assassination IF the VC wanted to assassinate advisors. One night he was sitting in the park in the center of the roundabout main entrance to Bến Tre. He was enjoying a glass of fruit juice in the cool of the evening when a stranger, Vietnamese, came up and sat down on the bench with him. He began talking to Norris in Vietnamese, obviously knowing who Norris was and that he spoke fluent Vietnamese.

The Vietnamese man introduced himself as "Ahn Hung" and said he was a VC and knew who Norris was. He told Norris he could kill him now or any time he or his colleagues wanted to kill him, but they would not do so. The reasons why—"they" knew Norris and other civilian Americans in his office had repaired the main city public swimming pool and were working on repairing a school. He named one of Norris's senior assistants and said he knew the two of them often took gifts to the orphanage. Then he got up and walked off into the night.

The VC had a widespread and efficient intelligence network and knew all of the American advisors. Like my friend telling me, "Everyone likes you, even the VC," they had very complete dossiers! And if "winning hearts and minds" is a trite and overused phrase, I firmly believe that doing exactly that, locally, out in the towns of rural Vietnam, probably saved untold advisors' lives over the long run of the war.

Con Dòi Outpost Operations, Then and Now

Just one day after I arrived back in Hàm Long the enemy pressed a strong ground attack against Con Dòi outpost, Phú Đức village, located very close to the Mỹ Tho River. The PF soldiers abandoned the outpost and fled to Tân Long outpost, a few kilometers to the northeast. This attack happened on a day when, by fortunate coincidence, the 18th ARVN Regiment was operating on the ground in eastern Hàm Long and western Truc Giang, so the regimental commander and his senior advisor were able to scramble a VNAF helicopter for a VR over the battle area. Trung-tá Sơn, Trung-úy Hương, Sergeant Bé, and I joined the ARVN regiment commander and his advisor to overfly the area around Con Dòi outpost and control air strikes.

We had met on the ground a few days earlier, and I had established my bona fides as a qualified advisor. Trung-tá Sơn had made it clear that he trusted and relied on me. I was grateful that the regimental senior advisor deferred to me in placing the air strikes where Trung-tá Sơn wanted them. It was an instant, intangible exchange of respect between two advisors who recognized that each shared the same level of commitment despite the difference in ranks. There was no conflict over senior privilege. I wonder how that might have worked out in a U.S. combat unit.

Thanks to the presence overhead of a Covey FAC and his quick contact with USAF aircraft, I was able to place several air strikes in and around the now-abandoned Con Dòi outpost. The FAC reported sighting eight VC killed, several fires, and one large secondary explosion. This was to lead to one of the more surreal experiences of my advisory career.

The 18th Regiment commander turned to me after an exchange of transmissions on his radio and shouted to us in English that he was talking with the NVA commander on the ground! Threats and curses got exchanged, and the most disturbing information was that the NVA offered a large reward if they would kill the advisors on the helicopter. Fortunately, the 18th Regiment commander and the rest of us were on the same side. Here's how I remembered it afterwards.

... The strange realities of an unreal war: riding in a Huey with the CO of the 18th ARVN Regiment, his advisor, and the District Chief while the NVA overrun Con Dòi Outpost and drive our soldiers out to Tân Long. The regiment commander getting the enemy commander on his radio, talking to him, jibing him when the air strikes come on target; the NVA's curses and the hatred obvious in his voice when he asks if an American is running the air strikes; and then his offer of a big reward if they shove us out of the helicopter. Happily the regiment commander did not want that big reward.

After we were back on the ground, Trung-úy Hương grinned at me and said, "Đại-úy, that VC does not like you." It had been quite a day at the office.

I had been to Con Dòi outpost during my earlier ten months in Hàm Long. The operation to Con Dòi outpost described here was conducted during that earlier period, approximately January 1972. I place that experience here to show the context of my relationship with the outpost and its men.

On that earlier day Sergeant Tu and I went on an operation commanded by Trung-úy Hương to the original Con Dòi outpost, in Phú Đức village near the Mỹ Tho River. On my map I could see the "blue lines" designating rivers and canals along the proposed route of march, so I knew it would probably be a wet day. Trucks took us out to Tân Lợi, and then we began patrolling north on a random route toward the outpost.

After a while we came to the bank of a swampy river. "Uh-oh," I thought to myself. "Đại-úy, we go on boat," Trung-úy Hương told me with a grin. Not a boat! Instead it was a flotilla of tiny ordinary sampans used mostly by families to cross streams or wide canals, for fishing and other watery chores, definitely not a large water taxi. Each little sampan came with a family member to paddle us along and across the river and then take their boat home.

At first I didn't even think I could fit myself into one of those tiny sampans. One of the soldiers showed me how to do it: just step into the middle of the boat and quickly sit down. He made it look so simple, but it was not so simple for this large, ungainly *cố vấn*. I dropped my rifle into the sampan, stepped in, quickly crash-landed on my butt and my back on top of the PRC-25, and managed to struggle to a sitting position with my legs stretched straight out in front of me, all without capsizing the sampan. Sergeant Tu and four other soldiers nimbly stepped into the sampan and either squatted down or sat with their legs crossed.

It didn't take long for all 20 or so of our operational force to get aboard the armada of sampans. Our hosts deftly paddled their heavy cargo onto the river with Hương pointing to the place on the other side where he wanted us to land. It was a swampy tidal area with narrow riverine arms as the sampans moved out of the main channel and stopped against a very low, marshy bank. Now, how was I supposed to get my legs under me, stand up in this wobbly little sampan, and step off onto dry land? Easy! Trung-úy Hương, standing regally dry on the bank, ordered four soldiers into the water, which was only waist-deep in the narrow little inlet, and they shoved the bow of the sampan up onto dry land all of two inches above water level. I literally crawled out of the sampan. Much laughter, but at least I didn't fall into the water, and both the radio and my rifle stayed dry.

Con Dòi outpost was another 200 or 300 meters further in from the swampy landing. The small force spent most of the day there while Trung-úy Hương supervised the soldiers to improve the bunkers and berm line (lots of mud available for that) and clear the brush back from the outpost to provide much better fields of fire against any would-be attacking enemy.

Around midafternoon it was time to patrol back toward Tân Lợi and return to the compound. I was relieved that I didn't have to try to

I don't know why these sampans didn't sink! The soldier at the bottom of this picture shows the correct way to get out of a sampan.

get into one of those tiny sampans again. We marched off in a different direction for several kilometers but then came to another riverbank. This was a bigger river, too big to wade or swim across. We waited while the soldiers commandeered several of the small-size water taxis as they chugged by. It was much easier to get in and out of a water taxi. Once across the river we returned to Tân Lợi and back to the compound with no further difficulty.

On the way back from Con Dòi outpost we waited for water taxis to get across this larger river.

But that was then, and now it was August 1972 and the tactical situation was much more dangerous. We wasted little time in getting started. Trung-tá Sơn wanted to begin rebuilding outposts that had been overrun or destroyed by the NVA. The first one of those he selected was to build a larger Con Dòi outpost closer to the Mỹ Tho River. I felt an affinity with the soldiers once assigned to build and man the outpost. Back then we had gone out there together, worked in the heat together to upgrade it, ate lunch together. They had survived through the heavy fighting in August, abandoned the outpost to the VC, and would soon be back to help rebuild the outpost in a different place. The task would take several days and certainly would draw quick attention from the VC/NVA. Province arranged with the Vietnamese Navy to provide patrol boats to escort an armada of large water taxis to transport the large force to the outpost location.

On 26 August 1972 we traveled by vehicles to the Tân Thạch ferry landing, where we met the Vietnamese navy patrol boats and four large water taxis to transport the men of *Liên Đội* 117 and the Hàm Long reinforced PF platoon who would man the new outpost. *Liên Đội* 117 was a province-level asset composed of three RF companies. Their missions were to secure the outpost construction site and conduct strengthened patrols around the area of the new outpost and the Tân Long outpost and destroy the overrun outpost. That part of the operation was planned for a minimum of one week, and fortunately, it was placed under Trung-tá Sơn's operational command.

Quickly everyone got aboard the water taxis, and we strung out in an armada of boats led by the navy patrol boat and two smaller VN Navy craft. It turned dangerous as we neared the location to disembark the boats. We realized we were under enemy attack only when some type of rocket round struck one of the water taxis behind the Navy patrol boat Trung-tá Sơn and I were riding in. The blast damaged but did not sink the boat, but it killed one RF soldier and wounded two others. The rocket was fired by enemy forces across the river in Định Tường Province. An escorting Vietnamese navy patrol boat returned fire, but the distance was too great to do any damage. Enemy casualties were unknown.

Along the way we stopped to pick up the demoralized soldiers who had abandoned Con Dòi outpost under heavy enemy attack, and then continued to the landing area and went ashore to build the new outpost. One company from *Liên Đội* 117 swept toward the old Con Dòi outpost site and found five more VC bodies and many blood trails. The air strikes I had coordinated during that helicopter ride with the ARVN regimental commander, including the time he spent on the radio with the enemy's ground commander, had done some good.

Trung-tá Sơn used the other two *liên đội* companies and the PF platoon to build this outpost rather than civilian manpower that was usually rounded up for outpost construction. The area was too dangerous for a large number of unarmed civilians. We stayed with the soldiers for the rest of the day. While we were occupied with the Con Dòi operation, Province directed a B-52 strike into the northeastern part of Hàm Long and northwestern Trúc Giang districts, with 9th ARVN Division units to exploit afterwards. It was the closest I had ever been to a B-52 strike, and I was impressed!

Trung-tá Sơn and I needed to be back at district headquarters, so late in the afternoon we used one of the water taxis to take the command group back to the Tân Thạch ferry landing. It was well after dark when we got to Tân Thạch. A check with the Trúc Giang District TOC and the advisors there confirmed that the highway was unsafe, so we spent several hours napping in the Tân Thạch village office. Long before dawn we loaded into jeeps and trucks and made a high-speed drive in the dark down the highway to the "Y" and out to Hàm Long. It was a bit dicey for me because the PSA had ordered that no advisors would drive the roads after dark. Regardless, I had to be with my counterpart, so Phi, Sergeant Bé, and I followed Trung-tá Sơn's jeep, careening down the road with a truck full of security troops behind us. We made it home without incident. Here's how I remembered that experience.

    .... *Getting back from a naval operation late, arriving at Tân Thạch ferry landing after dark, and wanting to be back home in Hàm Long. And so, running the road without headlights, at 60 mph. Not telling the TOC because they would order me to spend the night at the ferry site. Telling them only after I got back and enduring a terse lecture from the PSA—and getting a pat on the back from him the next time we got together.*

    I told Mr. Kotzebue that my place was with my counterpart no matter what the situation was. He agreed.

Working with Great FACs

    By this time in the war, the USAF FACs flew the OV-10 Bronco aircraft, which had split tail sections and had great maneuverability, as well as onboard weapons for defense against ground fire as well as to identify and attack enemy targets. FAC support for Kiến Hòa Province and most of the Mekong Delta came from the 21st Tactical Air Support Squadron (TASS). The tie between the 21st TASS FACs, call sign Covey, and the Kiến Hòa Province advisors was very close, based on mutual respect. We thought they were incredibly courageous to fly so slow and so low, close to enemy ground fire, braving rocket and antiaircraft heavy weapons fire, to support us with tactical air assets. They thought we were incredibly brave to go out into the field with our counterpart forces, a lone American with a small force of Vietnamese soldiers and no large Vietnamese or U.S. main force units nearby to come to our assistance. Both they, and we, responded the same way: "It comes with the territory."

The 21st TASS—Covey—headquarters was on Tân Sơn Nhứt Air Base, Saigon. Kiến Hòa advisors going to Saigon for administrative chores or going on R&R often stopped by to visit them to thank them for supporting us so well. Occasionally, we gave them souvenirs to thank them for saving our asses on so many occasions. They prized any equipment or weapons from the enemy, but SKS carbines, the only rifle that could be taken home as a souvenir, topped the list. We also passed along VC flags as well as small items of VC/NVA soldiers' equipment.

I visited their headquarters twice, received great hospitality, and met several of the Covey pilots who flew for us. They briefed us on their operations, and we gave them a lot of information about our life as advisors. The Covey pilots liked working for the Kiến Hòa Province advisors because we always had lots of good targets for them and, as one of them told me, "You have your shit together" in managing air strikes. Several of the Covey pilots came down to Bến Tre and visited the district teams that they supported. We never had them as visitors in Hàm Long, but several of them visited Mỏ Cày. The personal contact was a major boost to both sides, being able to see the faces that went with the radio call signs.

Two separate operations, at different places and different dates, show the importance of the FACs and their ability to control air strikes in support of the RF/PF soldiers. One such operation in September 1972 was successful because of the skill of the FAC and the quick responsiveness of the fast-mover aircraft. The district chief and I were airborne in the swing ship, in radio contact with both the FAC and the ground troops. The FAC's marking shot hit right where the RF commander requested, and once the tac air arrived, he told us where to move the attacking fire. The enemy forces were in bunkers built along a small jungle stream. One early round caused a secondary explosion, and the tac air caused enemy casualties and allowed the RF to advance across open ground and into the enemy-held tree line and small bunker complex.

… Unbounded gratitude to the Covey FACs and their boss, Covey 20, and their calm presence overhead. Giving them coordinates for seven separate targets in support of troops in contact, getting two more fighter-bombers to help on that memorable day when I delivered 26 separate air strikes to support the RF and PF; and the great line from Covey 20, Texas drawl and

all: "OK Babe, where do you want the next one?" And then him praising our soldiers.

On another day, with the same FAC pilot:

... Covey 20, out of fighters, offering to adjust artillery fire for us. Hàm Long's tubes firing a perfect line and the sound of amazement in his voice when Covey calls it the best shooting he's ever seen, anyplace. Then another laconic drawl: "Why don't you and those gunners go back outside and take a piss break." And then, barrel rolls and a loop over the compound and Covey 20's words "Tell those little guys that was for them." Grins at the artillery compound when I do.

I became a regular voice on the radio with several different Covey pilots. My Vietnamese counterparts had a full map of targets for air strikes against the emboldened local force guerrilla units, suspected bunker and hooch complexes. Those units had been reinforced by the invading NVA battalions, given new weapons and ammunition, and were individually and collectively a more robust force. During my earlier ten months in Hàm Long, they were not as strong and not considered a viable target for tactical air strikes. Now they were.

On another day a company of RF soldiers on a security clearing operation near their outpost called in a request for tac air in a very bad area of northern Thành Triệu village. They had taken a circular route around and through a large tree mass and were attacked on their return route to their outpost by an unknown-size enemy unit inside a heavy tree line. It was considered an emergency, and I was lucky to be in the air doing a VR and command and control flight with Trung-úy Liêm, the District S-3. After contacting the FAC and describing the situation, when called for, the RF popped smoke and asked for strafing runs or bombs into the tree line directly to their front. The air strikes killed and wounded enough of the enemy to drive them away. It was a very close thing because the enemy could well have attacked and overrun their outpost while so many of its defending force were in the field and blocked from returning to the outpost.

Heavy Operational Pace

The heavy operational pace continued throughout the rest of August and September. Every day I was either on a field operation or coordinating air strikes or both. Frequently I would be with Trung-tá Sơn on one operation, and soldiers on a different operation would request tac air support.

It was complicated, but we could do it since both he and I had radios. His ground commander would request support on his net, Sergeant Bé and I would be right next to him, and I would request a FAC and air support on our radio. Sometimes I had to relay through SFC Jones at the compound when I needed to talk to Province. But once a FAC came on station I could talk directly to him.

We continued to confront the enemy a little bit at a time, gradually pushing them back and regaining control of small areas at a time. I encouraged the district chief to go to the field more frequently, both to show the command flag and to assess the performance of his soldiers. Being there, I told him, would raise the morale of his forces, who had been stunned by the ferocity of the NVA invasion. He responded to my suggestions and, like the soldiers, I could see him regaining his prior confidence and command presence. The July–August offensive had cost lives and adversely affected the morale and courage of the survivors. Now things were improving more rapidly than I expected.

Even so, occasionally the VC had the advantage. Hàm Long's TOC and supporting intelligence information was never as good as it should have been. We never fully realized how close to the compound enemy forces could advance, even after the disastrous ambush in August that caused the death of Captain Chandler. On several days enemy formations were able to move within one kilometer or so of the compound and assault friendly forces that were deployed to provide security for the district headquarters. In early September 1972 for a few days in quick succession there was heavy combat within eyesight of the district compound, and it resulted in heavy friendly casualties almost literally in our backyard.

On 5 September one such difficult situation came up. Trung-tá Sơn raised a platoon-size security force, and we went out to check the district compound physical security (barbed wire, bunkers, lines of fire) between the compound and the Tre Bông River and to monitor an RF company operation in the dense coconut groves across the Tân Lợi road from the compound, on the east side of the Tre Bông River. Just past noon a large enemy force attacked the RF troops so close it was within easy earshot. A separate, coordinated, smaller enemy force attacked the command group from a tree line near the Tre Bông Bridge. We quickly found cover and returned fire. At the same time the district compound was mortared.

The RF company took casualties, but the company commander did a good job of pushing through the ambush, pursued the enemy forces, and re-established contact with the fleeing enemy several times over the next two hours. The smaller force firing on us quickly broke contact. Trung-tá Sơn led us across the road, where we gathered a few stragglers and began tending to the many wounded soldiers. A VNAF medevac responded, but it took three sorties to get the casualties to the hospital in Bến Tre. The results of the ambush and pursuit were six VC KIA, four weapons captured, but five RF soldiers were killed and 16 wounded.

Just a few days later almost the same thing happened. Trung-tá Sơn led a platoon-size unit of district headquarters' security forces that served as the left flank of a large RF operation just northwest of the district compound. One platoon from the 853 RF Company and one platoon from the 401st RF battalion (a Province formation that had one company detached to Hàm Long control) and our ad hoc platoon from district headquarters presented a lucrative target for the stronger local VC guerrillas.

Just before noon—again—the enemy ambushed us less than one klick northwest of the district compound. The enemy had been bold enough to set a platoon-size ambush, and there were heavy friendly casualties. Province was able to contact a Covey FAC for me, and I managed several air strikes, trying to locate and pound the retreating enemy forces. Neither the FAC nor the fighters were able to spot enemy forces in the heavily wooded terrain, but I had them bomb and strafe several potential rally points just in case. This was one of the several times when I directed fire and adjusted the tac air while in contact with the enemy. The Covey FAC was superb, moving the several sorties in the directions I thought the enemy might use for movement away from contact. It was a close affair since we also attracted mortar fire because of the large size of the friendly forces in the operation. Results of this operation were three RF KIA, 14 RF WIA, with unknown enemy casualties.

These two times were the closest the enemy came to making a ground attack against the district headquarters compound. Both times the enemy initiated contact in, and from, a dense mass of unkempt coconut groves and heavy undergrowth along the east bank of the Tre Bong River. The area had not been "checked out" by friendly soldiers in many months, and obviously the enemy had discovered an important area for launching a ground attack against the district headquarters. A very angry Trung-tá Sơn mustered the full RF company and a large contingent of headquarters' soldiers and put them to work with saws, sickles, and explosives and had a significant portion of that nasty grove of trees removed as potential cover for future enemy attacks. Even he and I took our turn on the opposite ends of a long crosscut saw to take down our share of the coconut trees.

17

Hàm Long Soldiers
Gain the Upper Hand

Opening the Road to Tân Lợi

It took a lot of artillery missions, air strikes, and a strong counter-attack by elements of the ARVN 9th Division before the Hàm Long RF/PF soldiers began to regain the upper hand. Several weeks after my return as DSA, Trung-tá Sơn determined that he had enough strength to clear enemy forces from the area between the Tre Bông Bridge and Tân Lợi. Trung-tá Sơn led an entire RF company for security, and we walked all the way to Tân Lợi without any enemy contact. We met with the PF from Quới Thành and then with the RF, PF, RD Cadre, and PSDF men who had repulsed the NVA attacks on Tân Lợi. The road to Tân Lợi was open. It never closed again during my time in Kiến Hòa.

When we arrived in Tân Lợi, I renewed my friendship with the village chief and the village military chief. As I gathered details about the battle for Tân Lợi, I felt increasingly incredulous as I saw the battle damage, walked the area of the fighting, and began asking questions about the battle. I was determined to tell their story!

The village chief gave me a copy of a Vietnamese newspaper article about the battle. I still have the article in my files today. With translation help from Sergeant Bé and from LTC Sơn and Lieutenants Hương and Liêm, I interviewed many of the men who had defended Tân Lợi from the NVA, and I got a translation of the newspaper article. The information I gathered formed the basis for the segments earlier in the book about the Battle of Tân Lợi. I wish more people could know the story of the courageous performance of this small group of defenders. I took pictures of the battle damage during the time we spent in Tân Lợi that one very special day. I would go to Tân Lợi on several more occasions during my time as DSA.

Starting at the entrance to Tân Lợi village and gradually moving back along the road toward the district headquarters compound, the district chief implemented orders from the province chief to cut vegetation back from the road to give a broad open view on both sides and thus reduce areas where the enemy could mount surprise ambush attacks, such as the August incident when Captain Chandler was killed. This policy had both good and bad aspects. The good, of course, was opening up the views in overgrown areas or where trees provided potential sites for enemy cover and ambush opportunities.

The unfortunate aspect was the destruction of well-tended coconut and other fruit groves. It was sad for me to watch the destruction of dozens of producing fruit trees, with the distraught owners of the property arguing without success to save those trees. In one of the few times when I actually argued with Trung-tá Sơn, I suggested that having grateful citizens along the road would provide adequate security. I urged him not to cut down the trees but to just do a thorough clearing of brush, grass, and smaller bushes in the affected orchards. My suggestion was in vain. He reiterated that he had been given a direct order to "clear back" everything from the roads in Kiến Hòa Province. Although the owners of the coconut trees received some compensation for their losses, it surely was not enough to cover the loss of income from lost years of fruit production. It was sometimes difficult to reconcile the need for security with the circumstances on the ground.

A Vignette, 23 Years Later

This is another of the few segments of this book where I describe things in postwar Vietnam. I include this vignette to underline the deep attraction I felt to "my places" in wartime Vietnam and my pride and respect in the local force officers and soldiers with whom I worked.

In 1995 I made my first return visit to Vietnam after the U.S. re-established diplomatic relations with Hanoi. Since then I have been back many times, enjoying what many Vietnam Veterans observed during the war: "This would be a great place for a vacation if there wasn't a war going on." In that and many subsequent trips I have traveled through Vietnam from near the Chinese border to Hanoi, through the mountainous northwest, south through the Central Highlands and coastal central Vietnam, and down through Saigon to renamed Bến Tre Province. On several trips I returned to Hàm Long and Mỏ Cày, where I had spent 18 of the most intense and memorable months of my life.

On that first visit I was surprised to find out that things really were "okay." The bountiful agricultural economy of the province was doing just fine. Areas closed to habitation during the war were reoccupied and replanted. There were no barbed wire barricades, concrete bunkers, or defensive fortifications, no mines, no booby traps. The road from Bến Tre to Hàm Long was still paved, but the former district compound was derelict. The dirt road to Tân Lợi was upgraded and wider. Side pathways were upgraded, and among them is a concrete road near Tân Lợi up through Phú Đức and Phú Túc villages and then east across to the main highway to Bến Tre. Productive rice paddies and fruit and coconut orchards were everywhere in what were once the most dangerous villages in Hàm Long.

To my delight when I got to Tân Lợi—now renamed Tân Phú—the village center in 1995 was almost exactly the way I remembered it in 1972. As I strolled through the market, a crowd of villagers quickly gathered around—foreign visitors were rare back then before heavy American tourism, and Tân Lợi was not on the tourist circuit. My interpreter and I took a seat in a small open-front shop house restaurant, ordered tea, and a group of curious onlookers immediately surrounded us. I told them of my former connection with Hàm Long and Tân Lợi, and wonderful conversations ensued. Tân Lợi's people are still friendly. No doubt many of the older faces that chatted with me had fought in the Battle of Tân Lợi, probably on both sides. Regardless of the changes wrought by modern history, Tân Lợi has always been a special place to me, as it has been to those who, in their moment of glory, defeated an enemy battalion to defend their homes.

Winning the Battle of Phú Đức

The Phú Đức battle in late September 1972 was, along with the Battle of Tân Lợi, one of the biggest fights while I was back in Hàm Long. I was not in the battle, however. I was with Trung-tá Sơn on another operation in a nearby village. A large VC/NVA force, possibly an understrength battalion, attacked the Phú Đức village office in broad daylight. Trung-tá Sơn asked for U.S. air support, and I was happy to oblige. A Covey FAC was soon overhead. He spotted the village and could see a large number of unidentified but uniformed people in the trees and in cleared areas on two sides of the village center. The RF company commander in Phú Đức gave us details on where the friendly troops were located. There was one group of soldiers in a well-fortified outpost, and most of the rest were in and around the fortified village office and nearby bunkers and defensive positions.

I had been to Phú Đức village many times either for HES Report interviews or on tactical operations, so I knew the layout of the village center, which consisted mostly of the PF outpost, the village office, several scattered mud and concrete bunkers, and a ramshackle Catholic church. A dozen or so homes were scattered around the center. More recently the soldiers had dug a network of foxholes and trenches with overhead cover. I was anxious to help the heavily outnumbered PF soldiers, but I had to be very sure not to accidentally kill any innocent civilians. Trung-tá Sơn assured me that all of the villagers had fled because they knew the enemy was coming and that all of his soldiers were under cover. Therefore, everyone the FAC could see on the ground in the trees were enemy soldiers. The FAC said he saw lots of them. The Phú Đức military chief provided good information. I gave the FAC target information, so he went ahead with the air strikes, primarily highly effective strafing runs against all those enemy soldiers not under cover.

The village military chief talked to the district chief on the Vietnamese radio frequency, Trung-tá Sơn and Sergeant Bé translated for me, and I talked to the FAC on my radio. The FAC placed quite a few air strikes and strafing runs over a period of about an hour. He kept asking for bomb damage assessments (BDA) because he was not sure the aircraft were hitting anything and he did not want to cause friendly casualties. The BDA response from the Phú Đức PF commander was succinct—one of the best reports I can remember:

> Keep shooting just the same, just the same, the ones that aren't dead are running around bumping into trees.

The VC retreated, a quick survey of the battlefield found something like 30 VC KIA; the village itself was not badly damaged. A good day!

The Constructive Side of Advisory Duty—Doing Good

Duty as an advisor in Vietnam meant fighting a war alongside Vietnamese counterparts, most of whom had spent their adult lifetime fighting the war and were far more experienced than any advisor. The secret to success was establishing a meaningful and mutually respectful relationship with counterparts at all ranks. I was able to do that.

A primary reason why I enjoyed my advisory assignment was that, in addition to the "destructive" element of war-fighting, we also participated in the "constructive" element of doing good and making things better—maybe only marginally so—for the Vietnamese people among whom we lived. Civic action—part of pacification—was too often overlooked in the Vietnam War but was vital if there was to be a successful outcome. Unfortunately, the U.S. leadership tended to overlook the importance of pacification—winning the hearts and minds of the people. I enjoyed that side of the war and did as much as I could to further this mission. This was so even during the three exhausting and dangerous months when I was back in Hàm Long as DSA. Despite constant combat operational activity, air strikes, and repeated field operations, there were a lot of good things needing to be done, and I was proud of that part of our job. Here are some examples.

... *Happiness Is Building the New Tre Bông Bridge.*

Just west of the district compound flowed the small Tre Bông River. Only about 50 meters wide but steep-sided, it was a major obstacle for travel to the western half of Hàm Long District. The bridge when I arrived was a rickety, narrow bridge made of coconut logs cut in half with the round side up, no railings, and it was quite dangerous to drive across. We could get jeeps, small trucks, and Lambrettas across this bridge but always with a guide walking backward in front of the vehicle to be sure the wheels stayed on the bridge.

Getting a new Tre Bông Bridge was a major development goal, but for the longest time there were no funds to pay for it—U.S. or Vietnamese. Then, in fall 1972, we learned that a U.S. Navy Seabee detachment was looking for a mission, so I asked if they knew how to build a bridge.

The old Tre Bông Bridge, just west of the district compound. Those coconut logs made for a very rough crossing!

Of course they did! We formed a troika: the U.S. donated the steel bridge framework, the Seabees assisted with know-how and engineering expertise and supervised construction of new abutments, and the district chief organized local labor to do the work and used our AIK funds to pay them. It took a while, but the troika worked just fine.

My thoughts, written then:

... Driving over the new Tre Bông Bridge, built by the Seabees, local labor, and AIK money. Looking at the incredibly rickety old coconut log bridge and realizing with a twinge of regret that the challenge of crossing the river was gone.

... Happiness Is Finally Getting the Dispensary Built.

One of the long-standing development projects the Hàm Long advisory team had been trying to complete was to build a new dispensary for the district. Major Kretschmar inherited the plan when he arrived and had spent more than a year standing in line for the monies required. He had applied for enough AIK money to purchase the concrete, sand, roofing, and wooden framing needed to build the building, as well to purchase an "opening supply" of medical equipment. The district chief said he had the labor, skilled and unskilled, all set. He had already allocated the land for the building in the complex of civilian offices across the road from the district compound.

Finally we got the funds. Labor arrived, a local engineer supervised, and the dispensary got built. Does the dispensary have a staff?—Check. Are medical supplies and medicines available?—Check. Finally, it was opened and operating. A real success.

AIK funds helped build other projects in Hàm Long. One was a new village medical clinic in Phú Long village; another was a two-story addition to the district high school. It always felt good to attend the small ceremonies when these new facilities were officially opened.

... Happiness Is Fixing the Boy's Face.

One of the most satisfying programs run by the American medical community in Vietnam was to repair children's harelips and cleft palates. The surgery was done at the U.S. Army 3rd Surgical Hospital in Saigon; volunteer American doctors came to Vietnam periodically for this project. Advisory teams were under instructions to keep our eyes open for children under the age of 12 with this facial deformity—surgery for younger children was much easier than for older people. "Doc," the province team medic, managed the program in Kiến Hòa.

One day, during an otherwise uneventful operation, we passed through a scruffy hamlet, and I saw a young boy with a harelip and cleft palate. He was standing off by himself, and I did not see any friends around him. When we got back to the compound, I told Trung-tá Sơn about the medical program and that we would be able to help the boy if he could provide security to go back to that village and persuade the family to let us "borrow" the child. Trung-tá Sơn assigned the S-5 to run the operation. I informed Doc by radio, and he was ready to go. If all went well, the district advisor (me) would obtain permission from the child's family and transport the child to Bến Tre. Doc would take the child to Saigon and turn him/her over to the doctors there. After surgery and a short period for recovery, Doc would return to Saigon and bring the child back to Bến Tre, and the district would do the rest. The hard part was persuading the family to let the child go alone. Most of the time when a Vietnamese of any age went to a hospital, one or more of the family went too, to help care for, feed, and look after the patient.

About a week later the S-5, Sergeant Bé and I, with a platoon of troops for security, went back to the hamlet and found the house where the boy lived with his mother and his blind grandmother. We tried our best to convince his mother that doctors in Saigon could "fix" the boy's face if they would bring him to the headquarters compound and trust us to get him to Saigon and back. Then we waited.

Sometime later, I don't remember how long, the mother arrived at the district headquarters with her son, clearly worried about turning him over to people she didn't know. The S-5 convinced her to trust us, and she agreed. He and I drove her and the boy to Bến Tre, turned the child over to Doc, and took the mother back to Hàm Long.

A while later Doc notified me that the boy was back in Bến Tre. Trung-tá Sơn quickly arranged a security operation. Sergeant Bé and I went into Bến Tre to pick up Doc and bring the boy back home. Then we walked with a platoon of security troops to take him back to his family. By then it had dawned on me that the operations to and from the boy's home hamlet had required a lot of security forces each time. Yes, it was a VC hamlet in a bad area, and the S-5 told me that the boy's father was a senior Vietcong officer. Maybe we won at least a couple of enemy hearts and minds.

My thoughts, written shortly afterwards:

...The small boy, aged 11, with the grotesquely deformed harelip and cleft palate. Explaining to his mother and blind grandmother that it can be "fixed." After weeks of waiting, getting permission to take him to Saigon for surgery. The S-5 asking if I knew his father was a senior VC, my surprised reply that I hadn't known and honestly adding that it didn't matter. Then joy when the boy returned with hardly a mark on his face, the tears in the

eyes of his grandmother when she feels his face with her fingers and "sees" the results.

Re-Establishing Phú Túc

One of the projects Trung-tá Sơn was most proud of was re-establishing a village office and volunteer residents in Phú Túc village. It was long the worst village in Hàm Long security-wise and was empty of an innocent civilian population—only VC and NVA and their supporters lived there. The success of the military push to oust the invading NVA regiment provided the opportunity to reopen a government presence there. It was a significant undertaking, as heavy equipment was needed to clear the tangled jungle-like terrain enough to enable villagers to create and tend vegetable gardens and small fruit orchards. Granted, the new village was makeshift, granted it was right next to the Mỹ Tho River, so the people, the officials, and the security force could quickly get away if a major enemy offensive came. But it was a start. It was also my last major project as Hàm Long DSA.

The project was in three phases. The first and most labor-intensive was clearing out a patch of several hectares of jungle to provide space for houses and gardens. It took over a month, by several RF and PF platoons, to get that done. Phase two was recruitment of new residents, who were given rudimentary temporary shelter huts and a plot of land for fruit or vegetable gardens. The final phase was building two facing rows of thatch and bamboo "houses" for the incoming residents, including buildings for the village office and billets for RF soldiers to provide security. I was able to contribute a significant sum of AIK funds to support the project.

Trung-tá Sơn and I, and a large group of district and province officials, rode from Tân Thạch in a small convoy of water taxis to attend the opening ceremony of speeches, distribution of land ownership certificates to each resident family, and a toast or three of good brandy. I was pleased with the results.

Improvement

By the end of September, Trung-tá Sơn had recovered his confidence and morale and was slowly gaining the upper hand. At the same time, I had to stay tuned to events in Mỏ Cày because Major Reed had to make trips back to the hospital for doctors to check on his wounded legs, and he was also due a much-deserved 30-day home leave. I went back to Mỏ

Cày as Acting District Senior Advisor for three weeks in late September and early October while Major Reed was away. SFC Jones and Sergeant Bé remained in Hàm Long to assist Trung-tá Sơn, with the understanding that if things got really bad again, I would return and a substitute officer would go to Mỏ Cày. This was because Mr. Kotzebue felt that it was me as a familiar face who was important to boosting Trung-tá Sơn back to his prior competent self.

SFC Jones did an outstanding job working with Trung-tá Sơn and his forces during the time I was away. Throughout Vietnam during the war years, there were many reports of difficulties between Vietnamese officers and lower-ranking U.S. advisors (including in Mỏ Cày), but this never happened in Hàm Long. LTC Sơn gave me every professional respect and personal courtesy despite my being two ranks junior to him. He did the same with SFC Jones during the three weeks SFC Jones was the Acting DSA. Had all ARVN officers been so professional and accomplished, perhaps the outcome in Vietnam would have been different.

After my three weeks back in Mỏ Cày, I returned to Hàm Long to finish up my work there. Mr. Kotzebue had told me that the tactical situation had improved enough that he wanted us to close out the team and return to our regular assignments as soon as possible. My analysis was that Trung-tá Sơn had regained his confidence and, with much better security after the Tân Lợi and the Phú Đức battles, he and his forces had control of the situation. I had spent a lot of time training Lieutenants Liêm and Hương on calling air strikes, and both of them spoke enough English that they would be able to communicate with American FACs. There was little remaining for me to do.

The Value of Tactical Air Strikes and B-52 Strikes

It goes without saying that we could not have ejected the invading NVA regiment from Hàm Long and re-established security without prodigious use of tactical air strikes and B-52 strikes. Trung-tá Sơn and I handled the tactical air strikes; the province chief and PSA handled the B-52 strikes. From August through early November we managed tactical air strikes against enemy personnel and facilities virtually every day. I kept a very informal log during my tenure, but I did not write down every single air strike. The total would have been in the several hundreds of separate tactical air and armed helicopter strikes. During my time in Hàm Long, there were, I think, a total of eight B-52 strikes along the northeast and northern parts of Hàm Long and western Trúc Giang District next door. There would not have been any improvement in the security situation without those strikes and especially without the work of those incredibly skilled and courageous USAF FACs from the 21st TASS.

Time to Leave

By November everyone in Hàm Long knew I was leaving and would not be back. Although the Paris cease-fire agreement had yet to happen, the ongoing talks in Paris were well known. In any case, they all knew I was scheduled to leave Vietnam on my new DEROS of 7 February 1973. Trung-tá Sơn arranged a farewell lunch for Sergeant Jones, Sergeant Bé, and me in a small restaurant near the compound. LTC Tausch came out from Bến Tre to join us for lunch, a gesture I deeply appreciated. The small restaurant was filled with three Americans, one interpreter, and dozens of my counterparts, from the district chief down to individual RF and PF soldiers. It was a tremendously emotional event for me.

A Very Unusual Final Dinner in Hàm Long

On the last evening before my departure, Trung-tá Sơn hosted a different sort of dinner for me. He had provided the three of us with most of our meals since August. In all that time he had not come up with anything "weird" to eat. But on this occasion he did. "We're having something interesting you should eat with us," he said. Sergeant Jones, Sergeant Bé, and I sat down at a large round table in the open area between our quarters and the watchtower. Many of the civilian Hàm Long dignitaries joined us.

Out came a cook with a huge, beautiful ceramic bowl filled with round brown things about the size of my thumb. "These are really good," Trung-tá Sơn said, and everyone started reaching for them with chopsticks and spoons. I did too. The brown things were soft but firm enough to grip with chopsticks. I popped one in my mouth. It had a strange, squishy texture, but I managed not to barf it back out. It actually tasted quite good, like young coconut. After downing several of the brown things, I asked what I had just eaten. Several of the guests began a discussion, but they had difficulty in translating from Vietnamese to English.

"It is a bug that lives inside coconut trees," Trung-tá Sơn told me. I got it right away. Not a bug, but larvae that occurred, like a butterfly, when said bug bored into the coconut tree, laid eggs, and the result mutated into fat, squishy larvae. We were eating stir-fried mutated coconut-tree-boring bugs! Lots of people thought I was telling a tall tale about this, so just to show it's real, I found the following material on the internet many years later as I wrote the drafts for this book.

> *Đường Dừa* is a form of beetle larvae. After the breeding season the beetle usually chooses a healthy coconut tree, pierces a hole on top and lays the eggs in it. After the eggs hatch, the larvae grow by eating the young shoot of the coconut tree until the tree is pierced through. Although the coconut is spoiled by *Đường Dừa*, the worms are delicious and are a delicacy in the coconut land of the Mekong River delta. Consuming them is believed to enhance men's sexual abilities. The coconut worm has long been considered a specialty food of Ben Tre.[1]

Trung-tá Sơn was doing us a great honor by providing this unusual and expensive dish for one of the last meals I was to eat in Hàm Long.

Quiet Recognition from My Counterpart

One of the last things that happened before I left Hàm Long was the surprise award of a Vietnamese medal. There was no formal ceremony. Trung-tá Sơn simply called me into his office in the afternoon on the day before I was to leave in November 1972 to return to Mỏ Cày. He had the entire district staff there standing at attention. I am very proud that he personally pinned the award—the Vietnam Honor Service Medal—onto my jungle fatigues. The Citation:

> John B. Haseman, CPT, SN 223-56-7019, U.S. Army. A U.S. officer well experienced in his specialty and displayed a high sense of service in a superior manner while serving as U.S. Sub-Sector Advisor in Hàm Long District, Kiến Hòa Province. Captain Haseman's exceptional understanding of the situation and courage in supporting sub-sector operations were invaluable assisting Sub-Sector Headquarters to eliminate the Communists with a great success and effectiveness toward the territory pacification program in Kiến Hòa Province.

It made it even harder to leave.

A Brave
Vietnamese Lieutenant

I was privileged to work with many talented, highly professional Vietnamese officers during my 18 months in Kiến Hòa Province. You have already met some of them—Lieutenant Colonel Cử, the heroic defenders of Tân Lợi. Here is another. Each of these stories tells of dedicated Vietnamese soldiers whose work and sacrifice is worth telling, especially to show that Vietnamese officers and soldiers could be at least as courageous and effective as their American counterparts.

This is the story of First Lieutenant Nguyễn Thanh Liêm, the S-3/Operations Officer of Hàm Long District.[1] I didn't notice the steel behind the smiling face the first time I met Liêm.

He was one of many officers I met in the whirlwind first day as an advisor in Hàm Long District. Liêm impressed me with his air of confidence, competence, and pride.

I quickly found that I was able to provide valuable assistance to my Vietnamese counterparts, but far more importantly, I found myself learning more than I taught—learning lessons in courage, character, and strength in a culture that has existed for over a millennium. Those lessons remained with me and strengthened me during the ensuing years of my army career and in the years that have followed. Liêm played a major role in my education.

Liêm knew his men and his tactics like the back of his hand. His duty performance won him the confidence of the district chief and a well-earned reputation as a good soldier. When I arrived in Hàm Long in July 1971, he had been the District S-3 for five years. He had seen a lot of American advisors come and go, and not all of them had been what he referred to as "friends of my country." Liêm was friendly to the Americans on our small advisory team, but as a newcomer, I could sense the reserve behind his eyes. The gaze said, "prove yourself worthy." As the weeks passed and I felt myself becoming accepted by my Vietnamese counterparts, he became more open.

Born in the nearby district of Mỏ Cày, Liêm's anti–Communist family had fled their home village to escape the Việt Minh. Liêm grew up in the city of Bến Tre. He was 30 years old when I met him, and he had 12 years of military service. By comparison, when I arrived in Hàm Long, I was 29 and had six years of service. He was a veteran of fighting in the infamous Iron Triangle north of Saigon and had helped repulse the VC battalions that had almost overrun Bến Tre during the 1968 Tết Offensive.

As the months passed, our mutual respect and friendship grew. His leadership ability, tactical knowledge, and courage under enemy fire made him the type of officer who is easy to follow, hard to emulate. He was a fine example of courage and character in an army that was too often criticized for its failures.

Though thoroughly a soldier, Liêm was no martinet. When interrupted at his work late at night, he had time to chat with a lonesome American friend. I remember the compassion in his eyes while he gave first aid to wounded soldiers, cradling their heads in his lap and comforting their wailing families.

He often talked about how things would be when the fighting ended. It was amazing to me that after spending all of his adult life at war, he remained confident of attaining peace. He was a realist; he knew peace would be achieved only at great cost and after a long delay, but he always felt that peace would eventually come.

In November 1972 my time as DSA in Hàm Long ended, and I returned to Mỏ Cày to complete the final months of my assignment. My last view of Liêm was blurred by the emotion of the

First Lieutenant Liêm after receiving a combat decoration.

moment, but I still remember it—a smile on his face and a shouted farewell on his lips. The steel was there too, well-hidden but known to those like me who had the privilege of knowing him well.

The so-called Paris peace agreement did not end Liêm's battle to save his country from the enemy. Treacherous breaches of the cease-fire continued long after the declaration of peace. On March 14, 1973, only a month after I left Vietnam, Nguyễn Thanh Liêm's long search for peace finally ended. Vietcong mortars fired on a small outpost in a jungle clearing, and a ground attack ensued. Liêm rallied the defenders, sprinting between bunkers to lead the defense against an attacking enemy company. But one shell landed too close, and Liêm, a survivor of a lifetime of war, died in the first months of "peace," his last act one of courage and sacrifice. He would have been proud to know that his outnumbered force repulsed the enemy and retained possession of Con Dòi outpost—a place you have already read about and one I saw on several occasions.

The details of Trung-úy Liêm's death were relayed to me in a personal letter from Trung-tá Sơn to tell me about the loss of my friend. He also told me that Liêm had been promoted to captain, but the promotion orders had not arrived before he was killed in action. He left behind a wife and six children. Only weeks later his widow passed away, perhaps from a broken heart. The children were raised by their grandparents. I was humbled to provide some assistance to the family, acknowledged with proud thanks by Liêm's father.

Nguyễn Thanh Liêm was neither famous nor high in rank. He was merely brave, loyal, a true leader of men, and an honest patriot. He was my friend and teacher, and I will never forget the honor of knowing him and what he stood for.

19

Final Return to Mỏ Cày District

I returned to Mỏ Cày for three weeks in late September 1972, leaving SFC Jones and Sergeant Bé in Hàm Long to support Trung-tá Sơn. Major Reed went to Saigon for a medical checkup and then on home leave, much deserved after the harrowing events of the summer. We had several days of turnover so I could be briefed on the enemy situation, the status of projects and operations, and all the key things Major Reed wanted me to be aware of. I barely had a chance to meet and talk with the new District Chief, Major Hoàng Văn Mạnh, who had recently arrived from the 7th ARVN Division. He was young, quiet and reserved, but I could sense a lot of strength there.

The enemy offensive in Mỏ Cày peaked in August and failed to achieve major objectives because of the enemy's inability to coordinate the actions of the many battalions operating in Mỏ Cày. That, and B-52 strikes against large concentrations of enemy forces in Phước Hiệp, Định Thủy, and Thành Thới villages in July and August caused heavy casualties to the NVA battalions in those bad areas. By late September, enemy strength declined as the invading NVA battalions were withdrawn from the district.

I assessed my position as a bit tenuous because of a new district chief who did not know me, as well as some changes in the district staff, and I therefore saw my role as caretaker until Major Reed returned. As it turned out, I did more than that because of a resumption of operation tempo as the enemy threat lessened somewhat. Thiếu-tá Mạnh was initially cool but polite toward me, which I thought might be attributed to a less-than-good situation with advisors in his prior assignment in the 7th ARVN Division. I was able to form a good relationship with him by simply being willing to go to the field with him. As it turned out, both Major Reed and I worked well with him, and when I returned to Mỏ Cày for good in November, our final two months together were very professional and pleasant.

... Happiness Is Getting the Grass Cut in Marlboro Country.

The main road in Mỏ Cày District was the highway from the Bến Tre ferry through Mỏ Cày District and on to Hương Mỹ and Thạnh Phú districts further down the lower island. Although paved, it was a rough ride because of weak pavement and poorly patched mine craters. About four kilometers south of Mỏ Cày town the highway crossed a small canal and then entered what we called "Marlboro Country," a dangerous stretch of road that passed through an area of open grassland before reaching the An Binh Bridge, the border with Hương Mỹ District. Each district maintained a small outpost at their end of the bridge. There was a long history of ambushes, mines, and sniper attacks on traffic through Marlboro Country.

It was particularly nasty on the Mỏ Cày side because—unlike along other stretches of road in Kiến Hòa Province—the grass and trees on either side of the narrow road had not been cut back to make a clear security zone. Soldiers feared the area was infested with antipersonnel mines and booby traps, and small bands of snipers made it too dangerous to send soldiers with sickles and machetes off the road to cut the grass. As a result, the grass had grown to great heights on both sides of the road. I guessed the grass "walls" to be six feet high along that stretch of road on the Mỏ Cày side of the An Binh Bridge.

A succession of advisors had implored the district chief to mount an effort to cut back the grass in Marlboro Country, to no avail. We advisors drove it frequently, and it was the only way for Hương Mỹ and Thạnh Phú advisors and their counterparts to drive to and from Bến Tre.

And for another reason. The Mỏ Cày and Hương Mỹ advisors, with bravado and perhaps foolishness, frequently drove to the An Binh Bridge to meet and trade movies that we received in heavy metal cases. When either district team had finished showing their three or four movies, we exchanged poorly coded radio messages and arranged to meet at the An Binh Bridge to trade movies. These trips were planned on the spur of the moment, and we always hoped our passage would be a surprise, should any VC be lurking near the road. We drove at a high rate of speed to the bridge, and whichever group arrived first would wait on "the other side" in the mud-walled outpost at either end of the bridge until friends from the other district arrived. After a quick chat, we traded movie cases and raced back to our compound, hoping that no enemy had noticed our trip and knew we would soon be returning along the only road.

Some thoughts I wrote at the time:

.... Wondering "what am I doing here?" driving through Marlboro Country with Tuyến just to trade movies with Hương Mỹ advisors at the An

Binh Bridge......Marlboro Country: that five klick stretch of road with the rough asphalt pitted with holes from land mines, lined by grass six feet high because it's too insecure for the troops to keep it trimmed down. And, after the first time, getting almost too used to driving the road for a silly reason.

The grass finally got cut, but it took a near-tragedy. The new District Chief, Major Mạnh, had been in Mỏ Cày for only a few weeks, and I had been down from Hàm Long for only a few days. The new Province S-2 was visiting the lower island districts on a familiarization tour. He stopped for the night in Mỏ Cày, and I met him at a party that Thiếu-tá Mạnh hosted. His small group went on to Hương Mỹ and Thạnh Phú. On the return trip a few days later traveling in a convoy of three jeeps, they were ambushed in Marlboro Country. Upon receiving word of the ambush and that the S-2 had been wounded, Thiếu-tá Mạnh quickly rounded up some soldiers and set off down the road with a three-quarter-ton truck. He did not tell me he was going—I found out from the commo NCO. I quickly grabbed Sergeant Bé, and we headed out in our jeep to join them. When we arrived at the ambush site, Thiếu-tá Mạnh was surprised to see me.

"I didn't think you would come out with me if there was a dangerous situation," he said.

Uh-oh! He obviously had come to Mỏ Cày with a negative view of American advisors formed during his previous assignments.

A jeep-eye view of the grass "walls" along the road through Marlboro Country.

"Sir," I said, "I'm your advisor until Major Reed comes back. You know much more than I do about this war, but there are many ways I can be helpful to you. When you go to the field, please do not leave me behind. I will go with you, dangerous or not."

Taken aback, he apologized, and we had a fine relationship after that. Back at the compound we had a chance to talk some more about the ambush. I told him that the stretch of road through Marlboro Country had always been bad because the grass was never cut back to afford a clear view on either side of the road. The troops were afraid of snipers and booby traps, I told him.

This is how I described the incident then:

... The new Province S-2 ambushed in Marlboro Country and the District Chief dashing off to help him without telling me. Chasing him down the road and catching him at the scene, arriving without a security force to escort me. His surprise that his advisor would go into a bad area without an escort. Helping get the wounded S-2 to the small Mo Cay hospital and calling a medevac chopper. Showing, in a small way, that a new district chief could depend on his advisors.

It took a new district chief and an important province-level officer's injury, but that was what was needed to get things started. Using a combination of three PF platoons, civilian workers, and engineers from province for mine detection work, Thiếu-tá Mạnh mounted a security operation to cut that grass. It took a week, and nobody was hurt—no booby traps or mines, no snipers. I guessed that the large number of soldiers had chased the VC further back into the jungle. From then on it felt very strange to drive to An Binh Bridge to trade movies with our colleagues. We could actually see a long way on either side of the road.

Perhaps it was no longer Marlboro Country.

A Lucky Near-Miss

I had one very close call driving back from (not in) Marlboro Country. Sergeant Tuyến and I had driven down to the An Binh Bridge, traded movies, and were on our way back to Mỏ Cày. We had just "cleared" Marlboro Country and were nearing Mỏ Cày town when suddenly there was a loud and powerful explosion right in front of us. A VC antipersonnel mine or bomb exploded behind or inside a small grass and wood coffee shack that sat right by the side of the road. Several soldiers were enjoying a morning coffee, and all of them were literally blown out onto the road. Instinctively—and failing to consider the dangerous situation clearly—I quickly stopped, and Tuyến and I ran to help the injured soldiers.

I had driven by that little coffee shack on countless occasions and had never given it the least bit of attention. The command-detonated explosion may well have been intended to hit the advisors' jeep, but the presence of several RF solders in the coffee shack might have caused the enemy to change the plan. Tuyến and I carefully lifted the two worst-hurt soldiers into the back of the jeep and set off for the Mỏ Cày hospital. We alerted other RF soldiers we saw along the road, and they ran to the scene of the explosion to take care of the other injured soldiers.

It took only a few minutes to reach the hospital, and I drove very fast (though at the time it seemed I was going much too slow), honking the horn continuously to clear people and animals off the road and also to alert the hospital. When we arrived, medics were waiting and quickly got the two wounded soldiers out of our jeep and into the hospital. A few minutes later a truck arrived with the other wounded soldiers and their platoon leader.

Then, back at the compound came the difficult task of cleaning the blood out of the jeep. I started shaking, suddenly realizing that if we had been only a few seconds faster on the road, that mine would have hit us. Maybe it WAS intended for us, and the enemy had mistimed it. If so, we were very lucky that the shack was full of RF soldiers. Sergeant Tuyến saw that I was not doing very well. He quickly came over to me, put his arm around my shoulders, and said quietly, "Don't worry, Đại-úy. You did good." Well, yes. WE did good.

At the time I remembered it this way:

… Driving through Marlboro Country to check things out, and on the return trip watching the world explode five seconds and 100 meters in front of us when a VC mine behind a coffee shack throws five RF soldiers into the road, wounded. Screeching to a halt before the reaction sets in, bundling the two worst-hurt into the back of the jeep and moving off to the hospital in Mỏ Cày. The sincerity of the thanks of the men's commander when he arrives by truck with the other three casualties. And then, the uncontrolled shaking a few minutes later, trying to clean the blood out of the back of the jeep, thinking of what might have happened.....and an understanding, steadying hand on my shoulder from Tuyến.

There were a couple of very important lessons learned from this incident. First and foremost, in retrospect I believe that the mine was intended to hit the advisors' jeep and whoever was in it. It could well have been the culmination of a long, well-thought-out plan. Otherwise, why would a rough small coffee shop be built immediately adjacent to the roadway, a good kilometer or more from the outskirts of Mỏ Cày town? It was not for the benefit of any RF/PF soldiers; there were no outposts or military camps anywhere nearby, and it was the only commercial operation between Mỏ Cày and the An Binh Bridge. I could not remember when the shop was built, but earlier photographs of the area did not show it. In my view the VC found a way to ambush the advisors—nobody else was regularly going to and fro on this highway.

Second, this was an intelligence failure. No Mỏ Cày intelligence personnel had checked on this little shop to see who was there and why it was built in relative isolation. Nor had any of the advisors or interpreters checked out the simply-built place.

Third, although the RF/PF soldiers knew about this little shop and patronized it, I could not recall seeing many other people there. The shop was too close to the highway to allow for space in front for chairs and tables outside and overhead shade, which was the common layout for coffee and tea shops.

And finally, the strange placement of the shop immediately adjacent to the roadway provided adequate concealment for any sort of mine or booby trap—or a small unit of VC assassins.

The blast destroyed the shop, and the only casualties were the five RF soldiers. There were no other civilians around that I could recall seeing. Nobody came to help Tuyến and me assist the soldiers. The "owner" and staff were nowhere to be seen. The ruins of the shop stood for several days and eventually fell down. I never knew if either military or police investigators looked into the incident. We were much more observant on future drives back and forth on this stretch of highway!

Break the Rules and Gain Trust

One of my most important experiences with a medevac flight took place in Mỏ Cày in October 1972, shortly after I came down from Hàm Long while Major Reed was on home leave. It happened on an operation in the western part of the district, the first time I had gone to the field on a major tactical operation with Thiếu-tá Mạnh. The operation plans called for a sweep west along a "road" (muddy, rocky) with security on both flanks, then a turn to the south and end up at the Mỏ Cày Grand Canal.

We were well into the operation when a soldier on the right flank hit a VC booby trap that blew off his foot and inflicted severe head wounds. Some of his buddies carried him to the road while Thiếu-tá Mạnh radioed the province TOC to request a medevac. But the Vietnamese TOC duty officer told him that there were no VNAF helicopters available.

So he turned to me: "Can you help?"

In addition to being a medical emergency it was also a test—could his advisor help when help was really needed? I knew it was a test, but there was no way the American personnel at the TOC in Bến Tre could understand that.

By that time, it was firm policy that U.S. medevacs would respond only to U.S. casualties; all Vietnamese casualties had to be evacuated by VNAF helicopters. The policy was implemented in an effort to force the VNAF to be more responsive to ARVN casualties. With a lot of last-minute policies, nobody apparently considered the implications on our counterpart soldiers. Policy or not, I would do everything I could to save one of "our" soldiers. In a fortuitous coincidence, I knew there was a MACV Inspector-General team from Saigon making an official inspection of the Kiến Hòa Province advisory effort, and they had a dedicated helicopter for transportation to visit the outlying districts. At the time they were in our next-door district, Hương Mỹ.

I called the U.S. side of the TOC and requested they contact the IG team's pilots and ask them to fly a medevac. By now they were well aware that the casualty was a Vietnamese soldier, not an American, so the TOC duty officer denied my request. I got angry and told them a life was in the balance and we needed that medevac. When denied a second time, I got really angry and demanded that they call the pilot for the Inspector-General team, which was only a short flight from our location, to ask if they would come in to pick up the wounded soldier. By this time, the advisory team S-3/Operations Advisor, Major Robert Stephens, who outranked me, was on the radio, and the back-and-forth radio transmissions were contentious.

Fortunately, the Hương Mỹ advisory team was monitoring the radio net. The DSA broke into the now-contentious radio transmissions and said he would ask the pilots. The pilots agreed to fly the mission, and within minutes a pilot contacted me on the radio. I passed him our coordinates, described the landing zone on the road where we had stopped and put out security. A soldier tossed a smoke grenade to show the wind direction and the exact location where we wanted him to land. I stood on the road with my rifle held horizontally over my head to guide him in. The helicopter landed, took the wounded soldier and two soldier escorts on board, and flew them to the Bến Tre hospital. Then they returned to Hương Mỹ and continued their administrative mission with the Inspector-General team. Thiếu-tá Mạnh and I continued the operation, which turned out to be an otherwise no-contact walk in the sun.

I knew I was in trouble. Senior officers do not take kindly to junior officers demanding anything. Besides, I had broken with an established

Major Mạnh is directly in front of me. Moments after I took this photograph, a soldier about 200 meters off to the right of the road hit the booby trap. This is almost the exact spot where the medevac helicopter landed.

policy by calling for an American helicopter to evacuate a Vietnamese casualty.

Several days later Thiếu-tá Mạnh and I went to Bến Tre for the monthly District Chief/ DSA meeting. I was sure I was going to get an ass-chewing from somebody. But unknown to me at the time, Thiếu-tá Mạnh, knowing I was going to be in trouble with my American team leadership, had already told the province chief about the entire incident, probably including a description of the contentious tone of voices on the U.S. radio net and what I had said and done. At the very start of the meeting the Province Chief, Colonel Kim, thanked me in front of the assembled American and Vietnamese officers for what I had done and praised the high level of the U.S.-Vietnamese counterpart relationship in Mỏ Cày.

Saved!

The PSA thanked me in public—and told me in private not to do it again. After the meeting, I visited the TOC to get up to date on goings-on in the province. The S-3 advisor took me aside and found a few minutes to "counsel" me in private on the proper way to speak to a senior officer. He was correct—I had been disrespectful and demanding on the radio. Now I was hot under the collar that I was being stood at attention again. I held my temper (fortunately for me), and I apologized for my tone of voice. I added, forcefully, that if similar circumstances came up again I would do the same thing again if need be. "I'm not letting a shitty policy deter me from trying to save soldiers' lives."

"John, you are my kind of officer," he said. "But you must pay more attention to your communications technique."

That was the very first time I had even met Major Stephens, who at that time was relatively new to Advisory Team 88. Major Stephens was on his second tour of duty in Vietnam. He had previously served in the 1st Cavalry Division and was wounded in action while a company commander during an air assault into the A Shau Valley. He had earned his spurs and the right to criticize.

Years later, by then a colonel, I was stationed in the U.S. Embassy in Rangoon, Burma, as the U.S. Defense and Army Attaché. Major Stephens had become Brigadier General Stephens and had recently arrived next door in Bangkok as Chief of the Joint U.S. Military Advisory Group–Thailand (JUSMAG-Thai). We had a reunion, and over time and later get-togethers, we enjoyed chatting about the "good old days" in Kiến Hòa Province. In the intervening years I had indeed worked on my communications technique and practiced it very hard on a daily basis during four U.S. Embassy assignments in Indonesia and Burma.

... Happiness Is Having Ha Xe and Mr. Bom on Our Side.

I was privileged to serve with many very brave Vietnamese officers and soldiers during my 18 months as an advisor in Kiến Hòa Province. Two of the most memorable of them were occasional operational colleagues. Each was different, but they had one thing in common—visceral hatred of the VC, which had killed family members or colleagues in terrorist incidents rather than in open battle. Both men had been VC and had changed sides by becoming *hồi chanhs*. They knew that their own lives would be forfeited if the VC won the war, and I imagine that they did not survive either the end of the fighting or the "peace" after 1975.

Mr. Ha Xe had been a Vietcong for nine years. Then he switched sides because he thought that his chances for survival and financial reward would be better. Ha Xe did not have too many friends among the Mỏ Cày RF/PF soldiers, or anyone else for that matter. He was a loner who commanded a special operations platoon at the Kinh Nhang outpost in a strategically important, insecure "D" village west of Mỏ Cày district town. His special operations team went on targeted operations against small VC/VCI units and leaders. He hated the VC, who had assassinated his uncle. He proved to be a very effective killer of VC and cultivated a particularly sinister personal appearance. He was a very good tactical commander and utterly ruthless in dealing with any VC who crossed his path.

Major Reed had met Ha Xe shortly after he arrived in Mỏ Cày, months before I moved down from Hàm Long. He told me a story about Ha Xe. During a visit to his Kinh Ngang outpost, Major Reed noticed that he had a big .50 caliber machine gun. When asked where he got it, Ha Xe said, "I bought it." He asked Ha Xe where he got the money to buy such a thing, since they were surely not for sale. Ha Xe replied, "There are many things for sale for the right price. I get much money when I capture VC."

A few days later Ha Xe appeared at the Mỏ Cày team house wanting money for 20 VC rifles that he had stacked by the door. (We paid a $20 reward for each VC rifle that was brought in.) Major Reed was skeptical and told him he wasn't paying for so many weapons because he did not think he had captured them on the battlefield. Ha Xe said, "Come with me," and took Major Reed about two miles out of town, and there in a field were 20 VC bodies piled up, men killed earlier in the morning. Back in front of the advisors' team house Ha Xe got his team into formation, and Major Reed paid him what amounted to $400 for this treasure trove. Ha Xe turned around and divided this bonanza among his men, keeping none for himself.

In January 1972, just before Major Reed left Mỏ Cày, he stopped to visit Ha Xe one last time. He asked him why he gave all of the money for those rifles to his men and didn't keep any for himself. Ha Xe's response was that they had ambushed a VC tax collection team. While his men were collecting rifles, Ha Xe was collecting knapsacks that were full of tax money that the VC had taken from the people. That was how Ha Xe had found enough money to buy a machine gun for his outpost ... and probably other things as well.

I admired Ha Xe for his courage and his abilities and was very glad that he seemed genuinely to like me.[1]

Mr. Bom was the Province Kit Carson Scout team chief. He had been a Vietcong, and like all of the KCS, he had "*chieu-*hoi-ed"—surrendered and switched sides—and then volunteered to be a Scout. You read a story about the tactical skills of the Scouts earlier in this book. The KCS knew they would never survive capture by the VC, and they were very tough guys indeed. The KCS unit worked both for the province military structure and for the province CIA chief, either as a small reconnaissance unit or on PH raids against VCI cadre. I was very glad Mr. Bom was on OUR side instead of still using his skills for the VC.

Police-Led Phung Hoang Raids

When I moved to Mỏ Cày, I worked as liaison to the PH program. The DIOCC was located in a nondescript police building in the center of

Mỏ Cày town. My PH counterpart was the Mỏ Cày National Police Special Branch Chief, Mr. Bee (not his real name). He was very active, and I went on several PH operations with him and his small National Police Field Force (NPFF) team. Unlike in Hàm Long, where all of the PH operations were run by the army, in Mỏ Cày they were almost all run by the police. Some of the PH raids I went on with Mr. Bee were successful and captured several VC cadre. I was a bit worried about going out into strange countryside with such a small force—never more than seven to ten policemen. Fortunately, we never ran into serious problems.

...Me and eight policemen hiding along a backcountry trail waiting for two VCI to come home. The NFPP Chief grinning like always, happy when they walk into his trap. Me, happy that it wasn't a VC platoon instead. Genuine concern and relief in the voice of the U.S. TOC radio operator when I report my return from another police operation. "What the hell are you trying to do, get yourself killed?"

Altogether I went on probably five or six PH operations with Mr. Bee. There was plenty of drama—never more than six or eight NPFF policemen plus me and an interpreter. Sergeant Bé and Sergeant Tuyến switched off, and neither of them seemed to be as confident with the NPFF as they did with the RF/PF soldiers that we went with most of the time. Mr. Bee never told me the details of his intelligence for each operation, but several of them were successful—by capture of VCI cadre rather than in

Sergeant First Class Bé after award of U.S. Army Commendation Medal, Hàm Long District compound, October 1972.

firefights. Nonetheless, I admit to being nervous on all of those PH operations because of the lack of information given to me and the suspense of whether or not we would encounter some number of armed VC rather than the usually unarmed VCI suspects.

This operation was one of the more exciting ones. On 15 November 1972 I drove our jeep with Mr. Bee and met a squad of NPFF policemen at the Hòa Lộc bridge, where we left the jeep at the PF outpost. We set off along a village trail from the bridge into some of the heavy growth between the main highway and the "road" to Đôn Nhơn District. It was not a long walk, and soon we were in an area of scattered homes and vegetable gardens. Mr. Bee led the police in surrounding one of the houses, and he called out for the people inside to come out. One person did so—the VCI suspect who was the target of the operation. So far, so good. But as we left the area to return to the Hòa Lộc bridge, we came under fire from what seemed to be a squad of VC. Perhaps they were security for the VCI suspect captured at the hut. Maybe there were more VC nearby; we did not know. We were far more concerned about escaping with our prisoner than shooting it out with an unknown-size enemy unit. It was a short firefight, and we quickly continued on back to the Hòa Lộc bridge, where Mr. Bee briefed the PF platoon on the contact area. We took the VCI suspect in my jeep and returned to Mỏ Cày.

Mr. Bee arranged for me to be awarded the National Police Field Force Medal of Merit, a gesture I appreciated. It meant I had done okay going on operations with them.

A Young USAF FAC Made the Supreme Sacrifice

We were very glad that most of our Covey FAC pilot friends lived to survive the war after all the risks they took on our behalf. But sadly, we had one tragedy involving a young Covey pilot. It happened on 26 September 1972. The Covey FAC was supporting a Hương Mỹ District operation along the Hương Mỹ–Mỏ Cày border. I was monitoring the province radio net when we received an alert to ask counterparts if any RF/PF units or outposts in the area had reported a plane crash. We were told that the pilot's last transmission was that he was preparing to dive and fire on a large enemy motorized sampan. Then nothing. The thoughts still bring tears to my eyes.

.... A young Covey flying his OV-10 into the swampy ground in the jungles of Binh Khanh supporting some little guys he never saw, for the advisors he never had the chance to meet. The Huong My DSA, anguish in every word, directing the aerial search from a VR helicopter vowing to "kill

those sons a bitches myself." And, giving lie to every snide comment ever made about PF soldiers, three different platoons of PF pleading to make the ground trip through the heavily booby-trapped area "to help U.S. pilot." A small Kit Carson Scout force was inserted into an un-reconned LZ to find and recover the pilot's remains. The poignant traffic over the net from the KSC commander: "This is Kilo 88. We found him. He's dead. Covey, I'm so damned sorry." And, the collective sorrow from every place, district after district checking in on the radio net, Truc Giang, Binh Dai, Thanh Phu, Giong Trom, Don Nhon; and especially we of Huong My and Mo Cay for whom he fought—Covey, we're so damned sorry.

This courageous FAC was 23-year-old First Lieutenant Vincent Craig Anderson. He served 162 days in combat. His last radio transmission indicated he was doing a strafing attack against a large enemy sampan. His aircraft was hit by heavy ground fire and crashed. Adding to the sadness of this event, the commander of the Kit Carson Scout mission who found and recovered his remains was a personal friend of Lieutenant Anderson.[2]

An Thạnh Village—An Island of Security in a Dangerous District

An Thạnh village was a special place for Mỏ Cày, and in a way, for all of Vietnam. An Thạnh was the second-largest town in Mỏ Cày District and was one of only two B-rated villages in the district. The other was Đa Phước Hội, the village in which the district capital city of Mỏ Cày was located. The road between Mỏ Cày and An Thạnh was the most secure stretch of road anywhere in the district, even including the main highway to the Bến Tre ferry.

Located along the south side of the Mỏ Cày Grand Canal about six kilometers west of Mỏ Cày town, An Thạnh was a quiet town with a very active daily market. Just a few kilometers south lay solid enemy-controlled villages that friendly forces could enter only with a large security force. The main road to An Thạnh was paved (but broken in many places) to the village, after which it quickly deteriorated to dirt and rock until all vehicles had to stop at a major river; the VC had destroyed the steel bridge many years before.

Although secure in 1972, it had not been secure for very long. As late as 1968 An Thạnh was widely known as "VC Market" and was totally under VC control. A concentrated effort to bring government security to An Thạnh had successfully pushed the VC out, and it was a very pleasant town that we visited frequently.

An Thạnh was the home village of Madame Nguyễn Thị Định, one of the founders of the Viet Cong movement in the south and of the shadowy National Liberation Front (NLF). One of the VC's most powerful and extraordinary women, she participated in insurrections against the French and against the regime of President Ngô Đình Diệm as well as the succession of governments after President Diệm was assassinated. She rose to become the deputy commander of the NLF, and after the war, she became a major general in the People's Army of Vietnam. Madame Định's former home in An Thạnh was used as the village office and the headquarters of the An Thạnh RF/PF military forces. She was so well respected that her house was kept immaculate. There was never a trace of anti–VC graffiti or personal insults on the pastel walls of the small villa, and even the pro-government propaganda posters were taped to the walls, not written in big ugly paint.

The An Thạnh village chief was a very able civilian whose performance of duty was far and away the best in the district. Personable and friendly to advisors, I always enjoyed going to An Thạnh during operations further afield or for HES Report interviews or other official meetings. His military commander was equally efficient and well regarded. I drove to and from An Thạnh on many occasions, always taking one of the interpreters and usually a compound RF soldier as well.

The revolutionary history of Mỏ Cày District was visible in many places along the main road between Mỏ Cày town and An Thạnh. Right next to the road was a Việt Minh/Viet Cong cemetery with a large entry arch. The grass was not cut regularly, but the tombstones were intact and unmarred. Nearby was a large, damaged concrete monument on which was painted the red and blue NLF flag with its centered yellow star. Toppled over but not destroyed, the flag was easily visible.

There was also a back road between Mỏ Cày and An Thạnh close to the Mỏ Cày Grand Canal. It was very narrow, barely wide enough for a jeep. I drove this road several times, usually with either Sergeant Bé or Sergeant Tuyến, all of us well armed, and never had any trouble. The countryside was different, raised higher than the nearby rice paddies with the spoil from Grand Canal construction. Instead of endless rice paddies or coconut groves, the land was planted with vegetable gardens, fruit orchards, and a lot of commercial tobacco and cassava. It was a very pleasant ride through the countryside, but we seldom met many people coming and going on the "road." That should have caused more anxiety than I felt.

As it turned out, the area was neither as secure nor as idyllic as I had thought. One evening Thiếu-tá Mạnh called me into his office. He told me that the VC knew when advisors were driving the back road. He went on to say: "The VC may be planning to capture you." He wanted me to stop driving the back road effective immediately. "Please consider this an order," he said, politely but firmly. We did as he asked. I always wondered what the source of that information was.

That the province and the district authorities allowed the Việt Minh/VC cemetery and the NLF flag to remain largely unharmed always was good for a lively discussion in the team house. Neither Major Reed, with his close relationship with LTC Cư, nor both he and myself with a good relationship with Thiếu-tá Mạnh, felt comfortable in raising what surely was a very important political issue, at least in Mỏ Càny with its long history as a revolutionary home base.

... Happiness Is a Three-Way Turtle Banquet at An Thạnh.

An Thạnh was famous for its turtle banquets. Always served as the midday meal, the banquets featured copious quantities of beer and brandy. Turtle was served three ways: turtle soup, stir-fried tiny morsels of meat, and stewed with vegetables and a sauce that was delicious and, apparently, only prepared for the turtle stew.

Like almost all the meals at official occasions, the turtle banquets began with beer and dried snacks—"French" fried potatoes, dried squid (which I avoided at all costs!), peanuts. When the main course was served, it was the unofficial signal to switch to brandy. One of my best and most expertly honed advisory skills was making my way through such gatherings with a minimum amount of alcoholic consumption—beer or brandy. But it was hard to do that in An Thạnh because Major Reed and I were always seated next to the village chief and the district chief, whose personal batman made sure that our glasses were always full. Neither of us could avoid achieving an alcohol level well in excess of the minimum.

On one occasion we tried to reduce the flow of alcohol into our glasses by pleading that we needed to be sober to drive our jeep back to Mỏ Càny. That did not work. The district chief called out to somebody not included at the banquet table, and a sharp-looking soldier instantly appeared in front of us. "He will be your driver," he said. Ah, well, we had tried.

An Thạnh—Base of Operations

Because of its location, high degree of stability, and transportation access by roads and canals, Mỏ Càny forces frequently used An Thạnh as a base for operations into adjacent, less secure villages. On one such operation Thiếu-tá Mạnh set up a field TOC in a tiny hamlet near An Thạnh so he could monitor and direct the larger nearby operation. The "field TOC" consisted of a high, three-legged stool for him and a regular chair for his S-3, set up on the well-swept front yard of a simple farmer's cottage. I made do with a low stool. "Nearby" usually meant Thành Thới village, which was a combination of fertile agricultural fields, not much population, and some very difficult jungle areas where the enemy had its own base camps. It was into Thành Thới that Trung-tá Cư led the operation that resulted in his death and Major Reed's wounding back in July.

I believed the enemy deliberately did not attack An Thạnh because they did not want to damage the home town of Madame Nguyễn Thị Định. And, most likely, the friendly-to-us population was largely pro–VC. An Thạnh was never attacked or mortared during my time in Mỏ Cày.

An Thạnh was also a base for operations into villages north of the Grand Canal and out into the Cổ Chiên River. Soldiers went by truck to An Thạnh, boarded a fleet of water taxis commandeered for the operation, and then did a modified amphibious assault into the target area. Operations in and near the staunchly pro-government Catholic hamlet of Rạch Dầu were almost always initiated from An Thạnh. I spent a lot of time going to, and being in, An Thạnh.

Northwestern Mỏ Cày—Again

In mid–December I accompanied Thiếu-tá Mạnh on another operation in far western Mỏ Cày. Because of the location almost adjacent to the border with Đôn Nhơn District, I was particularly concerned. VC/NVA units habitually created mini-base areas along province and district boundaries, where coordination between the GVN military counterparts was less than optimal. The area for the operation was in the same area where the invading VC//NVA E-2 Regiment invaded Mỏ Cày during the July–August offensive. As mentioned previously, the 15th ARVN Regiment was deployed to Mỏ Cày on 6 September specifically to locate and engage the E-2 Regiment, but "failed to find them." The E-2 Regiment left Mỏ Cày in late September. Since then, district forces hunkered down in outposts but only patrolled within sight of their outpost.

The plan for this operation was to land by water taxis with VN Navy supporting fires and patrol along the derelict road that led to Tân Thanh Tây village, where it intersected the rock road from Mỏ Cày that Major Reed and I had walked earlier in the year with Trung-tá Cư. Sergeant Bé and I went on the operation.

I was sufficiently concerned so that before the operation I established communication with the Đôn Nhơn District advisory team. One of my MASA Course classmates was the PH coordinator in Đôn Nhơn. We arranged for me to make a commo check every half hour on a "just in case" basis. I was not told what coordination, if any, had been made between the two district chiefs and did not know if Thiếu-tá Mạnh's RTO also made commo checks with the Vietnamese TOC in Đôn Nhơn or not.

The entire force of several RF companies left Mỏ Cày in the pre-dawn darkness, moved by truck to An Thạnh, and boarded a fleet of large water taxis. We sailed out into the Cổ Chiên River, then north past Rạch Dầu and unloaded at a point about 500 meters south of the Đôn Nhơn-Mỏ Cày border, where intel scouts had already located the "road" that formed the axis of advance for the operation. I was pleased that I was able to get in immediate contact with Đôn Nhơn using the long antenna on the PRC-25.

The operation turned out to be a quiet walk in the sun, although the area was as wild and unkempt as any I had been through in Mỏ Cày. I was nervous and anxious the entire morning, certain that if the enemy did not attack, they certainly knew we were there. It would have been a fine place for local force VC/NVA units to build mini-base areas. The command group walked along the rough trail that showed on maps as a road but which had not seen jeep or even motorcycle traffic in a very long time. Although there was no enemy contact, I continued to make the commo checks every half hour with my Đôn Nhơn counterpart and felt very good having that "back up" monitoring our progress. My friend told me that as far as his knowledge went, neither Đôn Nhơn nor Mỏ Cày forces had ever conducted a coordinated operation along that border.

By noon the command group arrived at Tân Thanh Tây village market—the same place Trung-tá Cư, Major Reed, and I had visited a few months before. If nothing else, we confirmed that there was no evidence of large enemy units in the narrow area we traversed on that "road" that was now a trail. We were delighted to find a fleet of trucks to ride back to Mỏ Cày instead of making that long, rocky walk again.

By now the progress of peace negotiations in Paris was well known. The upcoming Christmas period seemed to be an unofficial time to slow the pace of operational activity. It was a false perception, as it turned out only weeks later, but at the time it actually felt like a peace accord would be reached. As it turned out, this operation to Tân Thanh Tây market was my final field operation in Vietnam.

A Quiet Christmas

Christmas in Hàm Long, December 1971, had been very low key—except for the fantastic surprise visit from Martha Raye. Most people in Hàm Long were Buddhist; certainly the senior officers were. Somewhat to my surprise, there was a burst of activity for Christmas 1972 in Mỏ

Cày. The compound was decorated with lights, ribbons, wood and paper symbols.

A military jeep was transformed into a mobile Christmas float. Papier-mâché, wood, and paint became a small replica of the Grotto at Lourdes. The materials for these displays had to have been carefully stored away and brought out at Christmastime. While there was no Vietnamese Santa Claus, it was nice to have the spirit of Christmas all around the normally prosaic district compound.

A Pause:
The Importance of Trust

I was at the end of the U.S. advisory chain. The district officers were ARVN officers, but all of the soldiers were locally recruited Regional Force and Popular Force (RF/PF) soldiers, not regular force ARVN. We were very far away from any large conventional military force that could come to our assistance if the situation turned very bad. Everyone else was Vietnamese. All of them had more experience in combat than I had. How was I to advise them? Would they accept and trust me? Could I trust them—with my life?

I hope this book has told our stories well enough to answer those questions positively. Let me return for a moment to the time I returned to Hàm Long District, following in the footsteps of a friend and colleague who had been killed in action just days before. Now I am back as the district senior advisor. I felt reasonably comfortable but not fully comfortable. In the earlier ten months I had enjoyed excellent relations with my Hàm Long counterparts. But at that time I had been the *deputy* advisor. Now I was worried that while I had been effective as a deputy, how would I be received as the advisor to a much-more-senior Vietnamese officer? Would the two cultures and the difference in our ranks be a problem?

I need not have worried. "I am so glad they sent you back out here to help me," he said. "We know you and trust you, and we will work well together."

And so we did. Slowly but surely his troops stiffened and confronted the much stronger local VC/NVA units and guerrillas with the help of daily air strikes I managed for them. Although friendly casualties were heavier than before, confident RF/PF troops responded well against enemy ambushes and outpost attacks. After three months of heavy combat together, my counterparts had won and maintained government control of the district. Trust had overcome any cultural obstacles of rank and position that could, in another situation, have been difficult to overcome. The key to that success lies in the words of the previous paragraph: "We know you and trust you."

Trust.

Another example comes from my relationship with the new district chief in Mỏ Cày. You remember his response when I showed up at an ambush location where he had hastened to rescue the injured Province S-2. "I didn't tell you I was going out here because I assumed you would not go out to a dangerous area." We had barely known each other for a week! Then a short while later we went to the field, a soldier was badly wounded, and he could not get a Vietnamese Air Force medevac helicopter, so he asked me to help. I broke a standing policy, and I was forceful on the radio with a senior officer, but we got American pilots to bring the medevac and save a soldier's life. He trusted me to be there when he needed me.

And he saved me from some severe ass-chewing by telling the province chief the story, and the province chief's public words of thanks were a very clear signal of approval. I trusted him to be there when I needed him.

And here is one more example of the importance of trust when two cultures mix together. Recall the story of the boy with the cleft palate, whose father was a senior VC officer. The mother trusted a strange American with the life of her son. Why? There is no doubt in my mind that she discussed this with her VC husband, who no doubt asked his sources in the Hàm Long District headquarters about that American, who in turn surely told a worried father that they trusted that American. It took a couple weeks before the mother brought her son to the district headquarters and turned her son over to me. Wartime communications in a rural Vietnamese district sometimes take time. There was great trust exhibited in this humanitarian incident. A distraught mother trusted a stranger, that American, with the life of her son. A family in the enemy's camp trusted that their enemy would not betray them by harming their son. We all trusted that western medicine would make a big difference in the child's future life.

Trust, once earned, is good for the duration if one continues to perform as the supporting half of the team. My counterparts trusted me to be there when they needed me. I was able to help and trusted them to remember what I did.

No advisor can succeed without trust.

20

When a Cease-Fire
Is Not a Cease-Fire

After the surprise of Christmas celebrations on the Mỏ Cày compound, the rest of my time in Mỏ Cày returned to normal. The ongoing Paris peace talks seemed destined to go on forever, and there was no indication, at our level, of when things would end. VC/NVA attacks continued with vigor. The enemy objective seemed to be to capture and overrun outposts rather than to target tactical units. As was learned later, the change in tactics marked the start of steady VC/NVA territorial encroachment and seizure of outposts.

My memorable assignment as a district-level advisor came to an unexpected end. My adjusted DEROS called for me to leave Vietnam on 7 February 1973. After an exchange of letters with the MI branch assignments office, I received orders assigning me to attend Cambodian language training at the Defense Language School—East Coast, managed by the State Department in a high-rise office building in Arlington, Virginia. Then I would be assigned to Cambodia to serve in what was called the Weapons Delivery Team—cover name for military support and advice.

But world politics intervened. The Paris Peace Accords got signed. Among the provisions was a requirement that American, South Vietnamese, and "VC" military units observe a cease-fire in place, with no further efforts to expand the areas the respective units occupied. American military personnel and units were required to cease-fire "in place" and prepare to depart Vietnam. American advisors were required to be out of combat at the district level and regroup in a "cease fire posture" at the province level no later than 28 January 1973. Most would then be reassigned out of Vietnam.

Major Reed and several other Kiến Hòa majors with time remaining on their Vietnam tour of duty were assigned to the Four-Power International Commission of Control and Supervision (ICCS) monitoring team to complete their 18-month tour of duty. Major Reed was sent to the city of

Mỹ Tho. He and Sergeant Tuyến left Mỏ Cày in mid–January. Soon most district advisory teams in Kiến Hòa had closed up and turned their team house and property over to their counterparts. My friends in Hương Mỹ and Thạnh Phú closed out and were flown by helicopter to Bến Tre because of their longer distance from the province capital. A small province-level team, mostly civilians but including some military administrative personnel—but no tactical advisors—remained in Bến Tre.

Sergeant Bé and I were the last members of the Mỏ Cày District advisory team. I had been the last district senior advisor in Hàm Long, and now I had become the last district senior advisor in Mỏ Cày.

The Paris agreement called for a mutual cease-fire by both sides and no encroachment by either the VC/NVA or the Saigon military forces against areas controlled by the other side. But none of this occurred in Mỏ Cày. The home of VC leader Madame Nguyễn Thị Định was in An Thạnh village, and the VC/NVA forces were determined to give her home district to her, completely communist controlled, as a cease-fire present. There was no cease-fire in Mỏ Cày. NVA units attacked all across the district, overran outpost after outpost, pushed into areas previously controlled by government forces, and raised VC/NLF (not North Vietnam) flags to show geographic control. The Mỏ Cày RF/PF units fought back as best they could, but the NVA were winning. By the end of January, the enemy controlled most of the district, shown by hundreds of VC flags fluttering from coconut trees and telephone poles. They took control of the highway from Mỏ Cày to the Bến Tre ferry. Therefore, it was impossible for Sergeant Bé and me to drive to Bến Tre before the required date of 28 January.

Now my concern was getting to Saigon in time to leave on or before my DEROS of 7 February. I was notified that some U.S. official at a very high level determined that it was politically unacceptable for me to be evacuated by helicopter since the Saigon government had controlled the highway to the Bến Tre ferry until the NVA/VC cease-fire encroachment violations. Therefore I became a "ceasefire violation" by not leaving the field of combat by the prescribed date of 28 January 1973. The continued fighting in Mỏ Cày was reported all the way to the top of U.S. political and military levels in Washington, D.C., and in Paris (as well as in Hanoi). At some very high level in Paris or Washington, "somebody" asked if the U.S. advisor was still in Mỏ Cày.

Hell Yes, he was!

A policy decision was quickly made—the American tactical advisor would remain in Mỏ Cày as a political symbol until the security situation returned to *status quo ante*. In other words, the VC/NVA were required to remove their forces—and their flags—from areas seized during January in violation of the cease-fire agreement. That included removal of their forces from control of the main highway to the Bến Tre ferry landing. Only then would the last American tactical advisor leave the field.

I felt very lonely. I still had radio contact with Bến Tre, and everyone assured me that "everyone" was working on the situation. I was ordered not to give any tactical assistance to my counterparts. (What advice did they need from me in this situation?!?!) They assured me that "the very highest levels" were working to get a cease-fire in place in Mỏ Cày. The North Vietnam and communist country members of the ICCS (Poland and Hungary) assured everyone that they were in contact with VC/NVA forces in Mỏ Cày and had ordered them to observe the cease-fire provisions. But the fighting continued. Similar issues probably were taking place in other contested districts in the country, but I have never learned whether or not this was the case. At the time, I understood that I was the only district-level tactical advisor in all of Vietnam still at his district advisory post.

Then one morning in February Thiếu-tá Mạnh came to the team house and said, "Today you go Bến Tre." Needless to say, I was not too sure about that. He assured me that the VC/NVA had moved back to prior base camp areas and Mỏ Cày RF and PF soldiers had reoccupied all of the outposts along the highway up to the ferry. I had no knowledge of how the two sides in Mỏ Cày had worked out this solution, and I did not ask.

Sergeant Bé and I packed up, loaded our stuff into the trailer, and with some trepidation joined a small convoy—led by Thiếu-tá Mạnh—and drove unhindered to the Bến Tre ferry. The ferry boat had been held and was waiting for us. We both got out of our jeeps. Thiếu-tá Mạnh looked me in the eye and thanked me for all I had done for him and for his soldiers during my time in Mỏ Cày and bid me farewell. It was very low key— no hugs, no gifts, just a firm handshake. I thanked him for his support and wished him luck. I think we both knew there was not going to be a happy ending in Mỏ Cày.

Sergeant Bé already knew that he was going to be reassigned to an ARVN unit back in his home province of An Giang, and he was very pleased. I spent a few hours saying goodbye to friends in Bến Tre while I waited for a helicopter to come from Cần Thơ to pick me up. I lined up my collection of large ceramic elephants on the steel bridge to the helicopter pad and hoped they would all fit into the helicopter (they did) and that I could get them properly packed up in Cần Thơ (I did). Sergeant Bé and I exchanged a firm handshake and hoped we might meet again sometime.

The helicopter arrived, all of my stuff fit inside, and with very mixed emotions I left the place that forever after owned a part of my heart and soul.

I surprised people in Cần Thơ. "What are you doing here? You were supposed to be gone weeks ago." Well, yes, but the North Vietnamese Army had other ideas.

In no time at all I got all of my BUFEs (Big Ugly Fucking Elephants) packed and crated, my remaining stuff packed up, everything shipped off, and I was flown by helicopter to Camp Alpha at Tân Sơn Nhứt Air Base for final out-processing. I still had orders to Cambodian language school in Arlington, Virginia, so I flew to Washington, D.C., and joined my family for a happy reunion.

The MI branch personnel officer asked me what I wanted to do next since obviously I was no longer going to be an advisor in Cambodia. "Well," I suggested, "I'm here, I'm ready for language school; send me to the Thai language course." So they did.

I spent several months in the Pentagon waiting for my language class to start. I worked on the army's Operation Homecoming team, Office of the Assistant Chief of Staff for Intelligence (ACSI). We processed intelligence collected from the debriefings of the U.S. POWs coming home from Hanoi. My main contribution was a long, easily rolled-up time chart showing the movement of all U.S. Army POWs from date of capture to date of release. The details came from the reports of individual debriefings of the returning POWs as well as all of the existing intelligence on U.S. POWs captured and missing in action. The chart provided a graphic study that helped to identify when and where POWs mingled together and thus helped clarify some of the unexplained MIA cases.

My application to be accessed into the Regular Army was approved. The ACSI arranged for my father, Colonel (retired) Leonard L. Haseman, to swear me into the Regular Army, just as he had sworn me in as a second lieutenant prior to the graduation ceremonies at the University of Missouri ten years earlier.

Then I started "Chapter Next" in my career, preparing for assignment to Thailand. I ended up spending 18 years of my 30-year army career in Asia and learned three Southeast Asian languages to support my assignments. All of my post–Vietnam assignments were interesting and challenging. Southeast Asia had its hooks deeply embedded in me and would remain there for the rest of my life. But the memories of being an advisor in Vietnam have always been the most deeply felt, the most poignant, and the longest lasting.

21

Sergeant First Class
Hồ Văn Bé

Loyal, Reliable, Unforgettable

Written a few days before leaving Kiến Hòa:

.... Sergeant Hồ Văn Bé, whose loyalty to his advisor transcended any requirement of duty or position, the one man among many in Vietnam I proudly call friend, whose knowledge and dedication bridged the gap between nationalities and cultures, and made my job easier and richer every day, who turned down a transfer to his secure home district "until Đại-úy Haseman goes home too."

ARVN Sergeant First Class Hồ Văn Bé was a Hòa Hảo from An Giang Province in the western Mekong Delta. He was born in Thốt Nốt District, where the Hòa Hảo sect was first formed. Hòa Hảo is a Buddhist sect that eschews the lavishness of temples for plain structures in which to pray, and its members are fiercely anti–Communist.

I first met Sergeant Bé in 1968 when I was the 9th MI Detachment (Forward) commander at Dong Tam and he was one of the counterintelligence section interpreters. He was young, early 20s, and he spoke fluent English learned in school. Like all young Vietnamese males, he was drafted into the army and got assigned as an interpreter with the American military because of his English language skills. He was a good worker with a pleasant personality, and we got along well. He was an adept and aggressive interpreter for his American interrogator counterparts. Perhaps befitting his Hòa Hảo culture, his nickname among the Americans as well as his fellow interpreters was "Tiger."

Sergeant Bé was mature beyond his age and a leader on our team. When tasked to provide an intelligence NCO and an interpreter on temporary duty to the district advisory team in Cái Bè District, Định Tường Province, I selected Sergeant Bé to go with one of my counterintelligence

NCOs. They did an excellent job in a dangerous district, and Sergeant Bé was personally commended by the province senior advisor.

When the 9th MI Detachment joined most of the 9th Infantry Division's withdrawal from Vietnam in summer 1969, Sergeant Bé was reassigned to MACV Advisory Team 88 in Kiến Hòa Province and placed on the Giồng Trôm District advisory team. He was highly regarded as an interpreter but even more so as a courageous NCO.

I connected with a former DDSA in Giồng Trôm by email in 2016. He relayed to me a short description of Sergeant Bé's courage and loyalty to his advisors. They were part of a tactical operation by RF and PF soldiers in Giồng Trôm. When they were attacked by a larger VC force, most of the RF/PF soldiers fled. Sergeant Bé refused to run and remained at his advisor's side. Suddenly one American captain and one ARVN sergeant were alone on the battlefield. The two men were able to conceal themselves well enough to avoid discovery by the searching enemy forces. The captain maintained radio communications with friendly artillery units while his DSA and province-level advisors controlled a steady stream of tactical helicopters and tac air attacks against the VC. My interlocutor described Sergeant Bé's steady presence and recalled only one memorable comment from him: "Đại-úy, I think we die tonight." Happily, they did not.

Fast forward to July 1971 when I arrived in Kiến Hòa Province. Early on I learned that Sergeant Bé was an interpreter on the Giồng Trôm District advisory team. He had heard that I had been assigned to Kiến Hòa Province, and he was anxious to work with me again. I told Major Kretschmar that we should try to arrange a trade so we could have Sergeant Bé on our district team. On one of his visits for the monthly DSA/District Chief conference, the Giồng Trôm DSA brought Sergeant Bé along to meet Major Kretschmar. The Giồng Trôm DSA confessed that he was having a personality issue with Sergeant Bé, and he was happy to trade interpreters. The reassignments were quickly worked out with the province chief. Sergeant Hùynh went to Giồng Trôm, and Sergeant Bé came to Hàm Long.

I found Bé to be more mature than three years earlier; he had married and had a son. His family lived with his wife's parents in An Giang Province, far to the west of Kiến Hòa. When we closed out the Hàm Long advisory team in May 1972, I was concerned about Sergeant Bé's future since he could have been reassigned within ARVN to almost anywhere. I asked if he wanted to move to Mỏ Cày with me, and he readily agreed. Major Reed was happy to have a second interpreter, and there was plenty of room in the big team house.

When I was assigned to go back to Hàm Long as DSA in August 1972, Sergeant Bé went with me, and the two of us continued to work as an effective team during that hectic, dangerous time. At some point one of the Vietnamese officers asked Be when he was going to return to an assignment in his home province. He said, simply, "I stay with Đại-úy Haseman. When he goes home, I go home."

After the cease-fire agreement was signed, the VC/NVA continued their attacks in Mỏ Cày, and combat persisted for more than two weeks after the deadline for all American advisors to leave the field. Sergeant Bé remained with me in Mỏ Cày until we were able to drive safely to Bến Tre. I processed out of Vietnam, and Bé was reassigned to an ARVN unit in An Giang Province.

In May 1974 I stopped off in Vietnam on leave en route to my next assignment in Thailand so I could visit Kiến Hòa Province. I had stayed in sporadic touch by mail with Sergeant Bé and had contacted the new Kiến Hòa PSA by letter. He invited me to stay with him while I was in Bến Tre. I went out to Hàm Long and found out that LTC Sơn had been promoted to colonel and reassigned as province chief in neighboring Vĩnh Bình Province. I also went to Mỏ Cày, where Major Mạnh was still district chief and my friend and former counterpart as S-2 in Hàm Long, now Captain Hương, was the district S-2. Another ARVN interpreter had also been in touch with Sergeant Bé. The PSA radioed his counterpart in Vĩnh Bình, who quickly put me in touch with Colonel Sơn, who immediately invited us all to visit him.

My interpreter friend was able to contact Sergeant Bé and passed along the invitation. He and I took a civilian bus to Vĩnh Long. A convoy of jeeps from Vĩnh Bình met us at the Vĩnh Long side of the ferry and drove us to Trà Vinh, the province capital. Sergeant Bé arrived the next day, and we spent three days as guests in Colonel Sơn's official province chief's residence. The three of us spent the time catching up on the intervening year's activities and enjoyed Colonel Sơn's hospitality. He told me that the situation in Kiến Hòa and Vĩnh Binh provinces had improved considerably in the intervening year. We even covered the details concerning the deaths of mutual friends First Lieutenant Liem, former driver Phi, and more men who had lost their lives fighting off the VC/NVA during the "peace" since January 1973.

At the end of the visit to Trà Vinh, Sergeant Bé returned to An Giang, and Trung-tá Sơn sent me all the way back to Bến Tre in one of his jeeps. I took a bus back to Saigon and flew on to Bangkok to begin my assignment there.

The parting from Sergeant Bé was difficult. For the first time in the years we had worked together we gave each other a strong emotional hug. We had spent two and a half years in close daily contact, frequently sharing danger and risk, both of us lucky to be untouched by the enemy even though many colleagues had paid the supreme price. I was, presciently, quite sure we would not see each other again.

Sergeant Bé and I maintained sporadic letter contact for several months. He sent me a photo of himself sitting on some rocks during an operation in the Seven Mountains area almost on the Cambodian border.

Then the letters stopped.

After a long while, I received word that Sergeant Bé was killed in action during that same operation, not long after the photo was taken. I was devastated and still think about him all the time.

Rest in peace, my friend.

Remembering…

22

A Good Advisor but
Not a Hero

My 18 months as a district-level advisor was a life-changing period for me. I developed an expanded sense of confidence in myself established by the circumstances of combat, living in a different culture, and finding a deep sense of personal worth. Those 18 months brought me more fire-fights with the enemy, mortar attacks, and ambushes than I might have expected. But to be clear—I would never categorize my actions in any of our combat episodes as heroic. Most advisors I knew did a lot of brave things—that came with the territory as they say, all in the line of duty. Those 18 months changed me in many ways, gave me an enhanced sense of duty for my country, and made me far more mature.

The Combat Infantryman Badge

The best tribute I received came on my first Officer Efficiency Report (OER) wherein the Hàm Long DSA wrote, "Even though regulations prohibit its award to him, Captain Haseman has more than earned award of the Combat Infantryman Badge." Those regulations required awardees to have participated in armed combat against the enemy, be assigned in an infantry billet, and to be in the infantry branch. I met the first two requirements but as a Military Intelligence branch officer, not the third.

However, thanks to the strong efforts of John Paul Vann, Wilbur Wilson, and others, those regulations were changed to allow award of the Combat Infantryman Badge (CIB) to MACV advisors who were in non-combat arms branches but met all other requirements. The nomination and justification had to come from the PSA and be approved by the appropriate corps commander. I was carried in the DDSA slot (a combat arms billet) rather than in the Phụng Hoàng Coordinator slot (an MI billet), had attended the Infantry Officer Basic Course and earned the infantry officer MOS at Fort Benning, had experienced my share of combat, and had earned the confidence of two district senior advisors and of my PSA. With the waiver of the requirement to be in the infantry branch, I became eligible for the CIB. It was a surprise. Mr. Kotzebue called me into his office one day when I was visiting the province team offices and TOC, read the order, and pinned the CIB to my fatigue jacket. It has always been the award I am most proud of receiving.

The Respect of My Counterparts

The best reward I carried away was the respect of all the Vietnamese with whom I fought the enemy. Respect is not easily given in combat—it must be earned on the ground. Many friends have told me that they could not conceive of what it would have been like to go out into the field, expecting combat, as the only American with a small unit of Vietnamese RF/PF soldiers. I did not know either—until I went into combat with the Hàm Long RF/PF soldiers. I trusted that the Vietnamese soldiers would do well, trusted that they would not leave me behind to be captured or killed by the enemy and that I would be equally trusted and reliable to provide the combat multiplier they needed to succeed. I was able to do that by coordinating tactical air strikes, medevac helicopters, and by walking in their footsteps and facing danger with them.

Most district advisors I know were superb men who also did all of that, did not get awarded medals, just did their job. A few, always mentioned with scorn by Vietnamese colleagues, did not gain the trust of their counterparts and likely did not enjoy their advisory assignment. Gaining the respect of those soldiers was one of the highest honors I gained in 30+ years of military service. My departure from Hàm Long, from Mỏ Cày, from Bến Tre was a very bittersweet departure. I was going home to safety and, hopefully, a good career with interesting assignments. My Vietnamese friends, however, were destined to keep fighting until either they were wounded, killed, or defeated by the NVA. I think we all knew the ending was not going to be a good one.

For the Record

The military system smiled on me. In addition to the CIB, I was awarded the Vietnamese Cross of Gallantry with Bronze Star for Heroism in Combat, the Vietnamese Honor Service Medal, the Vietnamese National Police Field Force Honor Medal, two U.S. Bronze Stars (for service, not for valor) and two U.S. Air Medals (for all the time spent on those VR missions). Kiến Hòa Province Advisory Team 88 was recommended for the Presidential Unit Citation but, as far as I know, that paperwork was lost in the rush to get Americans out of Vietnam. I have a copy of the nomination, and reading it as a more experienced and more senior officer, I believe the award is justified and should have been made.

I spent 30 years on active duty and enjoyed all of my subsequent assignments. The U.S. Army's Foreign Area Officer program was established in 1972; at my request, I was accessed into the program in 1974. Counting my two assignments in Vietnam, I ended up spending 18 years in Asia and retired at the rank of colonel. I firmly believe that my performance of duty in combat in Vietnam established the base for my successful army career. It also prepared me for entrance into the Foreign Area Officer program in which I was assigned for the final 20 years of my career.[1]

23

The Aftermath

I am saddened that I do not know the post–1973 life experiences of many close friends and counterparts from Hàm Long, Mỏ Cày, and Bến Tre. Some of them are mentioned in this book, and the details I do know follow.

Colonel Nguyễn Văn Sơn, Hàm Long District Chief and Vĩnh Bình Province Chief, was arrested in May 1975 and spent 13 years in re-education camps. Though he survived, the experience destroyed his health. He came to the U.S. in the late 1980s through the Orderly Departure Program and lived in Washington state, beset with dementia/Alzheimer's disease and suffering from several internal ailments. He passed away quietly in the 1990s.

First Lieutenant Nguyễn Thanh Liêm, Hàm Long District S-3 and RF company commander, was killed in action on 14 March 1973. You read his story in this book. He was a worthy teacher.

I do not know the fates of the other Hàm Long District officers. I suspect, without any firm information, that among them were loyal men who may have been killed in action or who were arrested and suffered after 1975 and that also among them were longtime undercover VC assets who did just fine after the "peace." I would like to know their stories.

Major David Kretschmar, Hàm Long DSA, returned to the U.S. and was promoted to Lieutenant Colonel. He retired on the Eastern Shore of Maryland as an Emergency Medical Technician and volunteer ambulance driver. He passed away from a stroke and heart attack in 2007.

Sergeant First Class Huỳnh Đức Tuyến, loyal and courageous Mỏ Cày interpreter, transferred to the ARVN field artillery when the interpreter program ended. He was stationed in II Corps and became a father for the second time. I have had no contact from him since 1974 and do not know his fate.

Mr. Toi, Hàm Long PH interpreter, retained his deferment from military service and returned to his family in Biên Hòa. I have had no contact from him since 1974.

Sergeant Tu, Hàm Long interpreter, was reassigned out of Kiến Hòa Province, and I do not know his fate.

Sergeant First Class Hồ Văn Bé, loyal and courageous interpreter in Giồng Trôm, Hàm Long, and Mỏ Cày districts, was killed in action in 1974 during heavy fighting in the Seven Mountains area of Kiên Giang Province. You have read his story in this book. No greater friend and ally has graced my life.

RF Private Phi, the Hàm Long advisory team driver, was killed in action in 1974.

I do not know the fate of Major Hoàng Văn Mạnh, Mỏ Cày district chief, or the other Mỏ Cày District officers.

Major George B. "Byron" Reed, Mỏ Cày DSA, had a successful military career—a few instances of his professionalism, compassion, and courage are included in this book. He retired as a colonel after 27 years of active duty service. In civilian life he worked for Northrop Grumman as Director of Land Combat Systems, for Colsa Corp. as a member of its "Gray Beard" consulting team, and for Asbury United Methodist Church as Executive Director in Madison, Alabama. He is retired in Huntsville, Alabama, where he and Sue, his wife of 55 years, are busy with their grandchildren.

Colonel Phạm Chi Kim, Kiến Hòa Province Chief, was arrested in May 1975. In the aftermath of the war, I was told by a Vietnamese friend that Colonel Kim had been summarily executed by the arriving VC/NVA in April 1975, so for many years I had assumed that was correct and took no action to find out about his postwar situation. However, in mid–2020, to my great surprise and pleasure, I was put in contact with one of Colonel Kim's sons, and he brought me up to date on the real situation.

Colonel Kim was arrested in May 1975 and was sentenced to an indefinite stay in a re-education center, first in Châu Đốc Province but later further north. He spent 11 years in prison and was eventually released in 1986. He came to the U.S. in 1991 through the Orderly Departure Program. Around 2013 or 2014 he fell into ill health and told his sons he wanted to die in Vietnam. He returned to Biên Hòa (his wife's home) and passed away in 2015.

Colonel Kim and his wife had seven sons, one of whom was attending university in the U.S. in 1975. He remained in the U.S. Two brothers escaped to Malaysia in 1979 and came to the U.S. through refugee channels. In the ensuing years three more brothers came to the U.S.; one remained in Vietnam with Mrs. Kim, who never came to the U.S.

Lieutenant Colonel (retired) Albert L. Kotzebue, Kiến Hòa PSA, remained as PSA until mid–1973, when he was reassigned to Bình Định Province in MR II. He retired in December 1973 and moved to Carmel,

California, where he bought and managed a bed and breakfast. Restless in retirement, he returned to a CORDS assignment in Vietnam in late 1974, but that ended just before the April 1975 fall of South Vietnam. He purchased and managed a small motel in Inverness, California. Mr. Kotzebue passed away from cancer in 1987.

Lieutenant Colonel William Tausch, Kiến Hòa DPSA, was reassigned to Fort Bragg, North Carolina, and remained on active duty for several more years, then served for ten years with the Arkansas National Guard. He lived in North Little Rock. He passed away on 30 October 2001.

Mr. Norris Nordvold, Kiến Hòa DPSA, left USAID after serving two 18-month tours in Vietnam and returned to Arizona. Mr. Nordvold worked as a Research Staffer and then Senate Research Director for the Arizona State Senate for ten years. He and his wife, Brenda Young, left the senate position and were hired by a consortium of three American religious groups to serve as co-directors of a refugee assistance program in Somalia. Norris worked on this refugee project for two years and then worked for USAID in Somalia for five years on economic development programs in Northern Somalia, now known as Somaliland.

Mr. Nordvold served as the Chief Political Lobbyist for the City of Phoenix from 1987 to his retirement in 2006. During this time, he volunteered to work as a Short Term Election Monitor in approximately ten different Eastern European countries, including Russia.

Today Mr. Nordvold works on consulting contracts with Arizona Tribal Governments and is active in public affairs at the City of Phoenix.

Major Robert L. Stephens, Jr., Kiến Hòa Province S-3/Operations Advisor, left Bến Tre in January 1973 and, like several other majors, was assigned to the ICCS station in Vĩnh Long. He had a long and distinguished career after Vietnam. He was a battalion executive officer with the 101st Airborne Division and commanded a battalion in the 9th Infantry Division. As a colonel, he commanded a brigade-size task force and the 193rd Brigade (Separate) in Panama. He balanced field commands with several successful assignments on the Army Staff and with the Joint Chiefs of Staff. He was promoted to Brigadier General in July 1989 and was assigned to the Office of the Deputy Chief of Staff for Operations in the Pentagon. Then came a short assignment as Assistant Division Commander of the 9th Infantry Division at Fort Lewis, Washington. His next assignment was as Chief, Joint U.S. Military Advisory Group–Thailand in Bangkok, which became one of the family's favorite assignments. After two years in Thailand, BG Stephens was assigned as the Director of the Joint Military Armed Forces Inaugural Committee to prepare for and manage the inauguration of incoming President Bill Clinton. BG Stephens retired from the U.S. Army in May 1993.

BG Stephens did not really retire, though. In civilian life he served as Director of Personnel for the State of West Virginia for four years; then as Assistant and then Deputy Commissioner of Personnel Management for the State of Georgia. He then embarked on many years with Clayton State University as Visiting Assistant Professor of Management in the School of Business; as Executive Assistant to the University President; and University Vice President for External Relations. He is retired in Georgia and spends a lot of time on the golf course.

Captain Michael Delaney, MAT Team leader, Kiến Hòa Province field artillery advisor, TOC duty officer, and advisor to several *liên đội* operations, returned to the U.S. in October 1972 with orders to attend the Field Artillery Officers' Advanced Course at Ft. Sill, Oklahoma. Deciding to attend law school instead, Mike (somewhat to the chagrin of his career army officer father) resigned his Regular Army commission and entered the University of Kansas School of Law in August 1973. He graduated at the top of his law school class in 1976 and began a 38-year practice as a management labor and employment trial lawyer with a leading Kansas City, Missouri, law firm, where he served as a practice group leader and as a member of the firm's executive committee. Mike's work on behalf of his clients led to his election as a Fellow of the prestigious College of Labor & Employment Lawyers, the Litigation Counsel of America, and the American Bar Foundation, as well as to repeated recognition in such publications as "Best Lawyers in America," "SuperLawyers" and *Human Resource Executive* magazine's list of the "Nation's Most Powerful Employment Attorneys."

In 2014, after retiring from the law practice, Mike and his wife, Kathy, bought a 150-year-old historic home in Lawrence, Kansas, where he embarked on a third career, teaching courses in labor law and collective bargaining as an adjunct law professor at his alma mater. Mike also became an active member of the local historic preservation community and has served as the President of the Douglas County Historical Society/Watkins Museum of History, Chair of the Douglas County Heritage Conservation Council, a member of the board of the Lawrence Preservation Alliance and a Trustee of the Freedom's Frontier National Heritage Area.

Also in 2014, Mike and Kathy traveled to Vietnam, spending several days in Bến Tre and visiting the site of the Con Ho Training Center at the mouth of the Hàm Luông River, where his Vietnam service began more than 50 years earlier. Mike and Kathy's three children and two grandchildren all reside in the Washington, D.C., area.

Captain William Chandler, Kiến Hòa Province S-2 Advisor, was killed in action on his second day as district advisor in Hàm Long District, as you learned in this book. His remains were repatriated to the United States, and he lies in hallowed ground at Arlington National Cemetery.

In February 2019 I learned from Mike Delaney that Bill's hometown American Legion Post in Springfield, Pennsylvania, had contacted him to advise that the Post has a tradition of honoring a hometown son or daughter killed in action in America's wars each year on Memorial Day. Springfield chose Bill Chandler to honor in 2019; he was the last son of Springfield to be killed in Vietnam. Mike Delaney, Brian Valiton, and Ed Blankenhagen, all close friends on the Kiến Hòa Province advisory team, and I, who had the honor of following in his footsteps as DSA in Hàm Long, provided information, personal memories of Bill, and photographs to the Springfield American Legion Post. The memorial celebration included a parade with the honoree's family members and a memorial service at the Legion Post.

All four of us quickly determined that we wanted to join in memorializing our friend, so we "Four Captains" of Kien Hoa Province Advisory Team 88 met in Springfield, were invited to join in the parade, and were recognized for our friendship and service with Bill at the memorial ceremony. We met Bill's widow and daughters, other family members, and many of his friends dating back to childhood. It was a deeply emotional day for me and the others, one we felt privileged to experience and one we will long remember.

Major Roger Donlon, DSA Binh Dai, was medevacked to Bangkok in August 1972 with a detached retina. He traveled to a hospital in Saigon, then in Bangkok to join his wife, Norma, then to the U.S. for further treatment, and finally to Walter Reed Army Medical Center. Doctors saved his eye, and he returned to his assignment in Thailand. By then, he and Norma had three adopted sons, two of them Thai children. Subsequent assignments included Fort Benning, where Roger and Norma celebrated the biological birth of their fourth son. Assignment to Panama as a Special Forces battalion commander and then back to Fort Leavenworth followed. Just as he was promoted to Colonel he got the welcome news that his daughter from his short-lived first marriage wanted to reunite with her father at his promotion party. After three years at Fort Leavenworth, Roger was reassigned to Japan, giving Norma a chance to visit her roots and introduce the children to a new culture. After 32 years of active duty service, Roger Donlon retired in Leavenworth, Kansas.

Roger's personal character; support from his wife, Norma; and the stature of his Medal of Honor gave the Donlons the opportunity to enter a new phase of service. They became active in the People to People International organization. Roger became an early and respected advocate of reconciliation with Vietnam, and in 1993 People to People organized a

Mission of Understanding to Vietnam and other Southeast Asian countries. He was able to include a trip to Nam Dong, where he found the graves of his deceased Nung and Montagnard soldiers. The cemetery was unkempt, with grass hiding the gravestones of his men. He was determined to find a way to keep the grounds neat and tidy.

In 1995 he was able to arrange a second trip to Vietnam. This time I was honored to be one of the four friends he invited to go along. For me the arrival in Hanoi was surreal, but aside from curiosity, I detected no feeling of enmity or dislike. When we arrived at Nam Dong, we walked the ground where the Special Forces outpost had been located. There were no remnants to be seen, but Roger knew the ground.

The five of us puzzled for a time as to the identity of our senior escort officer, who was introduced as the Chairman of the Thừa Thiên/Huế Province Veterans Committee. We soon discovered that he had been a senior Political Officer and had supervised the Vietcong side of the Battle of Nam Dong! Following along as those two elderly military veterans discussed the details of the battle was an important experience for me. Lunch followed, where we found that our lunch companions had all been Vietcong. By the end of lunch and a beer or three, lots of tears, and good food and conversation, we parted not as enemies but rather as respected friends representing two countries' best professional soldiers.

At the end of that trip, I spent several days on my first return visit to Hàm Long and Mỏ Cày, which I had last seen in February 1973. Since that trip I have returned to Vietnam over a dozen times, but none of those trips were more memorable than that one day at Nam Dong and the first visit to what is now named Bến Tre Province.

Colonel Donlon became the first Executive Director of the Westmoreland Foundation, which awards academic scholarships to exemplary Vietnamese youth. He is also affiliated with Children's Library International, which builds libraries in small, remote towns all over the world. This gave rise to Roger's third return to Vietnam, to attend the dedication of a community library in Nam Dong. Once again I was honored that Roger invited me to go along. The beautiful two-story concrete and wood building came complete with computers and books.

Roger and Norma Donlon have maintained an exhausting schedule over the years, as Roger has accepted hundreds of invitations to speak at military units, schools, university ROTC corps, and government organizations. He has been given many honors, but perhaps the most meaningful might be the naming of the Headquarters, 7th Special Forces Group, at Eglin Air Force Base, Florida, as the Roger H.C. Donlon Hall. He donated his Medal of Honor to the Group's museum, where it rests around the neck of a bronze bust of his likeness.

Now slowed by Agent Orange-related Parkinson's Disease and advancing age, Roger Donlon spends his time at his home overlooking the Missouri River in Leavenworth, where he and Norma live close to their children, grandchildren, and (as of this writing) their first great-grandchild.

Sergeant Robert Isenhour, Kit Carson Scout Company advisor, asked me to respect his privacy concerning the details of his life after Vietnam. I can say that he served honorably in the U.S. Army, filled important civilian jobs after retirement from the army, and has served his country well. He is, simply, one of the finest NCOs I have had the honor to serve with.

Captain John B. Haseman, Deputy District Senior Advisor in Ham Long and Mo Cay Districts, later District Senior Advisor in Ham Long, had a long and interesting military career. He spent 30 years on active duty and enjoyed all of his post–Vietnam assignments. The U.S. Army established the Foreign Area Officer program in 1972, and he was one of the first to request accession into the program, as a Southeast Asia Foreign Area Officer. Counting two and a half years in Vietnam, he spent 18 years in Asia and spent the last 20 years as a Southeast Asia Foreign Area Officer. Details of his military career are at Appendix III. He earned two masters' degrees, in Public Administration, University of Kansas; and Military Art and Science, U.S. Army Command and General Staff College. He achieved the rank of Colonel in 1987 and retired from the U.S. Army on 31 January 1995, having received more than 20 awards for exemplary service in the U.S. and five Asian countries.

Since retirement, he has lived in Grand Junction, Colorado. He is widely published on Southeast Asian political-military issues as author or co-author of four books (you hold his fifth book as you read this one), numerous book chapters, and more than 250 published articles about Southeast Asia political-military affairs. He is the national Membership Officer for Counterparts, an organization of former advisors in Southeast Asia (www.counterparts.net). He is serving his fourth three-year term as an elected member of the Foreign Area Officer Association Board of Governors (www.faoa.org). In 2011 the Defense Intelligence Agency inducted him into the Defense Attaché Service Hall of Fame.

Appendix I

Citation for Award
of the Silver Star

to Major George Byron Reed
for Gallantry in Action

Major George B. Reed, Jr., distinguished himself by gallantry in action on 17 July 1972, while serving as District Senior Advisor, Mo Cay District, Kien Hoa Province, Republic of Vietnam. Major Reed, accompanying a four-company operation in Tan Thoi [*sic*] Village, came under intense enemy small arms, automatic weapons, and mortar fire. While his counterpart marshaled his troops into a defensive perimeter, Major Reed called in tactical airstrikes on both flanks to prevent an enemy attack. During the ensuing fire fight, the enemy was seen forming to his front for an attack on the position. While still controlling the tactical airstrikes, he engaged the enemy, killing several charging enemy at close range, and knocking out a machine-gun position which was inflicting serious casualties on his unit. When his counterpart, the Vietnamese district chief, was hit by an enemy B-40 round, Major Reed was himself painfully wounded by its fragments. Disregarding his own personal safety, he continued to expose himself to enemy fire to give first aid to his mortally wounded counterpart. Having directed the fires of several Vietnamese soldiers in stalling the enemy attack, he then began withdrawing, with the unit, to a more secure position. During the move, Major Reed continued to place accurate fire on the regrouping enemy, personally accounting for several more enemy casualties. On reaching a relatively secure area in the vicinity of a friendly outpost, Major Reed refused medical evacuation until the position was reorganized and the seriously wounded had been evacuated. Major Reed's heroic actions were in keeping with the highest traditions of the United States Army and reflect great credit upon himself and the military service.

249

Performance Evaluation Reports

Then–Captain John B. Haseman

Officer Efficiency Report, Hàm Long District

Rater: "CPT Haseman is an outstanding officer. He has performed every task given him to the highest standards. Initially prepared to function as the Phung Hoang Coordinator for a district advisory team, CPT Haseman was assigned to this reduced team and immediately took over the position of Deputy District Senior Advisor. CPT Haseman worked long hours and with great tenacity to learn the details of the Hamlet Evaluation System (HES), Territorial Forces Evaluation System (TFES) and the many other responsibilities of a District Advisory Team. He became qualified to control U.S. air assets; attack helicopters, troop carriers and tactical air, and he commanded such assets successfully on several occasions while accompanying Vietnamese commanders on tactical operations. Despite regulations preventing its award, CPT Haseman has 'earned' the Combat Infantryman Badge. He sought always to expand his knowledge and to improve his techniques as an advisor working with Vietnamese military, police, and civilian personnel. CPT Haseman was totally dedicated to the accomplishment of the district team mission, but possessed that unique trait required of an advisor, the ability to resist discouragement when advice is not taken. On two occasions, CPT Haseman served as the Acting District Senior Advisor for extended periods, earning the praise and respect of all who worked with him. I can think of no other man I would rather have assigned with me in this situation. I have urged CPT Haseman to apply for a Regular Army commission and would recommend him without hesitation should he choose to apply. I would consider it a distinct pleasure to serve with him in some future assignment."

/s/ David A. Kretschmar
MAJ, AR
District Senior Advisor
1 June 1972

Senior Rater: "I have known and worked with some 40 plus DIOCC advisors in Kien Hoa over the past 3½ years. CPT Haseman is far and away the finest, judged against any criteria or personal and professional characteristics. The same is true of his performance as a deputy DSA, even when rated against combat arms officers. This fine young officer's potential is unlimited, in whatever field he may eventually choose. Every effort should be made to see that he chooses the U.S. Army."

A.L. Kotzebue
FSR-3
Province Senior Advisor
3 June 1972

Officer Efficiency Report, Mo Cay District:

Rater: "CPT HASEMAN performed all of his duties in an outstanding manner. He established immediate rapport with the people and commanded the respect of his Vietnamese counterparts. As Deputy District Senior Advisor in Mo Cay, he advised military operations, intelligence collection, and the Phung Hoang Program. He participated in tactical operations with both military and police agencies. He was selected to be Senior Advisor in Ham Long District when that area was invaded by an NVA regiment. He provided outstanding leadership and reassurance for his distraught district chief. His aggressive direction of airstrikes was a primary factor in driving the NVA from the district. He was responsible to a great degree for reestablishment of viable government and military security in that district. CPT HASEMAN has unlimited potential and should be integrated into the Regular Army."

George B. Reed, Jr.
MAJ, ADA
District Senior Advisor
11 Feb 1973

Senior Rater: "CPT HASEMAN was the most outstanding captain to serve on the province team during my two years as DPSA. No task was insurmountable and consistently was accomplished in a cheerful, expeditious, and professional manner. His tenure as Senior Advisor in Ham Long was the significant contributing factor to the restoration of confidence of the District Chief and retention of GVN control of the district. His career should be closely monitored, to insure proper assignments commensurate with his unlimited potential. I would be happy to have him serve with me in any capacity."

William A. Tausch
LTC, IN
Deputy Province Senior Advisor
11 Feb 1973

Post–Vietnam Career Assignments and Awards

Colonel (Retired) John B. Haseman

Assignments

Feb 73–Jul 73 Operation Homecoming, Office of the Assistant Chief of Staff for Intelligence, Department of the Army, The Pentagon

Jul 73–Apr 74 Thai Language Course, DLIEC, Arlington, Virginia

Apr 74–Jul 74 Counterintelligence Division, Detachment K, 500th MI Group Bangkok, Thailand

Jul 74–Nov 75 Commander, Udorn Field Office, Detachment K, 500th MI Group Udorn Thani, Thailand

Nov 75–Jul 76 Red Wargaming Team, Combined Arms Center, Fort Leavenworth, Kansas, Promoted to Major

Aug 76–Jun 77 Student, U.S. Army Command and General Staff College, Fort Leavenworth, Kansas. Distinguished Graduate, #15 in Class

Jul 77–Jun 78 Indonesian Language Course, Presidio of Monterey, California

Jul 78-Jun 80 Chief, Training Section, U.S. Defense Liaison Group Indonesia, U.S. Embassy, Jakarta, Indonesia

Jun 80–Jun 81 Chief, Army Division, U.S. Defense Liaison Group Indonesia, U.S. Embassy, Jakarta, Indonesia, Promoted to Lieutenant Colonel

Jul 81–Jul 82 Allied Activities Chief, Office of the Class Director, U.S. Army Command and General Staff College, Fort Leavenworth, Kansas

Aug 82–Jul 85 Assistant Army Attaché, U.S. Embassy, Jakarta, Indonesia

1984–1985 U.S. Army War College, Distant Learning

Jul 85–Jul 86 Senior Southeast Asia Analyst, Foreign Intelligence Division, Office of the Assistant Chief of Staff for Intelligence, Department of the Army, The Pentagon

Jul 86–Apr 87 Burmese Language Course, DLIEC, Arlington, Virginia

Apr 87–Jul 90 Senior Defense Official/Defense and Army Attaché, U.S. Embassy, Rangoon, Burma, Promoted to Colonel

Jul 90–Jul 94 Senior Defense Official/Defense and Army Attaché, U.S. Embassy, Jakarta, Indonesia

Aug 94–Jan 95 Staff Officer, Department of Joint and Combined Operations, U.S. Army Command and General Staff College, Fort Leavenworth, Kansas

31 January 1995 Retired, 31½ years active duty

Significant Honors

Inducted into the Defense Intelligence Agency's Defense Attaché Service Hall of Fame, 2011

Inducted into the University of Missouri ROTC Hall of Fame, October 2014

Awards and Decorations

Colonel (retired) John B. Haseman

Combat Infantryman Badge
Army Staff Badge
Defense Superior Service Medal w/Oak Leaf Cluster
Legion of Merit w/Oak Leaf Cluster
Bronze Star Medal w/2 Oak Leaf Clusters
Defense Meritorious Service Medal
Army Meritorious Service Medal
Air Medal w/Oak Leaf Cluster
Joint Service Commendation Medal
Army Commendation Medal w/3 Oak Leaf Clusters
National Defense Service Medal w/Oak Leaf Cluster
Vietnam Service Medal w/8 campaign stars
Humanitarian Service Medal w/Oak Leaf Cluster
Armed Forces Reserve Medal
Presidential Unit Citation (Army)
Joint Meritorious Unit Award w/Oak Leaf Cluster
Meritorious Unit Commendation
Army Service Ribbon
Overseas Service Ribbon, 6th Award
Korean Service Ribbon
Republic of Vietnam Gallantry Cross Unit Citation with Palm
Republic of Vietnam Civil Actions Unit Citation
Republic of Vietnam Campaign Medal

Republic of Vietnam Cross of Gallantry with Bronze Star
Republic of Vietnam Armed Forces Honor Medal, 2 awards
Republic of Vietnam National Police Field Force Honor Service Medal
Republic of Indonesia Yudha Nararya Medal

Military Terminology

AIK—Assistance in Kind, funds advisors used to support civic action projects

aka—also known as

ARVN—Army of the Republic of Vietnam

CAG—Combat Aviation Group

Co Lac Bo—Vietnamese term for recreational club

Co Van—Vietnamese term for advisor

CORDS—Civil Operations and Rural Development Support. Responsible for the province- and district-level advisory effort and the overall pacification mission.

CP—Command Post

DDSA—Deputy District Senior Advisor

DIOCC—District Intelligence and Operations Coordination Center

DPSA—Deputy Province Senior Advisor

DSA—District Senior Advisor

FAC—Forward Air Controller. A U.S. Air Force pilot who controlled air strikes.

FAO—Foreign Area Officer, my military specialty the final 20 years of my career.

GVN—Government of Vietnam

HES—Hamlet Evaluation System. The single most important monthly report, prepared jointly by district senior advisor and district chief.

Lien Doi—Vietnamese army unit composed of two or more RF companies. The concept came fairly late in the war and was designed to provide province chiefs and district chiefs a larger tactical unit and simplify the chain of command.

MACV—Military Assistance Command Vietnam

MASA—Military Assistance Security Advisor Course, taught at Fort Bragg, North Carolina

MATA—Military Assistance Tactical Advisor Course, also taught at Fort Bragg

MAT Team—Mobile Assistance and Training Team. Usually five-man teams to train RF, PF, and other low-level military units. Could be subordinate to province senior advisor or district senior advisor. Most had been removed by mid–1971 as U.S. manpower levels decreased dramatically.

MEDCAP—Medical Civic Action Program, visiting villages to provide medical assistance.

Medevac—Medical Evacuation by helicopter

MI—Military Intelligence, my basic branch of service

MIA—Missing in Action

NCO—Non-Commissioned Officer, ranks from Private through Sergeant Major

NLF—National Liberation Front, the political arm of the communist movement in South Vietnam

NPFF—National Police Field Force, paramilitary arm of the National Police

NVA—North Vietnamese Army

OJT—on-the-job training

PF—Popular Force. Soldiers recruited within their home district.

POW—Prisoner of War

PRU—Provincial Reconnaissance Unit, highly trained, small tactical force with intelligence collection and offensive mission against Viet Cong Infrastructure targets.

PSA—Province Senior Advisor—the senior U.S. officer in the province

PSDF—People's Self-Defense Force, village-level militia

R&R—Rest and Relaxation—what all American soldiers valued!

RD—Revolutionary Development Cadre

RDC—Rural Development Cadre

RF—Regional Force. Soldiers recruited within their home province.

RVN—Republic of Vietnam

S-1—Personnel Officer and/or Staff

S-2—Intelligence Officer and/or Staff

S-3—Operations Officer and/or Staff

S-4—Logistics Officer and/or Staff

S-5—Civil Affairs and Psychological Operations officer and/or Staff

Slick—The ubiquitous UH-1 helicopter configured for air movement; unarmed (thus it was "slick" without rocket pods or other externally mounted weaponry). It depended on the crew chief and gunner, each armed with a bungee-cord mounted machine gun for defense against enemy ground fire.

TASS—Tactical Air Support Squadron

TFES—Territorial Forces Evaluation System, the military corollary to the HES

TOC—Tactical Operations Center
VC—Vietcong
VCI—Viet Cong Infrastructure—the enemy's local governmental
  organization
VNAF—Vietnam Air Force
VR—Visual Reconnaissance by helicopter

Officer ranks, from low to high, with equivalent and pronunciation in Vietnamese

2LT—Second Lieutenant—Thiếu-úy (tee-you wee)
1LT—First Lieutenant—Trung-úy (trung wee)
CPT—Captain—Đại-úy (die wee)
MAJ—Major—Thiếu-tá (tee-you tah)
LTC—Lieutenant Colonel—Trung-tá (trung tah)
COL—Colonel—Đại-tá—(dye tah)

Non-Commissioned Office Ranks, from low to high, most frequently encountered in the CORDS advisory system

CPL—Corporal
SGT—Sergeant. In the U.S. Army, the rank E5. Also a generic term for all
  sergeants.
SFC—Sergeant First Class, the rank E7

Chapter Notes

Chapter 1

1. Vietnam War Allied Troop Levels 1960–1973, at https://www.americanwar library.com/vietnam/vwatl.htm, viewed 17 Dec 2020. The figures given are as of December each year.

2. MACV Advisory Team 88 Alpha List of Military Personnel, undated.

3. MACV Advisory Team 88 Alpha List of Military Personnel, 7 September 1972. This is the last roster I saw before departure from the team in February 1973.

Chapter 4

1. *cố vấn* has usually been translated as "advisor." A more literate translation is "trusted friend," which actually is a better description of the relationship between Vietnamese officer or soldier and the American "advisor."

2. James N. "Nick" Rowe told his story of time in captivity in *Five Years to Freedom*, Little, Brown & Co.; First Edition (January 1, 1971), with a later edition, same title, Presidio Press (March 9, 2011). Rowe was promoted to major during his captivity. I was privileged to get to know Nick Rowe while we were both attending the Military Intelligence Officer Advanced Course, Fort Holabird, MD, in 1970–1971. In a subsequent assignment he was credited with developing the rigorous U.S. Army Survival, Evasion, Resistance, and Escape (SERE) training program taught to high-risk military personnel (such as Special Forces and aircrews) and the U.S. Army doctrine

that institutionalizes these techniques and principles to be followed by captured personnel. In 1987, by now Colonel Rowe was assigned as army division chief, Joint U.S. Military Advisory Group–Philippines. On 21 April 1989, while being driven to work in the morning, his armored vehicle was ambushed on the streets of Quezon City, Manila. A single bullet entered through an unarmored door seam and struck Nick in the head; he was killed instantly. The insurgency organization New People's Army (NPA) admitted responsibility. In 1991 two members were tried and convicted of Colonel Rowe's murder and sentenced to long prison terms. Thanks to Wikipedia for the detailed information on this distinguished U.S. Army officer's career. https://en.wikipedia.org/wiki/ James_N._Rowe.

Chapter 6

1. James Patrick Coddington's name can be found on the Vietnam Veterans Memorial Wall, Panel 06W—Line 47. http://thewall-usa.com/info.asp?recid= 9617.

2. "Cửu Long" is derived from the Sino-Vietnamese and literally means "nine dragons," referring to the Mekong River, known in Vietnamese as the "River of Nine Dragons." Vietnamese military operations in the Mekong Delta were often given the name "Cửu Long." https://en.wikipedia.org/wiki/C%E1% BB%ADu_Long_Province.

3. The excerpts from this report are taken verbatim from the "flimsy" copies

of all such reports submitted during my assignment. All descriptions of contact with the enemy in this book are taken from similar reports, all of which I retain in my personal files.

Chapter 7

1. SFC Hồ Văn Bé to the author. For more detailed information, see John B. Haseman, "The Hoa Hao: A Half-Century Of Conflict," *Asian Affairs: An American Review*, July/August 1976.

Chapter 8

1. The details of the *dình* celebration I saw firsthand; I visited the *dình* on two consecutive evenings. I later did a lot of research on the historical background of the *dình* from local officials and subsequent academic research. See John B. Haseman, "The Dinh at Tien Thuy," *Asian Affairs: An American Review*, January-February 1978.

Chapter 10

1. See Roger H.C. Donlon with Warren Rogers, *Outpost of Freedom*, New York: McGraw-Hill Book Company, 1965, for Roger Donlon's childhood, education, early military career, and the stirring account of the defense of Nam Dong by U.S. Army Special Forces Team A-726. Two later books expand on *Outpost of Freedom* and the Donlon family over more than 50 years since the Battle of Nam Dong. See Roger H.C. Donlon, *Beyond Nam Dong*, Leavenworth, KS: R & N Publishers, 1998; and Chuck Theusch, *Return to Nam Dong, Legacy of the Green Berets*, Milwaukee, WI: Children's Library International, Inc., 3rd Edition, 2016.

Chapter 14

1. The details of this battle were provided to me in an eight-page letter from Sergeant First Class Hùynh Đức Tuyến dated 20 June 1973, and an email from Colonel (retired) Reed to the author on 8 July 2021. The two missives were written 48 years apart but contained virtually the same details, written in much different styles.

2. Major Reed's Silver Star Citation is at Appendix I.

3. See John B. Haseman, "Nguyen Van Cu, The Maverick of Mo Cay," *Vietnam Magazine*, October 1992.

Chapter 15

1. Much of the information for this segment came from the author's discussions with defenders in Tan Loi, with the help of Sergeant Bé and Hàm Long's district chief and staff. For more complete details, see John B. Haseman, "The Battle of Tan Loi," *Vietnam Magazine*, August 2004.

2. All three principals involved in this incident—LTC Sơn, Mr. Kotzebue, and CPT Chandler—have passed away. These details were provided to me personally by LTC Sơn in August 1972 after I arrived back in Hàm Long as DSA.

3. William Gary Chandler's name can be found on the Vietnam Veterans Memorial, Panel 01W—Line 62. http://thewall-usa.com/info.asp?recid=8678

Chapter 16

1. I recognized many of the names he gave me, which included officers and soldiers at both the district and province levels. However, in the absence of further confirmation, I do not mention any names.

Chapter 17

1. https://www.huffpost.com/entry/specialties-in-vietnam-horrify-visitors_b_8660250; http://english.vietnamnet.vn/fms/society/139406/photos—ben-tre-bans-breeding-of-coconut-worms-as-food.html

Chapter 18

1. For full details, see John B. Haseman, "Looking Back: A Lesson in Strength," *Infantry* magazine, March-April 1983.

Chapter 19

1. I am grateful to Byron Reed for the story about Ha Xe. I knew him as well but had met him only at his outpost; I had heard many stories about him but had not gone on any operation with him.

2. Much of this information comes from the Forward Air Controller Association website: https://www.fac-assoc.org/memorial/memorial02b.html.

Details also provided by then-Sergeant Robert Isenhour. First Lieutenant Anderson's name is on Panel 01W 075 of the Vietnam Veterans Memorial.

Chapter 22

1. See career details in Appendix III.

Index

Numbers in **bold italics** indicate pages with illustrations

263